Receiving *Grace*

By

Ellen Sherrill

The Love Meadow Series

Volume 1

The Love Meadow Series- Volume I: Receiving Grace

 All scripture references are taken from the New King James Version of the Holy Bible.

ISBN: 978-1-937250-64-5

Acknowledgements

Special thanks again to my dear friend and faithful editor, Gayle, to JP for creating another beautiful cover for this book, and to my great-niece, Kathryn, and her husband, Andrew, for allowing me to use their engagement photo for the cover.

I don't have the words to express my appreciation to my son and daughter-in-law, Jeff, and Carol, for supporting me in every way as I was completing this book.

And most importantly, I give thanks to the Creator for giving me this story in a dream as I napped one afternoon.

Getting this book to the state of being published has been a struggle of several years, but I have been determined to get the message of this story to my readers…that God does bring good out of our trials. He is ever faithful to love us and be with us every step of the way. I hope you find encouragement and enjoy it, too!

Ellen Sherrill

Receiving *Grace*

CHAPTER 1

"Thank you for your patience, everyone." The airline employee's voice sounded as tired as the group of people who had been waiting through several delays.

"The plane for your flight to Houston has now arrived. If you can bear with us just a little longer, we'll need a few minutes to freshen the cabin and get a crew aboard. Anyone requiring special care in boarding should make your way to the gate at this time. We're looking at approximately thirty minutes before take-off.

"Again, we apologize for the delay and want you to know that we really do appreciate your flying American Airlines."

With a sigh Grace Morgan fluffed her long, blonde hair and reached into her purse for her cell phone. She felt guilty that her friend would have to drive to the airport to pick her up in the wee hours of the morning. At least the delay would allow Karen to sleep a little longer. She had assured Grace that she didn't live that far from the airport.

Pushing the speed-dial number, Grace waited for the always up-beat sound of her southern friend's three syllable, "Hell-o-o." It came after the second ring.

"Hey, it's me again. They just told us we should be leaving in about thirty minutes."

"Okay, Girlfriend. Any more delays and you'll get to experience Houston's early morning work-day traffic."

Grace chuckled. "Have you forgotten I live in LA?"

"Oh, yeah, well, I guess you should feel right at home."

The fleeting thought in Grace's head questioned the probability that she would ever feel "at home" again, but she refused to follow that train of thought now.

"I really do appreciate this, you know."

That irritating lump in the throat that showed up so frequently these days threatened to cut off her sentence mid-stream.

Karen's voice softened. "Hey, what are friends for?"

Grace swallowed and managed to eke out, "Yeah. I'd better get my things together here. You get some sleep and I'll see you in a few hours."

Taking a deep breath that put her back on an even keel, she added, "I'll treat you to breakfast."

"That's a deal. You get some sleep, too. I've got things planned for us to do…can't let you snooze all day."

Grace groaned. "You and your limitless energy! Anyway, I'll see you soon. Bye."

She clicked her phone off and set it to airplane mode. Not in the mood to get caught up in the line of passengers waiting for others to load their overhead baggage, she gathered up her things, but remained seated.

"We're now boarding all passengers on flight 1016 to Houston Hobby…all passengers to Houston Hobby boarding now at gate five."

When the line of boarding passengers was down to four, Grace joined them. Within moments her boarding pass was scanned, and she made her way down the tunnel to the plane.

Trying not to bump passengers already seated in aisle seats, Grace pulled her carry-on behind her as she balanced purse and tote bag. The number on her boarding pass read 21F. That would be a window seat…and way back in the rear of this smaller plane.

Row 19…20…21. The passenger in the aisle seat looked up as she hesitated.

'"You need in here, Ma'am?"

Grace nodded toward the window. "Yes, I think that's my seat."

Grace met the gaze of the man whose western-cut shirt, Levi's and boots shouted, "Cowboy!" She couldn't look away. In an instant she saw in those brown eyes kindness, warmth, and something else…pain?

"Uh…can I help you get your bag up there?"

Grace suddenly realized she'd been unmoving…staring at the man. Her face flushed.

"Yes, I'd really appreciate that." And she meant it. Ever since her baggage had gotten lost on a flight, she always kept a small piece of luggage with her. But that bag was loaded and heavy. She hadn't considered the fact that she'd have to lift it over her head when she kept cramming just one more item into it.

The cowboy started to rise, and Grace tried to move back to give him more room. But passengers on either side were still placing bags in the overhead bins, so when he stood Grace was close enough that she could feel the warmth of his tall, lean body. He reached down for her carry-on and she caught a scent of cologne that hinted of the fresh outdoors, deep and woodsy …totally masculine.

She felt the flush rising to her face again and hoped he didn't notice. He was standing aside now, waiting for her to move past him to her seat. He must be at least six-three, she thought, slipping into the seat as quickly as possible.

Grace snapped the seat belt into place just as the airline hostess made her way down the aisle checking the overhead bins and making certain passengers were buckled in. She gave Grace a thumbs-up with a smile and moved on.

Trying to stash her tote bag and purse under the seat in front of her, Grace could swear that the cowboy's eyes were on her. Why did she feel so clumsy? She sat back in her seat and took a deep breath.

Now came the part she dreaded…taking off. That was only a little less frightening to her than landing. Too nervous to sit still, she fidgeted, adjusted the seat belt, and pulled her jacket closer. Embarrassed when she realized her hands were visibly shaking, she grabbed her right hand with her left.

Normally, she would have prayed and found peace to make it through the flight. But she wasn't praying these days. Not for the past ten months, in fact.

The scene that tormented her flashed into her mind now. Her handsome husband with the scantily-dressed, red-haired glamor girl on the furry, white rug in front of the fireplace.

He hadn't expected Grace home from visiting her parents so soon. What if she'd waited that extra day? Would she be on this plane now, or would she still be in Los Angeles, busy with her duties as the pastor's wife, and blissfully ignorant of her husband's infidelity?

In spite of how desperately Grace did not want to cry, tears began to flow down her cheeks. She turned to the window where in the darkness lights from the crew on the ground guided the pilot to position the plane on the tarmac.

Would she ever feel God guiding her again? Likely not if she wasn't talking to Him. That thought filled her with loneliness like none she'd ever experienced.

Grace had given her heart to the Lord at the age of six and had loved Him all her life. Even through the teen years when several of her friends had chosen to experiment with things of the world, Grace had drawn closer to God. She knew in her heart that He had a plan and purpose for her life, and she had found that purpose as a pastor's wife.

But that choice had brought her to a place she never dreamed she'd be. She had counseled many women whose husbands had been unfaithful. She had given them the best advice she could find in the Bible and in books. Now, she realized how little she understood of the pain those women were dealing with; it was certainly different being on the other side of that desk.

Grace's face burned now beneath her tears as she remembered the times she had listened to some broken woman's story while thinking how different her life was, and how blessed she was that her own marriage was solid. How wrong could she have been?

She now realized that Damien's affair must have been going on for some time. She recalled the day months ago when she'd unexpectedly stopped by his office. Damien's secretary appeared very uneasy as she notified him that Grace was there. It was only a minute or so before Cici Jacquess sauntered out of Damien's office with a smirk on her face. It was obvious his secretary knew what was going on. Did other people at the church know of Damien's affair before she did?

Shame and embarrassment overwhelmed her again. All that time Grace had loved him, feeling she was being the wife he needed as a man of God. What a skilled traitor he was. He had never stopped being intimate with her, even as he was obviously giving the same attention to his mistress. How could she have been so stupid not to know?

"Stop it, Grace!" she silently ordered herself. She had to think of something else before she totally lost control. The plane was now in place for take-off, waiting for the tower to give the pilot the go-ahead. There was no stopping the shaking hands now, so she reached down and took a magazine from her tote. Maybe turning pages would cause the shaking to be less noticeable. She could do this. She had no choice; just as she'd had no choice in the break-up of her marriage.

Once the truth was out Damien had wasted no time resigning the church and moving out of their home, leaving Grace in shock. Lost, abandoned, and in more pain than she knew a person could endure, she no longer had a church family either because she was too embarrassed and ashamed to walk into that sanctuary again.

As pastor of one of the largest mega-churches in Los Angeles, Damien Vincent was well known by the media. Always impeccably dressed, handsome and charismatic, he was one of the most popular religious figures in the city.

Now he was at the center of the most popular scandal being broadcast several times daily on every television station in the area.

Photos, first of Damien and Grace walking out of the large, beautiful church, were on all the TV stations. Those were soon replaced with juicier, more news-hungry pictures of Pastor Vincent and his paramour, Cici Jacquess.

Totally slanderous headlines in cheap-shot magazines cast aspersions on Grace as a contributor to the pastor's downfall, and paparazzi followed her everywhere.

A couple who were faithful friends opened their home to her. providing a safe place to shelter for several weeks. Another friend was a dresser for stars in Hollywood and gave Grace a complete make-over. Her clothing was changed to a more youthful, edgier style, and her hair was lightened from the brown she'd naturally been all her life to an attractive highlighted blonde shade. A trendy hair style completed the new look and Grace had hardly recognized herself when she looked in the mirror.

The paparazzi didn't know her either, so all of them were wondering where Grace Vincent had disappeared to. She had taken back her maiden name to avoid any connection to Damien, but still took precautions to avoid the public when she could. Choosing the red-eye flight to Texas was part of that plan as she felt there would be less chance of her being recognized with fewer people in the airport.

A new name, a different look, obviously a different life before her...she was no longer a pastor's wife. Grace Morgan had no idea who she now was.

"What is going on with you?" Zach Clayton asked himself silently in a self-condemning tone. For the three years since his beautiful wife, Sasha, had died from cancer, not one woman had caused him to take even a second look, though a number of them had put a lot of effort into trying to make that happen.

But in the past ten minutes it was as though someone had turned that "Off" switch to "On," and at full current. The pretty blonde that sat on the other side of the empty middle seat had affected him far beyond what he was willing to acknowledge.

He didn't want a woman in his life. Sasha had been everything to him. There was no way he'd ever love another woman the way he'd loved her…still loved her…and it wouldn't be fair to involve a woman in his life when he couldn't give her his heart.

Curiosity drew his gaze toward the woman in the window seat again. Something was going on with her. She was literally trembling, her hands shaking. Zach pretended to be looking past her, out the window, but caught a glimpse of her face, shining with tears that fell onto her smart black leather jacket. Immediately, his heart was filled with concern.

It didn't seem to matter that Zach was through with ministry…done with reaching out to hurting people. He was the one hurting now and didn't have anything to give. Still, that old stirring and compassion for the suffering and broken hearted sprang up at times without warning, and this was one of them.

"Help her," Zach heard that inner Voice say.

"How in the world can I help her?" he argued. "I can't even help myself. Besides, I don't know anything about her."

"I know everything about her; she's one of mine," the Voice continued.

Zach glanced at her again, so frightened, and helpless looking. Was this God wanting him to help her, or was it his own desire? Did it really matter? She could refuse his overture if she felt uncomfortable with it. From the way she had gasped when the plane began to speed down the runway it seemed that she was afraid of the plane's taking off. They'd be lifting off the ground any second now. He turned to her and extended his hand.

"Hey, can we get through this together?" He smiled. "I hate taking off and landing."

Dark blue eyes sought Zach's brown ones as the pretty lady grabbed Zach's offered hand. Tears still shone in her eyes as she softly said, "Thank you. I'm…I'm grateful."

Zach wrapped his large hand around the small trembling hand clinging to his. Again, he felt a desire to shield this woman from the pain that she had obviously endured.

Surprisingly, he wanted to hold her until the pain went away. Where did that come from? No woman had stirred those feelings in him since Sasha.

But he hadn't been able to make the pain go away for his precious Sasha, nor drive away the cancer that wreaked havoc on her body, taking her away day by day. He could only pray that God would heal her, but that hadn't been enough either, because now she was gone.

Zach became aware that his companion was looking at him and realized that he was holding her hand very firmly. In embarrassment, he eased his grip.

"I'm sorry. I was kind of lost in thought. I hope I didn't hurt you."

She smiled. "You didn't hurt me…in fact, it felt really nice. But the plane's in the air now. I think I'll be all right. How about you?"

He gave her a crooked grin. "I don't know; I think we ought to wait until the pilot gives the okay."

When she laughed and didn't pull her hand away, Zach brought their hands closer, resting on the seat between them.

"I guess if I'm going to hold your hand you should know my name. I'm Zach Clayton."

"I'm Grace…Morgan."

Zach's brow lifted involuntarily at Grace's hesitation in speaking her last name. She noticed and blushed.

"'Sorry, 'getting used to a name change."

With that, Zach felt the wall come between them. He released her hand just as she drew it back and turned her face toward the dark sky outside the window. Zach suddenly felt more alone than he had in months, with the warmth of Grace's small hand achingly still present in his.

CHAPTER 2

Grace joined the group of sleepy passengers at the baggage claim just as the chute started spitting out bags. She'd marked hers with red and white polka dot ribbon to spot them easily among the multitude of black luggage. Trying not to be obvious she casually looked around the group, hoping to see Zach somewhere in the crowd. Just as she spotted him, she heard a familiar voice behind her.

"Hey, Girl!"

Grace turned to see Karen waiting with a wide grin on her face. Oh, it was good to see her friend!

"You haven't changed a bit," she said as she hugged Karen warmly.

"Well, we certainly can't say that about you, can we?" Karen said, lowering her voice. "You look fantastic. Where have you been hiding this hot chic all these years?"

She stood back, looking Grace over from her new blonde hair color to the smart black boots she wore. Karen's blunt-cut auburn hair swung from side to side as she shook her head.

With a twinkle in her green eyes, she said, "I wish ole Demon Damien could see you now. He'd drop that cheap red-head like a hot potato…not that you'd take him back anyway!"

"You're right about that," Grace agreed. "He did see me once since my make-over. We had to meet at the attorney's office for the final wrap-up of the divorce."

"And what was his reaction to the 'new you'?"

Grace smiled. "He didn't recognize me for a few seconds. I think the blonde hair really threw him for a loop. When he realized it it was me, the expression on his face was priceless."

Karen smiled. "I bet he was having second thoughts about his actions."

"He stared at me the whole time we were there," Grace said. "His attorney had to keep repeating things he had said to him." Grace suddenly felt sad. "He's lost so much more than I have, Karen. I don't know if he'll ever recover his reputation or his ministry. so many people were hurt by this."

She spotted her be-ribboned luggage coming their direction and positioned herself to take it from the carousel.

"I'll get the big one," Karen said.

It took a few minutes to get all the baggage situated, but eventually, they headed for the exit. Just before they reached the sliding doors Grace spotted Zach. He was shaking hands and sharing a hug with a man who was dressed just like him—all western. They were smiling as though they knew each other well.

He looked up and caught her eye, and it seemed that a host of questions passed between them. Then the moment was gone, and Grace was left with a sadness that those questions would never be answered. They hadn't spoken again on the plane other than her thanking him for retrieving her carry-on from the overhead bin. Grace had slept, even through the landing. In the hustle and bustle of leaving the plane a connection just hadn't happened.

From across the airport Zach saw Grace as she and another woman got her bags and started toward the exit. He had the feeling that he should run after her. There were too many things he didn't know about her.

But he loved Sasha. He shouldn't be chasing after any woman. When Grace looked his direction and their eyes met, he couldn't deny that something passed between them. Zach was both sorry and relieved. He wasn't ready to deal with the emotions this blonde had stirred in him.

He lifted his hand in a rather weak kind of wave, and at least, she returned it before tucking her head and leaving with her companion. Zach got the impression that she wasn't interested in a man any more than he wanted another female in his life. If he could just get his insides to agree with his head!

As he watched her walk away, he felt the same twinge of loneliness as he had when she had withdrawn her hand from his.

"A-hem," the cowboy at Zach's side woke him from his reverie. "She's certainly an attractive woman. Somebody you know?"

"Oh…uh…not really." We just sat in the same row on the plane."

Jim Sheridan nodded and smiled. He was glad to see that his friend was at least *noticing* a woman. Zach had been so imprisoned by love for his deceased wife that Jim and his wife, Susan, had made him a regular on their prayer list. It hurt them to see this man who had been so full of love and life simply existing without purpose day by day.

Picking up Zach's bag and heading for the exit, Jim grinned. "Well, did you get her phone number?"

Zach blushed and shook his head.

"What? You let that good-lookin' woman get away?"

"You know I'm not looking for a woman, Jim. Anyway, I get the feeling she's not looking for a man either."

Knowing his former pastor's ability to pick up on hurt in people, Jim sobered. "That bad?"

Zach nodded. "I don't know who, or what, has crushed her, but she's hurting inside. Just sitting across the seat from her I could feel it."

They had reached Jim's truck now and tossed his luggage in the bed. They didn't speak as they got settled in the cab and buckled up.

As he pulled out onto the roadway, Jim asked, "So, what are you going to do about this woman? God didn't make you aware of her need for you to do nothing."

"Aggh!" Zach practically growled. "I don't want to be aware of her need. I don't want to know about anybody else's pain and heartache!" He spoke with more fervor than he intended. But this was Jim, his friend who was closer than a brother. He knew that nothing he said would go further than the cab of that pick-up truck.

Jim waited a few moments, then gently spoke. "God never said we get to stop ministering to the wounded just because we become one of them."

Zach turned his face to the darkness outside the window. "But I don't have anything to give them."

Jim hit the steering wheel with his palm. "Well, where do you get off thinking that YOU ever had anything to give? Are you saying that all that healing, compassionate ministry at Cornerstone Cowboy Church was solely the awesome capability of Pastor Zach Clayton who performed wonderfully as long as his own life was A-okay? Boy, you sure had me fooled!"

Zach looked at his friend in surprise. The emotion in Jim's voice was as close to anger as Zach had ever heard. As the full impact of Jim's words hit his exhausted brain Zach shifted uncomfortably in his seat and sighed,

"I guess I had that coming."

"Yes, you did, and more."

"If I'm guessing right, you're just itching to give me the more, too."

Jim reached over and slapped him on the arm. "You are brilliant, cowboy!"

"All right, you're not going to be happy until you say it," Zach said.

With a look at his friend to see if he really meant it, Jim took a deep breath and in a gentler tone he said, "The church needs you, Zach. The people need their shepherd.

"I agreed to step in for a while so you could heal and allow God to bring you through the terrible loss of Sasha. But you're not going 'through.' You have allowed the enemy to keep you stuck in the middle. So, nobody's making progress, not you, not me, not the church."

Jim re-situated his Stetson. "Don't get me wrong. I love those people, and I'm doing everything I can to guide them. But I'm not a pastor, Zach. That's not my calling. I can be the best helper a pastor ever wanted…that's my place, but I don't receive that insight for the people's needs that a true pastor gets."

"You don't understand, Jim. You still have Susan."

"I know I can't understand fully, Bro, but I know this much; God didn't take Sasha to Heaven and leave you here on earth to live like a dead man. That means he's not through with you."

Zach felt the sting of truth in Jim's words..

Jim continued. "I know that Sasha wanted you to keep on living, Zach, to find someone else to love and to keep on working for the Lord. She said that to Susan and me…even made us promise we'd use the hot-shot rod on you if we had to. I guess you could say that's what I'm doing now. You have to agree, we've been pretty easy on you 'til now."

Zach had to smile, but took a deep breath before quietly saying, "I don't know how to do it without her, Jim. I don't think I can."

"I'm not saying that any other woman could ever take Sasha's place, but God can bring the helpmate you need into your life."

"I can't just marry someone because I need a ministry companion," Zach said.

"Hmm, seems like I remember you preaching about God being able to meet ALL our needs. You think He can't bring someone that you can love and who will also have the heart to love your people?"

"I suppose so, but that means I've got to let Sasha go. "

"I hate to remind you, Zach, but Sasha's already gone. You're not being disloyal to her by loving someone new. She would hate the way you're living now."

Zach was saved from having to reply to that by their arrival at Jim's ranch. He lived in an apartment that Jim had built over the barn for whoever might drop in needing a place for a while, like Zach. It worked out great for him because He could keep a few horses and the fifty or so head of cattle he owned there with Jim's herd.

Jim parked the truck in the pole barn and shut off the engine. "Hey, I was so busy preaching to you I forgot to ask about your dad and the wedding. How'd it go?"

Zach smiled, glad to have a change of topic. "I guess it was all right. It's weird to go to your parent's wedding. Dad's new wife is nice, friendly, and seems to genuinely love him. They go to a church nearby and have a lot of friends. It appears that his later years will bring much more happiness than the previous forty."

"I'm glad to hear that. Your dad's a great guy." He paused a minute. "Are we all right, Bro?"

'"You mean, am I mad at you for preaching at me all the way from the airport?" He grinned. "I probably needed it."

"Probably?" Jim punched him on the shoulder and headed toward the house. He turned back around and yelled, "But I still can't believe you didn't get that blonde's phone number!"

"I can't either," Zach muttered to himself as he climbed the stairs to his apartment. Once inside he dropped his bag and stood looking around the place he called "home." He'd gotten used to the spacious one-room design. The living room, kitchen, and bedroom were separated by half-walls with rows of cedar posts reaching to the ceiling. Only the bathroom was enclosed with a walk-in closet across from it. The casual look had been designed by Susan, Jim's wife, and the feeling was open, but cozy.

Zach plopped down on the king-sized bed and took off his boots, stretched out, and jammed a couple of pillows behind his head. Even as tired as he was, his mind wouldn't shut off. Neither would his heart.

The image of Grace Morgan, trembling with tears streaming down her face wouldn't go away. He kept hearing the Voice saying, "*Help her, she's one of mine.*" He could feel her pain, deep inside him, where his own heartache had taken up residence.

"So, I'm carrying pain for two now, as though mine wasn't enough," he thought wryly.

"I carried the pain of the world," the Voice spoke.

This was a fact Zachary Clayton knew very well. How many times had he preached that from His pulpit? That Jesus Christ bore our sorrows, even those as agonizing as losing someone you loved with all your being. It was so much easier to say those things when he'd never had to live them out. How many times had he encouraged people to make a decision for Christ…to believe that Jesus truly was the Son of God and would be faithful to perform the promises in His Word?

Suddenly, Zach felt that everything depended on his faith this very moment…his whole future, his relationship with the Creator, and any other relationship that he might have. He had a decision to make.

He could either stay mad at God for Sasha's death and live this miserable, bitter life without joy, or he could decide to practice what he had believed for years to be true…that God brought good out of sorrow, that His plan was always in the best interest of His children, and that His grace was always sufficient to bring them to victory. He'd been able to believe that for the people of his congregation, but could he believe those things for himself?

Zach thought of the scripture that clearly states God is not a respecter of persons. One incident after another came to his mind as he thought of the people of Cornerstone Cowboy Church who had faced insurmountable problems and had seen God come through for them. He and Sasha had believed with them and had rejoiced in their victories.

Was his faith only valid if Sasha was at his side? What did that say of him and his walk with God?

Something began to break inside Zach. The wall of bitterness and rebellion started to crumble. He could not live one more day with the turmoil of the war between truth and lies that was destroying him.

"Oh, God, I'm sorry," he groaned. "I'm so sorry."

He found himself face down on the floor, repenting with everything that was within him, and for the first time in longer than he could remember, he wept. Like a cleansing flood, the tears washed away the heartache of losing Sasha, his bitterness toward God for not healing her, the sorrow of his own decision to step down from his church, and any hurt that action may have brought to his people. Finally, he lay spent, emptied of the weight he'd been carrying for so long.

It was then that Zach felt the Presence…flowing over him like a healing balm, loving him to the depth of his being.

"My grace is for you, too, my son," the Voice so gently spoke. *"I couldn't give it until you were willing to receive it."*

"I receive it, Lord, but I don't know what to do now."

"Just walk with me; I'll guide you as I always have."

Suddenly, the image of Grace Morgan came to mind. Zach felt the pain of not doing all he could to help her.

"I missed it with Grace, Lord. I probably should have prayed with her, but I wasn't in the spiritual place to minister to anyone else. I have no idea how to reach her, but if You still want to use me in her life, bring her to me and I promise, I'll be obedient."

When he laid back down on his bed the peace that comes from a clean heart drew him sweetly into rest. For the first time in three years it wasn't Sasha's dark hair and smiling face that flitted through his mind just before falling asleep, but the frightened blue eyes and flowing blonde hair of Grace Morgan.

CHAPTER 3

Grace and Karen stashed all the luggage into Karen's Subaru and exited the parking garage. Now that she was clearly off airport property Grace felt that she had arrived. She took a deep breath and forced herself to relax.

"Are you still up for breakfast?" she asked.

Karen cocked her head and with a shrewd look at Grace said, "I think that question would more appropriately be addressed to you, my friend. You look beat. Why don't we have hot chocolate and a piece of toast at my place, get some sleep, and save eating out for lunch?"

"That sounds good to me," Grace told her.

"Wait 'til you sleep on the new bed I bought for your room. Now *that* is wonderful!"

"Oh, I get to break it in?" Grace asked.

"Well, I didn't say that. I had to test it to see if it was worthy of my BFF."

Grace giggled. It was great to be with Karen. Her lighthearted personality could cheer the worst grump. Maybe she'd move to this area to be closer to Karen. She certainly needed cheering.

"How are things at the university?" Grace asked.

"Everything is going well. I've got five professors in my department now and every one of them is actually intelligent and possesses common sense, too."

"What? No nutty professors? That must be dull."

Karen chuckled. "It's actually quite nice, and it certainly makes my job easier. When I have to be out of town for a few days I don't have sleepless nights wondering what kind of mess I'll have to straighten out when I get back."

She stopped abruptly… "Oh, did I tell you I have to be gone for three days next week?"

"Yes, you did," Grace assured her. "And I'm a big girl, I'll be all right on my own."

"By that time, you'll know your way around to the most important places, but before I leave, we are going to explore some of the tourist attractions the locals never go to."

"No amusement parks, I hope."

"I will spare you that," Karen said. "Mostly because I hate them myself. "She clicked on her right turn signal and soon pulled into a gated community. The sleepy-eyed attendant spotted her sticker on the windshield and opened the gate with a lack-luster smile.

"This is nice," Grace said, noting the beautiful landscaping of the community.

"I like it," Karen agreed. "I really enjoy someone else keeping my yard mowed and the flower beds weeded. I don't really know my neighbors, but we wave and share a little small talk when we happen to be outside at the same time. I feel that I could call them if I needed help with anything."

"That's not the way it is in LA," Grace said wryly. "Everyone there is afraid of being hit with a lawsuit if they get involved in anyone else's situation."

Karen rounded a curve, pushed the garage door opener, and pulled into a driveway where the door was already sliding up. Soon, they were inside, Grace's bags were in her room and her cute boots were off her tired feet.

She loved the bedroom Karen had prepared for her. The sea blue, white and gray shades were soothing. It was decorated with just enough accessories to be pretty.

She couldn't resist plopping back onto the bed and found it to be everything Karen had said it was. She was tempted to stay there, but the smell of chocolate drew her like a magnet to the kitchen just as the toast popped pertly up in the toaster.

Sitting at stools at the counter they buttered the toast and blew on the chocolate to cool it.

"I really like your house, KK," Grace told her, using the nickname she'd given Karen years ago. "It's just like you…warm and inviting, peaceful, and then there's a quirky piece of art that makes it all fun."

Karen smiled as she stirred the melting marshmallows into her hot chocolate. "I didn't realize how good it would feel to own a home. I liked most of the apartments I rented except…

Grace chimed in…" The one on Fifth and Ontario Drive!"

They laughed together. "Gosh, that place was a nightmare," Karen admitted, remembering the housing they tolerated while in college because the rent was low.

They nibbled toast and sipped the sweet chocolate, then Karen said seriously," All right, you're here now, Gracie. This is your best friend talking…how are you?"

Grace took a deep breath, then spoke, "As far as Damien goes, his betrayal is still really painful. I think that I've put it behind me and then some reminder brings it all back and I'm in tears again."

"And your relationship with God? Some things you've said have me concerned," Karen said gently.

"I wish I could say I have that settled, but truthfully, I still have a long way to go. I've lived my life to serve Him and help people. It just doesn't seem fair."

She looked up at her friend as her eyes filled with tears. "I don't know how to live without God, KK. He has been the center of my life since I was six years old. I miss our sweet fellowship so much, and I know the separation is all on my part. But when I think of Damien with that woman I feel as angry at God for allowing it to happen as I do Damien."

"And all the time knowing that's totally ridiculous," Karen said, leaning toward her. "Damien did what he wanted to do. I know God must have spoken to him not to go that direction. He doesn't let me get by with anything. If I've been missing my time in the Word and get irritable with people, God doesn't excuse my behavior. The Holy Spirit keeps reminding me of it until I apologize to them and repent to Him. You know, Grace that Damien is no exception. So please don't waste your anger on God."

Grace nodded. "I know you're right. I'll work on it."

"You're not entertaining any of the devil's lies that if you had done something differently, cooked better meals, made love better, kept the house cleaner…any crazy thing…that Damien wouldn't have been looking elsewhere, are you?"

Grace shook her head, "Those thoughts came to me when I first learned about his affair., but I know that I was as good a wife to Damien as I could be. I always put his needs before anything else, in every way.

"I tried to protect him from the pressures of the pastorate when things got hectic. He even said that to me the day he left. He stopped at the door and said, "Grace, this is not your fault, you've been a good wife."

She gave a bitter laugh, "And of course I jumped up in glee and said, 'Oh, goodie! I'll go my merry way now, seeing how much fun I can have putting my shattered life back together."

Karen smiled at Grace's attempt to lighten the remembrance of that dreadful day. She reached over and gave her a swat on the knee.

"You're a trooper. You know that, kiddo?"

"No, I don't know that. I never wanted to be anything but a pastor's wife and I'm certainly not that now. I guess that's the biggest thing I'm angry with God about, allowing that to be taken from me."

The last few words came out in a deep sob as Grace covered her face with her hands. Tears streamed out through her fingers as she wept deeply.

Karen was immediately beside her, holding her close. "Oh, Gracie, I'm so sorry. You are a beautiful person with a heart that radiates love to everyone around. This season won't last forever…you'll see. Do you honestly think God would prepare and train you to do the work of the ministry, and then when you get really good at it, He'd sit you on the bench because your dodo husband went dorky?"

Karen shook Grace's shoulders gently, and with a goofy voice asked again, "Do you? Do you really think that?"

When she got a smile out of Grace she went on. "Who knows, maybe God brought you to Texas to give you a cowboy. Wouldn't that be a switch from Damien in his thousand-dollar suits?"

"I don't know, though," she chuckled. "These cowboys can sink a fortune in a pretty pair of boots and a Stetson. And hey, I'll warn you ahead of time…don't ever mess with a cowboy's hat—not if you want to live!"

They laughed together and Grace dried her tears with the Kleenex Karen handed her.

"Did you notice that I am prepared for tears?" she said, sweeping her hand around the room.

Grace looked around and saw that there were boxes of tissues at every place a person could possibly sit.

"You expected me to use all these?"

"Well, I didn't know how cried out you'd be, so I wanted to be prepared."

Grace reached out to hug her. "You crazy, wonderful friend. What would I ever do without you?"

"I'm sure I don't know," Karen said with a yawn, "but can we think on that tomorrow…well, actually later today?"

"Thanks for picking me up in the middle of the night."

"Anytime, Gracie Lou. 'Sure you have everything you need?"

"Well, I'm absolutely sure I have enough Kleenex!"

Karen laughed as she turned out the lights. "See you in a few."

Minutes later Grace sank into the wonderfully comfortable bed and gave a sigh of pleasure. It felt good to be here. Better in fact, than she'd felt since…she didn't have a name for it. The Disaster, the Shattering, the Betrayal…who could even find a horrible enough word to describe all that the situation encompassed? But here in the warmth of Karen's home, for the first time in months, she thought that her unknown future might possibly hold something good.

It was then that she was reminded of the handsome cowboy with pain in his nice, brown eyes. Zach Clayton. Who knew what his story was? It was highly unlikely she'd ever see him again, but she really hoped that he would somehow make it through whatever was troubling him.

Grace stretched out her hand as she had done when Zach helped her through the take-off. Her mind perfectly recalled the strength of that hand and its warmth as it curled around hers. The memory comforted her, and with a sigh, she drifted off to sleep.

CHAPTER 4

Despite his late night, Zach awoke at daylight with the sense that something important had taken place the evening before. He lay still, allowing his memory to bring up the source of this feeling that things were good in his life…something he hadn't felt in an exceptionally long time. His heart quickened with joy as he remembered making things right with his Lord. The image of a pretty blonde with blue eyes appeared—Grace Morgan, the woman from the plane. The positive feeling was immediately followed with a sinking sensation. He had no idea how she could be contacted.

"But I don't want to contact her!" he said out loud, swinging his long legs out of the bed and heading to the bathroom. He lathered his face with shaving cream then met his eyes in the mirror.

"All right…I would like to see her again, but only because I know I missed God last night. I was supposed to talk to her, pray with her…I don't know…help her in some way."

Still, a sense of loss created heaviness in his heart as Zach made coffee. He waited impatiently for it to brew then opened the patio doors to the balcony that overlooked several acres of pasture where horses were already grazing in the early morning light.

This scene always brought him pleasure and this morning was no exception. Frequent rains in the past few weeks had produced lush green grass for the livestock. This helped in reducing the feed bill and created a beautiful landscape as well.

Zach thought back to the conversation with Jim on the way home from the airport. He knew his friend would stay on as interim pastor if he felt it was the Lord's leading, but his fervency last night that Zach needed to be back in the leadership role of the church caused fear to grip Zach. He wasn't ready to be in the pulpit and he couldn't handle dealing with the needs of a congregation yet. As he had told Jim, he didn't know how to do it without Sasha. She had been a natural with people, always willing to hear their problems and so good at receiving wisdom from God to help them.

He and Sasha had gone to seminary together, started Cornerstone Cowboy Church together. He simply couldn't imagine pastoring alone. The thought terrified him. But he couldn't see himself pastoring with any other woman either, so he still came up blank.

"Remember our conversation last night? the Voice interrupted Zach's thoughts.

"Did you not agree to trust Me?"

Zach sighed, "Yes, Lord, I did."

"Then…Amen."

He couldn't help smiling, "Yes, so be it, Lord."

Setting aside his coffee cup Zach reached for his Bible that he kept on the small table there. It was obvious that it had been unused for a while. Ashamed, he wiped off the accumulated dust and opened it at random. An underlined verse stood out—Psalm 42: 11.

"Why are you cast down, O my soul" And why are you disquieted within me? Hope in God; for I shall yet praise Him, the help of my countenance and my God."

Tears filled Zach's eyes as the truth of the words filled his heart. "I *will* trust You, Lord. You have been my hope since long before I met Sasha. I don't know why I had to lose her, but I set my heart in agreement with the scripture that I will yet praise you, that I will live in joy and fulfill Your purpose in my life…whether alone or with a mate."

He felt hope rising within him, and again the face of Grace Morgan filled his thoughts.

"Whatever her situation is, Lord, please bring hope to her, too."

Zach felt drawn to his guitar. It too, had been gathering dust, at least the case was. He had spent untold hours through the years playing that old Gibson, worshiping the Lord, both privately and with others. Shamefully, he tried to remember the last time he had played it. Probably not long after Sasha had been diagnosed with cancer because their lives had gone crazy after that.

""Sorry for neglecting you, ole buddy," he said as he lifted the guitar from the case. He walked back to his chair on the patio then winced as he strummed a chord.

"You are some kind of out of tune, Gib!"

Within a few minutes he managed to bring the old strings into an acceptable state of pitch and began to softly sing worship songs.

The sweet presence of the Lord filled his heart with a familiar healing joy.

Finally, he just sat and looked up to the heavens. "Oh, God, I didn't even realize how much I missed this. Thank You for giving it back to me. How did I ever think I could live without Your presence in my life?

Zach continued to play softly as the melody in his mind flowed to his fingers. It had been years since he'd written a new song, but he could feel it coming. He hurried into the apartment and returned with pen and paper. He wrote the lyrics that were coming so quickly, sang them, fitting them into the melody that was also flowing unbidden.

An hour later it was finished, and he sang and played it altogether:

I don't know just how You do it
Lord, I stand amazed
You take my broken pieces
And make me whole again
I won't make You promises
That I fear I cannot keep
But I trust You Lord to be here
Beside me when I'm weak.

For unlike me, You are faithful
Unlike me, You are strong
Unlike me, in my weakness
You still love me when I'm wrong

How could I think You'd leave me
In my time of greatest need
Why did I doubt Your presence, Lord
When the path I could not see
For You are love personified
Your grace so full and free
And I'm so glad, I'm so glad
You're unlike me

* * * * *

Grace smelled the coffee before opening her eyes. She turned over and snuggled back into her pillow. This bed alone had been worth coming to Texas for, and she wasn't ready to give it up yet. She dozed lightly for another few minutes, then decided she may as well get up; there would be no more sleeping.

She could hear Karen's printer from across the hall, so she was obviously already up and busy. Out of habit Grace turned and made the bed as soon as she was out of it. Arranging the throw pillows she gave the bed a final pat.

"You and I have a date for tonight," she told it.

A few minutes later she joined Karen, who was now pouring coffee for the two of them.

"Good morning. I heard you up and around," Karen said with a smile.

"'Morning to you, too. You were not kidding about that bed. I've never slept on one so comfortable." She slid onto a barstool as Karen placed a cup of coffee in front of her.

"I knew you'd like it. So, now what? 'Still up for lunch out?"

"Yes, I'm hungry."

"I thought I'd take it easy on you today, let you get over jet lag from your flight. After we eat, I'll drive you around and show you any businesses you might need while I'm gone. Maybe we can find a few sales we can't resist."

"I'd like that," Grace said. A shadow crossed her face. "I've been lying low in LA just to avoid the paparazzi. I need some summer things. I've dropped at least ten pounds during this nightmare."

"I'm so sorry you had to go through that," Karen said. "Hopefully, it won't happen here. I know the garbage has been broadcast all over the country, but you really do look different. Going blonde was a good move."

Grace nodded. "My friend, Marla, puts together wardrobes for stars there in Hollywood. She got me out of the tailored pant suits and into things with a younger look. I haven't been recognized or bothered since the makeover."

"Good!" Karen said. "Hey, how about having a movie marathon this evening like we used to do? I've got Netflix with an endless supply."

"Got popcorn and junk food?"

"Are you kidding?" Karen opened the pantry door and began to name off all their favorites from years ago plus several new ones. "And there's ice cream in the freezer."

"You did this just for me," Grace said with a scolding look at her friend. "I know you don't eat this way anymore."

"No, but I have to admit, I got excited at the thought of a chocolate sundae with nuts and whipped cream. We can celebrate you coming here and get it all out of our systems!"

Grace rolled her eyes. "I probably shouldn't buy any smaller clothes. I've got a feeling I'm going to put those ten pounds back on before you leave for your trip."

"Well we don't have to eat all this stuff. I guarantee you; my students will scarf up any leftovers in no time. I keep a big jar on my desk with snacks in it. I know some of them are working their way through school and don't have much money for food. I've never forgotten what that was like."

Grace cocked her head and smiled at her friend. "Do they call you 'Professor Softie?'"

"Not to my face," Karen smiled back, "but it does seem to promote a positive student/teacher relationship."

"I bet it does." Grace drained her coffee cup and set it on the counter. "Okay, I'm headed for the shower. 'Leave here in about forty-five minutes?"

"Forty-five works," Karen nodded.

* * * * *

"Oh, that was good!" Grace said, pushing her empty plate away as she held her stomach. "I did everything but lick the platter."

A pleasant waitress approached with a coffee pot. "Would you like more coffee, Ma'am?"

"Yes, please. "Grace pushed her cup toward the girl. "And please tell the cook that I really enjoyed my breakfast."

The girl smiled. "Yes, Ma'am."

"I love this Southern graciousness," Grace said as the server walked away.

"You're not insulted by the 'Ma'am?" Karen asked. "Some women are. They think it insinuates that they're old."

"Well, I think it's sweet and polite." Grace leaned back in her seat. "So, what have you got up your sleeve for tomorrow? You hinted at things to come."

Karen pushed her plate aside and finished her orange juice. "Let's see…tomorrow's Friday…oh, yes, this should be fun. She pulled a brochure from her purse. "I have signed us up for a tour of Galveston's most interesting tourist attractions, ending with a cook-out on the beach with a moonlight sing-along around a campfire."

"That does sound like fun. We'd best not forget the sunscreen, though. 'Looks like a lot of time in and out of the sun before the moonlight arrives."

"We're to meet the tour guide at one o'clock, then go by bus to the various places of interest, have some free time for lunch and shopping, then ride to the beach for a steak dinner and the campfire/singing time, then back to our vehicles."

"That will be a full day. I've always wanted to see the historical mansions here. My only real time spent in Texas was in the Dallas area when…Damien…we...came to a ministerial conference."

She unconsciously put her hand on her heart. Would it ever stop hurting when she said his name?

Karen leaned toward her. "Are you all right?" She asked softly.

Grace took a deep breath. "I will be."

CHAPTER 5

The cloudless blue sky gave promise of a beautiful afternoon as Karen and Grace drove toward Galveston Island. The traffic was light on the causeway and the sun sparkled like floating diamonds on the calm water of the bay.

"This is so beautiful," Grace murmured.

Karen nodded. "You know, I've lived in Friendswood for five years and I've only driven over to Galveston twice. I have always said I wanted to do the tourist thing and see the historic homes, but not badly enough to come alone. The friends I've made here have all been so many times and don't want to pay the fees just to accompany me." She reached over to take Grace's hand. "So, I'm glad you're here, Gracie Lou."

"Grace squeezed her friend's hand. "I'm glad I'm here, too. I feel like a huge weight has been lifted from my shoulders."

"You are welcome to stay with me as long as you like, Grace. My place is open to you permanently if you want it. Even if you don't stay with me, I'd be thrilled to have you in the area. There are lots of nice rentals and homes for sale, too."

"Thanks, Karen. It's nice to feel that I can just 'be' for a while. I know this won't last forever…I'll be wanting something to do, some direction for the future, but at least the hounds are not after me and I'm not constantly reminded of the horror of these past few months."

Grace was interrupted by the female voice of the GPS giving Karen driving directions. As they exited the causeway, they could see the lime green tour bus with pictures of tourist sites painted on it. "Sunshine Tours," and a smiling, bright, yellow sun completed the advertisement.

Karen pulled into a parking space in the area signed as "Tour Parking," and fit the sunshade over the windshield.

"I have the bag with our water and sunscreen," Grace said as she opened the car door.

"I guess we'll need our purses since we're expected as tourists to spend money," Karen quipped.

Grace laughed. "I've got mine, though I did try to lighten it before we left."

They joined the growing stream of people headed toward the bus and the man taking tickets or money. He wore a ball cap and tourist guide vest, but Grace thought there was something familiar about him. Surely not, she didn't know anyone in Texas except KK. He was making change for a customer and then looked up at the man, smiling as he gave him his money.

Grace froze, grabbing Karen by the arm.

"Karen! It's him, the man from the plane…Zach Clayton!"

Grace had not mentioned Zach to Karen, so she was surprised at her friend's reaction to seeing the man.

"Hmm, 'you been keeping secrets from me, Gracie Lou?"

Grace had turned her back to the bus and its owner and her face was flushed. "He…he…held my hand…just to help me through take-off." She took a deep breath. "He…was…nice."

Karen pursed her lips and shook her head. "Just…nice…and you're shaking like a leaf. If he had that kind of effect on you, I think I'd better go check him out. After all, we're going to be spending the entire day with him."

"Wait, KK!" Grace held onto her friend. "I didn't think I'd ever see him again. We didn't exchange any contact info or anything."

'Well, well. This is interesting. I can't wait to see his reaction to your showing up. Come on, all the other people have gone to the bus and he's looking at us like he's wondering what we're up to."

"Ooh, is my face still red?" Grace asked and smoothed her hair.

"Only a little," Karen fibbed.

Grace turned around and they started walking toward Zach. He had a smile on his face – an "I'm a friendly vendor and you're a customer," smile.

Grace couldn't look at him, but Karen saw it all. The shock, the pleasure, then something she couldn't quite define…guilt?"

"Grace?" he started walking toward her.

"Hi…umm…hi, Zach. "This is your business?"

"Yeah…my…business…I didn't think I'd see you again."

"I know…me either."

The awkward silence gave Karen an opportunity to move things along.

She extended the tickets. "Hi, I'm Karen Scott, Grace's friend. I bought us tickets for the tour today."

"Oh, yes, the tour." Other customers had come to stand behind them, so Zach shifted back into the tour guide mode.

"You can choose seats on the bus if you like. We'll be pulling out in about twelve minutes," he said with a glance at his watch. His face softened, "I'm really glad to see you again, Grace."

Grace couldn't help looking up into those kind brown eyes. "Me, too, Zach," is all she could manage to squeak out.

As they walked away Karen could hardly contain her excitement. "I love it, love it, love it!" she said under her breath. "From the look on his face I bet he's been kicking himself for not getting your phone number, and then you show up to take his tour! This is too good." Reaching the bus, she said, "Let's see if the seats right behind him are taken."

"No, Karen, that's too obvious!" Grace protested.

"What is obvious, is that he is really glad you're here and will be delighted to have you nearby."

Most of the tourists were already seated when they boarded the bus, but no one was in the seat directly behind the driver's chair.

"See, it was meant to be," Karen whispered as she slid into the seat and over to the window.'

Grace sighed as she settled in. "You know I didn't come here looking for a man. I'm not ready for that, and I don't know if I ever will be."

Karen just looked at her. "And sometimes God has other plans."

They could see Zach talking to customers and watched him through the window.

"I would never have guessed him to be a tour guide," Grace said. "A ranch foreman or full-time cowboy maybe. I wonder how he got into this. "

"Maybe we'll get a chance to ask him sometime today," Karen mused.

"Just don't get too personal. I've got a feeling he's been through something really painful."

"Aha, that compassionate sensitivity is still at work, I see."

Zach's face brightened when he saw them in the front seat "Hi, again. 'Glad you're here, "he said as his eyes met Grace's.

Then he addressed the bus load of people, getting a head count for future reference.

"Thank you all for choosing Sunshine Tours for your introduction to Galveston. We'll be going directly to some of the historical homes, but then we'll stop for lunch in an area where you can take your pick of several restaurants and shops. We'll set a time to meet back at the bus, and in fairness to everyone else, I'll only wait for ten minutes past the set time if we have any stragglers, and then we'll be moving out. I hope no one gets left behind, but if you do, it will be up to you to find a way to reconnect with us or get back to your vehicle."

He grinned at the group. "This lime green bus is pretty visible, (the people laughed) so you could likely find us on the beach."

Zach reached into a box near his seat and pulled out several watches. "Is there anyone who doesn't have a watch or a cell phone for the time?" No one lifted a hand.

"Okay, 'no excuses for getting back to the bus on time, then."

Even though Zach made his point clearly, he did it with a smile and a manner that wasn't like laying down rules. She liked that. She also liked the sound of his voice as he gave historical information about Galveston over the intercom as he drove. Several times she looked up and met his eyes in his rear-view mirror. Why did that cause a reaction in her insides?

Zach drove the bus down Seawall Boulevard to give the tourists a look at the seaside businesses and the beautiful gentle waves that seemed to go on forever. Then he took them to the historic Bishop's Palace and the Moody Mansion.

Grace tried to focus on the information about the lovely old building, but despite her efforts, her mind was always aware of Zach's presence and the sound of his voice.

She loved the way his expression could go from sober to an instant smile that lit up his eyes. She didn't think she was imagining that he was looking at her as frequently as she was at him.

Often, he was at her side, taking her arm and gently directing her to some interesting exhibit. She found herself wanting to slip her hand into his, as though it belonged there. Once his hand brushed hers as they walked, and it felt as though he almost took it…like the night on the plane. Her heart leapt at that memory.

…Karen…where was she? She needed her friend's solidarity. Grace looked around and spotted her across the room, reading a posting of facts about the building. She made her way over to join her.

Karen took one look at her and said, "Why don't we get some fresh air?"

Outside they found a bench and sat down. "Okay, give …you look as frazzled as a Raggedy Ann."

"It's my reaction to Zach," Grace said quietly. "I swear I feel like a teenager with a movie-star crush. I didn't even act like this over Damien. When he comes close to me my heart pounds so hard, I'm afraid he can hear it."

Karen grinned. "Oh my, you do have it bad."

"What am I going to do?"

"You're really asking me? Just see where it goes, I guess, Gracie. You know…God just may be in this. You met a stranger on a plane, never expected to see him again, neither of you has any way to contact the other, and yet, here you are together with sparks flying like fireworks."

"That's not true!"

"Yes, my friend, it is. A person would have to be blind to miss it, and even then, they could feel the heat. Tell me — if you can get past the outward jitters to the root of these feelings, what do you sense? Is it good; does it feel right?

Grace sat quietly for a few moments, then looked up at Karen. "Yes…it does," she said, in surprise.

"Well, let me share some advice I heard from a speaker at a Christian singles' conference once. He said that when the possibility of a new relationship presented itself, instead of running away from it, he moved toward it. He said if we run away because of our own hang-ups we'll never know if that relationship could be the one God was bringing to us. Moving into the relationship will help us to know that person and find out if we have something to build on. If you see early on that there's not enough there to continue, he advised ending it so there's less hurt for everyone."

"That sounds reasonable," Grace agreed. "I just don't know if I'm ready for this."

"One step at a time, friend – forward."

They looked up to see people from their tour group approaching. "There you are!" One of the ladies said, "I think Zach was looking for you."

"Oh, I'm sorry," Grace said, standing, "I'll go find him."

Grace went quickly back into the building and looked around for Zach. When she found him, he was peering into a hallway and didn't see her. "Zach," she called.

He wheeled around and relief filled his face. In a moment he was in front of her and took her by the arms.

"Grace, I thought I'd lost you."

Seeing his genuine concern, Grace apologized. "I'm so sorry, Zach." I didn't mean to cause you to worry. Karen and I went outside to wait for the rest of you. I won't do it again."

"Nonsense." Without thinking he pulled her into a quick hug, then felt awkward." I'm the paranoid one."

Seeing his embarrassment, she touched him on the arm.

"You're just being a good tour guide…watching out for your tourists. Let's go join the others."

"Okay, folks, I found our lost tour guide," she called when they joined the group. Everyone laughed as they began to walk back to the bus. Zach drove to a central location on the strand and stopped for them to disembark.

Bending his head to stand, he gave instructions for the return time.

"There are all sorts of restaurants and interesting shops to occupy your time and spend a lot of your hard-earned money. I have to park the bus on a side street, but I'll pick you up at this intersection at…what time?"

"Three-thirty!" the busload of people answered back.

"You got it. See you then." He turned to Grace, "Will you ladies be all right?"

Grace smiled. "I see stores—we'll be fine."

That smile flashed again, and his eyes rested on her face.

"I'll miss you," he thought, then blushed as he stepped back to let them pass. "Have a good time. "See you at three-thirty."

Karen and Grace watched the bus pull away. "He's got it even worse than you, Gracie. I wish I knew his story. You're going to have to get it out of him. We should have more time down at the beach."

"But that means I'll have to tell him mine, KK. I'm just not sure I want to do that yet."

"Well, let's choose a place to eat…my stomach's growling."

"Mine, too. Let's go."

They walked for a bit, taking their time choosing a place to have lunch. They finally decided on a fresh-looking diner with an outdoor seating area. It was too lovely a day to give up the beautiful outdoors.

Grace had seen a server deliver a beautiful chef salad to another customer, so she quickly made that her choice and laid aside the menu. As she looked up, she saw a familiar figure entering a bar down the street.

"Karen!" She grabbed her friend's arm.

Surprised, Karen looked up. "What?"

" I just saw Zach entering that sleazy - looking bar down the street."

"Karen followed her gaze and softly said, "Wow, I didn't see that coming. He didn't seem the type. You know, he's going to be driving us around for a few more hours. I don't know about this."

The server came to take their order then, but Grace couldn't shake the disappointment she felt. This whole Zach situation was too new to even think about what she expected from him, but drinking was certainly not in the picture. Why did she feel this ache inside at the loss of something that had not even begun?

* * * * *

Zach squinted as he entered the darkness of the Beachside Bar. How he hated coming into this place! If he wanted to see his mother though, it meant coming here because this was her hangout from mid-morning until the bar closed. At least the regulars were kind to her, and someone always saw her home safely.

Zach barely remembered his little sister. He wasn't quite four when she had died from pneumonia. Never an emotionally strong person, Amelia Clayton had found the loss of her baby girl a tragedy from which she could not recover.

Zach just remembered that his once happy mother stopped smiling, laughing, and living. Friends from the church they attended came around at first, but when Amelia's depression deepened none of them knew how to deal with it. Her constant rejection of their efforts to comfort her finally drove them away.

After a few years of this despondency she had found relief in alcohol. It's addictive tentacles quickly entangled her and brought an end to any sense of normalcy for her family. Mostly for Zach's benefit his father forbade her to drink in the home. Still a caring husband he did everything he could to help the woman he loved, but there was no desire on her part to live without the substance that eased her private pain.

After years of living with the shame of a wife who spent most of her waking hours in a bar and came home every night inebriated, he had divorced her. Surprisingly to Zach, Walter Clayton had signed up with an online dating site for seniors and had found love again with a kind woman who also served the Lord. It was their wedding Zach had attended in California when he met Grace on the plane.

Grace…what would she think of him if she saw him now? What would she think of his mother? Sasha had been kind to her, but Amelia only let her in to the point of acknowledging that she was married to Zach. It seemed she wanted no relationships other than those of her drinking friends.

Even Zach felt that she only tolerated his visits. Perhaps he was a reminder of her failures and the guilt was too much. Whatever the source of her distance, Zach felt the responsibility of checking on her regularly and seeing that she had what she needed.

He saw her now, in the farthest booth. *Her* corner, she called it, and rightfully so because she got there early and stayed. She had certainly spent enough money on drinks through the years to have purchased that small area.

There was little semblance now of the beautiful woman Amelia Clayton had been as she lifted her beer with a trembling hand. Zach wondered how much longer her body could tolerate this abuse.

"Hey, Preacher," Joe, the owner of the bar called to him. Zach's presence there always seemed to make the patrons a little uneasy, but they also respected him for coming to check on his mother.

"Hi, Joe, 'you doing all right?" Zach smiled at him.

"Every day without a hurricane is a good one," Joe said.

"I can surely agree with that," Zach agreed, shaking his hand.

The summer months always brought the threat of hurricanes in the Gulf and the island city of Galveston knew from experience the devastation that could bring.

Zach made his way to the corner, hating the stench of liquor and the cigarette smoke he was forced to breath.

Amelia looked up and recognized him as he neared her.

"Hello, Son," she said, her eyes already bloodshot. Her hair was almost totally gray now with only a few strands of the pretty blond it once was. Little effort had been taken to make it neat. There had been a time when she would never step outside her home without every hair in place and her make-up done. That remembrance brought pain to Zach's heart.

He bent down and kissed her cheek. "Hey, Mom, how are you?"

"I'm fine," she replied, her voice as shaky as her hands. She motioned to the seat opposite her. "Have a seat."

"'Need something to drink, Preacher?" Joe called.

"Sure, I'll have a Coke…and one of those premade sandwiches you've got. I don't care what kind."

Amelia smiled. "You never were a fussy eater…you ate everything in sight."

"I was a growing boy, Mom."

"That you were, and you didn't stop 'til you outgrew your dad."

Zach smiled. "That had been a big day for him, the day he measured a half inch taller than his dad on the kitchen doorframe.

"Thanks, Joe," he said as the bar owner placed a chicken salad sandwich, a Coke, and a bag of chips in front of him.

Amelia took another drink of her beer. "Did you go to your father's wedding?" she asked.

Zach finished chewing the first bite of his sandwich before swallowing and replied, "Yes, I did."

"What's she like?" Amelia asked.

Zach knew she was referring to his father's new wife.

"She seems nice. We didn't have much time to talk. There were a lot of friends there that she and dad fellowship with."

She gave a wry smile. "He always wanted us to have friends. I ruined all that. But I'm glad he's happy; he deserves it. Your father is a good man."

"Yes, he is." Zach laid down his sandwich and reached across the table to take his mother's hand in his. "Mom let me take you out of this place…out of this life. I'll get a bigger place and we can live together. I'll take care of you."

"I can't, Zach," Amelia said, looking him in the eyes. "I can't live without the bottle. You're a preacher. It's bad enough that I'm in your life at all. I won't bring shame to you by bringing this into your home."

"But Mom…."

"Enough said, Zachary!" Amelia's voice was sharp now. "Find

you another nice wife and forget about me."

"Neither of those things is easy to do," he said.

"Perhaps not, but they're not impossible. Now eat your sandwich. Do you have a tour to get back to?"

"Yes, in an hour or so."

"That gives you time for a nap before picking up your tourists."

For a few minutes they sat in silence as Zach finished eating and Amelia finished her beer. Rolling up his napkin and chip bag Zach looked up at his mother.

"How about I come one day next week and take you to lunch someplace nice?"

Amelia sighed, "Don't bother, Son. I don't have any interest in going anywhere and I don't like you coming here. You don't belong in this place."

Zach stood and bent to kiss her forehead. "Neither do you, Mom. I love you." He dropped several twenties on the table, then turned and quickly walked out before the tears came.

He felt so helpless. He'd do anything to bring his mother up out of the cesspool of her life, but she didn't want help from him or anyone else.

When he got back to the bus Zach changed his shirt then headed for the seashore and sat on a bench. The wind would hopefully blow the bar stench from his hair.

CHAPTER 6

The group of tour passengers were gathered at the meeting place when Zach pulled up in his bus just before three-thirty. Most were carrying packages…some people more than a few. Zach pushed the doors open and stepped down to the curb. His eyes moved over the group of tourists until they rested on Grace, then he blushed as though he'd been caught. He busied himself with helping package-laden passengers to board the bus.

Grace and Karen had both found a couple of summer blouses which only required one bag each. As the moving line brought Grace to where he stood Zach steeled himself to keep interaction with her casual. Was he imagining that he felt a distance originating from her, too?

"Did you enjoy your time, Grace? He took her hand to help her board. Though Grace had already decided that there could be nothing between them his touch produced a spark that ran all the way up her arm and left her feeling breathless. She could barely answer as she met his eyes.

"Yes, uh…it was fun."

"Karen. I see you found something," he said, pointing to her bag. He gave her a hand-up as well.

Karen smiled. "I did indeed, Zach."

After everyone was seated Zach did a head count and found all tourists accounted for.

"All right, folks," he said into the microphone. "Are you ready for a little pirate history?"

The reply from the passengers was positive so he began to tell about the French pirate, Jean Lafitte and his role in Texas and Louisiana history. He confessed that as a boy he and his friends spent their summers seeking for Lafitte's buried treasure rumored to have been hidden in many places along the Gulf coast.

"If you're wondering if we found any of that gold…just remember, I'm the owner of this old green bus, telling you stories for hire!" He smiled good naturedly as the people laughed.

Grace met his eyes in the rear-view mirror and almost started at the connection that she felt. Although Zach was laughing and Smiling for his passengers, Grace could see the pain in his eyes. She couldn't help herself, she wanted to reach out and touch him…to somehow ease that pain. Dropping her eyes before he read her thoughts, Grace struggled to concentrate on the historical sites of interest Zach was pointing out. She lost track of time as she gave in to the soothing sound of his voice, hoping she'd never have to repeat the information he was sharing.

The spell was broken as Grace realized Zach was slowing the bus. In moments he had driven off the pavement and onto a narrow dirt road that led to a rock-lined cove.

"I'm trusting that you all live somewhere else and won't be coming back to crowd my favorite beach spot," Zach said, "but I'm willing to share it with you for a few hours."

He turned off the motor and stood. "I'm sure you're ready for a break from both my voice and my bus. It will take a little time for me to get things set up and your steaks going on the grill. I'm shooting for dinner to be served at five-thirty, so enjoy God's beautiful outdoors.

"I'll have lawn chairs out in a bit," he continued. "You can set them up here and watch me work or take them down to the water's edge so the waves can lap your feet. Remember that the tide is coming in, though; you may have to move your chairs back before you find yourselves in the Gulf! If that's your desire and you brought swim wear, you may change in our enormous bus restroom."

Everyone laughed, knowing the size of that facility.

"Gotta get busy now. Walk the beach if you like…just don't be late for dinner." Zach started to exit the bus. "I don't want your steaks to be overcooked."

With a grin he was gone, but not before giving Grace a hand as she rose and walked down the bus steps.

"Enjoy the beach," he said, his eyes lighting up as they met hers.

Grace blushed as she shook her head in agreement and Zach reached to give Karen a hand.

Grace and Karen walked toward the beach. "So, what's it going to be, Gracie Lou? We didn't bring swimsuits, so we can sit by the water, or walk a bit."

"Is there any chance I might find a sand dollar?" Grace asked. "I've always wanted to find one, but never have."

"We can give it a try. A few pretty seashells might add to the décor in your room, too."

As they walked Grace glanced back over her shoulder to make certain they were out of Zach's hearing. He saw him hurriedly unloading coolers from the open cargo side of the bus. Unlike his normal easy-going attitude, he seemed harried.

"I don't know, Karen. I don't believe Zach has been drinking. I was close enough to him that I think I would have smelled it. But what reason would he have had to go to that bar?"

Karen shrugged. "Things aren't always how they appear. Maybe we should give him the benefit of the doubt until there's reason to do differently."

"Well, it certainly didn't change his effect on me. I nearly melt when he touches me. This is crazy!"

She looked back and saw that Zach was still quickly moving things from the bus and then going back to check on the grill. Suddenly, Grace stopped and put her hand on Karen's arm.

"KK, he needs help. I…I know it in here. "She put her hand on her middle.

Karen had years of seeing that look on Grace's face and had never known her to be wrong. Turning around, she grinned. "Then, let's go."

Quickly they walked back to where Zach stood looking down into a cooler as though he'd never seen its contents and hadn't a clue what to do with them.

"Hey, Mr. Tour Guide/Chef! We've seen sand and water and thought it might be more fun to come back here and see if you could use a little help." Grace smiled up at him.

The look on Zach's face was priceless, almost like a little boy when something he'd hoped for comes true.

"You are definitely angels," he said in relief. Then he swallowed deeply and met Grace's eyes. This is the first time I've tried to do this without my wife…my late wife."

"Oh, Zach," Grace almost whispered. So, this was the pain she had seen in his eyes. She couldn't help reaching out to touch his arm.

"I'm so sorry, Zach," Karen said gently. "I'm sure it will take both of us to do what she did but point us in the right direction and we'll get this thing rolling!"

Karen's upbeat approach was just what they needed.

"I guess the first thing is to get the tables set up for the food." Zach said. "The menu list is inside that clear plastic tub…well all kinds of lists…things that need to be set out."

"We can handle the tables, Zach," Grace said, seeing the lightweight folded tables propped against the side of the bus. "Where would you like them?

"Anywhere in this area for the food, paper goods and utensils," he pointed, "and just a little further over for everyone to sit and eat."

"Gottcha!" Karen called as she and Grace headed for the tables.

Within minutes the tables were up, covered with cloths and waiting for the food that would be set out closer to serving time. Charcoal was heating in the grill as Zach rubbed down the steaks with his own special seasoning mix.

Soon the smell of steaks cooking on the grill filled the air as Zach carefully tended them to make certain he had the right number cooked to the tourists' preferences. He would never have been able to do that and set everything up, too. As they worked Grace looked up several times to see his eyes on her and his appreciation was evident.

There are desserts in that cooler over there, Grace," he called to her, nodding his head toward the appropriate container.

"Okay," she called back and headed for the cooler. Opening it, she exclaimed," Oh my! Karen, look at these."

Karen joined her and looked into the cooler. There were individually sized pies in at least six different flavors. "I think I'll skip the steak and go straight to dessert! I wonder who made all this wonderful food for Zach. Somehow I don't see him in the kitchen."

"He does look cute in that apron, though," Grace whispered, sneaking another peek at Zach flipping steaks in his barbecue apron.

Karen shook her head. "You are done for, Grace Morgan."

Grace giggled and lifted out a box of the pies and Karen took another. They arranged them at the end of the table and covered them with a cloth. Karen checked the list that included all the tasks to be accomplished before eating.

Folks who had been walking the beach were returning now as it was getting closer to mealtime. Karen found a couple of men who were glad to oblige her request to move the drink container. Grace walked over to the grill and offered Zach a bottle of cold water which he gladly received.

"How're you coming there, Chef?"

After downing half the bottle of water, Zach smiled and handed it back to her to hold. "We're close."

Checking his watch, he put on the last four steaks. "These are the rare steaks, so we'll be eating soon…thanks to you and Karen. There's no way I would have made it without your help. This whole thing would have been a disaster. I don't know why I thought I could manage it alone."

"We were glad to help. Actually, it was fun." Grace meant it. She had enjoyed herself immensely. For the first time in months she felt she was filling a need, and that brought her pleasure.

Suddenly, a blur of little boys in swimsuits crashed into Zach and nearly knocked him down.

"Pastor Zach!" All three of them were grabbing him at their own levels and hugging him for all they were worth.

"We've missed you, Pastor Zach!"

"Where've you been, Pastor?"

"I got a new bike for my birthday. You've got to see it!"

To Grace's surprise Zach was grinning from ear to ear as he pulled each of the little boys up to his chest and hugged them warmly.

"Robbie, you've grown a foot since I saw you last."

"Max, where are your front teeth?"

"How's your Little League team doing, Carson?"

A young couple walked up then, also in beach attire. "'Sorry for the attack, Pastor Zach. When the boys saw your bus there was no stopping them." Both of them came closer and hugged Zach, too.

"It's good to see you Lana…Bruce." He looked at them for a moment then gathered them into his arms again. "Really good." There were tears in his eyes when he let them go this time, and Grace saw that there were also tears in theirs.

"We've really missed you, Pastor. How are you?"

"I'm making progress…in fact, this is my first tour since…" He stopped and the couple nodded knowingly.

"But I never would have made it without the help of these two ladies." He looked over at Grace and Karen who were a few feet away. "Grace, Karen, I'd like to introduce you to my friends, Lana and Bruce Caldwell and their boys…who are already headed for the water…Carson, Max, and Robbie."

Lana was a pretty young woman with light brown hair and large hazel eyes. She stepped up to Grace and Karen and took each of their hands. "Thank you so much for helping Pastor Zach today. He's a very special person to us."

Bruce, too, had a genuine smile as he shook their hands.

"Oh, my," Zach exclaimed. "I forgot I have rare steaks on the grill. Excuse me, ladies, I'd better check on them." Bruce followed him and Lana checked on their sons with a quick look toward the water.

"So, Zach is your pastor, Lana?" Grace asked.

"Yes…well, he was…I guess you could say he still is. He stepped down for a while when his wife, Sasha, died from cancer, but it's been three years now. None of us thought it would be that long. We're all really concerned about him. Pastor Jim Sheridan, his associate, has been filling in for him, but has us to pray for Pastor Zach every service. We are all still feeling a little lost without him. You'll never find a better pastor. You can see how my boys love him."

Grace laughed. "I didn't know what had attacked him at first."

"What's the name of your church, Lana?" Karen asked.

"It's Cornerstone Cowboy Church, out on Fryer Road, "Lana said. "I'd love for you to come to our church, Grace, and Karen. Do you live in this area?"

"Yes, I've been in Friendswood for five years. Grace and I met as college roommates and have remained friends. This is her first extended visit to Texas."

"I'll have to admit, I'd like to visit a cowboy church," Grace said.

"Please come. Our Sunday service starts at ten-thirty. Maybe you could get Pastor Zach to come with you."

"Uh…I really don't know him. That might be a bit awkward, don't you think? The people might not appreciate a woman other than Sasha being with him."

Lana laughed. "Most of our people would be delighted to see our pastor with a woman in his life, to help him heal. The only ones who would resent you are the ones who want to be that woman themselves!"

"And are there very many of those? Karen asked.

"Several," Lana emphasized. "A few very determined ones, but Pastor wasn't the least bit interested."

They were looking now at Zach as he turned steaks and talked to Bruce.

"Well, he *is* an attractive man, and I've already seen that he's kind."

"They just don't come any better," Lana said.

As if he heard their conversation, Zach turned and met Grace's eyes. He smiled and her heart did that crazy flip again.

"Are you girls ready to eat? I think these steaks are just about perfect."

The ladies walked over to join the men at the grill.

"Bruce…Lana, you guys want to join us for dinner?" Zach asked.

"Thanks, but the boys are all excited that we're roasting wieners and marshmallows after some playtime in the water. We'll let you get back to taking care of your tourists," Bruce said. He and Lana shared hugs with Zach again, telling him how good it was to see him.

"I'll be looking for you at church," Lana told Grace and Karen. Zach's eyes opened wider at her comment, but he didn't say anything.

"Is this a good time to set out all the food?" Karen asked.

"Perfect time," Zach answered.

Within minutes of his ringing the dinner bell the line had formed at the grill where the tourists were picking up their steaks.

Karen and Grace stood behind the table aiding anyone who needed help scooping food or carrying plates. When everyone was seated, they fixed their own plates and picked up their steaks from Zach at the grill.

"Save me a place: I'll be right there," Zach told Karen.

Moans of pleasure were heard up and down the table as people took their first bites of steak. Everything was delicious…the salads, homemade rolls, and the mini pies were a favorite with the guests.

A sing-along by the campfire was included in the tour package, so Zach enlisted the help of willing fellows to build the fire while he went for his guitar. Karen and Grace cleaned up the tables quickly, placing the left-over food back in the coolers. It was all practically done when Zach returned from the bus with his Gibson.

"Wow, you girls are something else!" he exclaimed when he saw them folding up tables. "Leave those and I'll get them later. I need you to come and help me sing."

He pulled up three lawn chairs and motioned them to sit. He took the third chair and checked his guitar for tuning. After a few tweaks he started strumming. The people were situating themselves around the campfire and looking to Zach with anticipation.

Grace couldn't help smiling with pleasure as he began to sing a familiar camp song. His smooth baritone voice was like warm honey flowing over her. She joined him with higher harmony and Karen filled in with her rich alto. The tourists either sang with them or simply listened to the beautiful trio they made.

No one seemed to object when Zach slipped into familiar Christian songs that some might know. The music seemed to rise and float out over the water in praise to the Creator. Tears of worship flowed down Grace's face as she felt the presence of God bringing healing to her battered soul.

"I'm so sorry, Lord, for not trusting You," she spoke in her thoughts even as she sang.

"I'm sorry I blamed You for Damien's sin. I need You now more than ever and I want you back in first place in my life."

Zach was playing a progression of soft chords with his eyes closed. Grace sensed that he was asking the Lord for direction. Then he began to speak:

"I know this may be more than you bargained for when you signed up for my guided tour of Galveston. I don't mean to be offensive to anyone. You may have beliefs that differ from mine about God, but I feel I need to share some things with you.

"My dad raised me to know God. I accepted Jesus as my savior when I was ten years old and never looked back. I thought that living for Him was the best thing ever, and when I graduated from college I went into seminary to become a pastor. Not long after I completed that schooling, I started my own church.

"Things went well for a few years and then I experienced a shattering life-blow that knocked me out of the game. My beautiful wife who had been beside me throughout this journey died with cancer. I began to doubt the God I had trusted all my life, left the ministry, and began a miserable, Godless existence that held no joy, no life, and certainly nothing that benefitted others."

"I have recently come to grips with my sin of unbelief and I am beginning to take steps upward, out of the pit, you could say. I'm putting my faith out there again, trusting that God's amazing grace is going to completely restore me."

Grace was so moved by Zach's willingness to be vulnerable to a group of strangers, to openly confess his faults to them. She looked over the crowd and saw that there were tears in the eyes of a few of them.

Zach continued. "Maybe you've had a life-devastating blow as well. Perhaps you've never trusted in God's salvation. I'm telling you, close to Him is the safest place we can ever be, even when life happens with all its fury. We may never have the answers we seek…the why's we can't figure out…but we can have His presence to carry us through.

"We're going to sing this beloved old hymn, Amazing Grace, and as we sing, maybe you've got some things you'd like to make right, just between you and God."

Turning to Grace, he said, "Would you take the lead on this one?"

Grace did so and Zach joined Karen in harmony as he played his guitar. The people around the campfire joined in the beautiful sound uniting them in worship. Only God knew the personal decisions made that night, but Grace knew she'd never forget the powerful sense of God's love that fell over that varied group of people from several different states that summer evening on a Texas beach.

Loading all the equipment went quickly as several people volunteered to help. Grace heard several tourists thanking Zach for the special time around the campfire, some mentioning that they had needed the talk he gave. Others expressed sympathy for his loss and the difficult time he'd had. He graciously thanked them all.

Zach and Grace stood together as the last of the tourist boarded the bus. He took her hand and spoke earnestly. "I can never thank you and Karen enough." He paused… "I have to get everyone back to their cars, but can we talk when I don't have deadlines?"

He looked relieved when Grace said, "Yes."

"I need to talk to you about something. Could I call you tomorrow morning? If you wouldn't mind giving me your phone number."

"Sure," Grace said. She gave him her number and told him she would look forward to his call. He stood looking wistfully at her. The thoughts that insisted on racing through his mind were not things he should be thinking, he told himself.

Grace seemed aware of his struggle and spoke up. "Well, everyone's aboard but you and me, Captain. We'd better go." She turned and started up the bus steps.

"All right, folks," Zach said cheerily to the people as he stepped in behind her. "This is our last stage of the Sunshine Guided Tour.

Enjoy the reflection of the moon and stars on Galveston Bay and take that memory home with you."

It was indeed beautiful as they drove back along the waterfront. Grace couldn't quite describe the emotions she felt as she watched the glittering reflections on the water. She knew that this day had changed her somehow for the better.

In the darkness of the bus she looked freely into the rear view mirror at Zach. Once, when lights from nearby businesses made it light enough to see well, Grace met his eyes in the mirror. He looked away, but not before she saw the loneliness and sorrow.

Sitting in the front seat, Grace and Karen had no excuse to linger, so they were some of the first passengers to exit the bus. Zach stood at the steps to give them a hand but released Grace's quickly.

"I'll call you in the morning. Thank you again for everything."

"Goodnight, Zach. It was a lovely day," Grace said.

"Karen, I can't thank you enough for your help. You and Grace saved me." Zach said as he helped Karen from the bus.

Karen laughed. "I can't say it's what I had in mind when I booked this for us, but it couldn't have been any better. I hope things work out well for you, Zach."

She and Grace walked to her car in silence. They were off the beach front and on the causeway toward home when Grace finally spoke. "As my grandmother used to say, 'My, oh my! What a day this has been."

"That's for sure," Karen agreed. "You don't think this is all coincidence, do you?"

Grace laughed. "I think it would take more faith than I have to believe that. I mean…of all the flights between LA and Houston we flew the same flight, sat in the same row…you book tour reservations with an unknown company and it just happens to be owned by the man from the plane who just happens to be a pastor in limbo who just happens to have lost his wife."

Karen added, "And according to Lana, he's had no interest in any other woman since his wife died, but he is definitely interested in you! And you, who wanted nothing to do with another man, especially a preacher, are going teenaged bonkers over *him!*

Grace groaned, holding her head. "Don't remind me!"

"Oh, yes, I will, because I'm delighted that you are not drowning in sorrow over Demon Damien, holding out hope for reconciliation with him!"

"Zach's calling me in the morning," Grace said dreamily. "He said he had something to talk with me about."

"I think he's going to propose."

"Karen!" Grace hit her on the arm. "You are nuts."

"Well, if not tomorrow, soon. I think you, City Girl, are going to be the pastor's wife of a cowboy church."

"I'm not equipped for that. I'd have to become a cowgirl, learn to ride, rope and sing country."

"That's all possible," Karen nodded.

Grace let out a deep breath. "All jesting aside, what do you really think about all this, KK?"

Karen paused a moment before answering. "I think just about everything we've said in jest is exactly the direction God is leading you. I have to admire Zach for opening his heart and telling everyone where he has been in his own walk with the Lord tonight. To share his brokenness took a lot of courage.

"You know, Grace, there was no way to know how many of those people were, 'Church folks.' Zach didn't know, but he was willing to be vulnerable to possibly reach others. And any man who can lead a group of people who were possibly unbelievers into the glorious worship we experienced on that beach…Gracie Lou, that's about as safe as they come."

Grace shook her head slowly. "That was the one thing that concerned me about Damien for years. Worship really didn't mean anything to him. He tolerated it because it was an expected part of the service for everyone else. He stayed in his office practically until time for him to preach. He was always on the worship leader's case to shorten the worship service."

She chuckled. "There were times that the people were so involved in worship that Kevin just couldn't move on. The Holy Spirit found ways to keep it going, even taking it out of Kevin's control when one of the anointed praise leaders would step up with a special song to the Lord. Damien always acted like he agreed with what was happening because he recognized it was the Holy Spirit working, but I knew he was seething inside. I'd hear about it on the way home."

"You mean, even knowing it was the Holy Spirit directing all that, Damien still thought his way was best?"

"He did, indeed. Pure arrogance, huh?"

"Is it any wonder he fell into sin?" Karen mused.

"I'm just sorry that so many people were hurt by his fall. Thousands of people left the church . I don't see how the ones still there can keep things operating. I know they had to let go so many of the staff."

Recalling her ex-husband's tastes, she continued. "He does like to live well. I don't think he's ever had to be concerned about finances, but that may have changed unless his new lady is lining his pockets. Thanks to my efficient attorney his alimony payments to me are not a small sum, so I can't help wondering how he's coming up with it."

"Wouldn't it be payback for real if he's having to get money from his red-headed girlfriend to pay you for cheating on you with *her*?" Karen said, laughing.

Grace laughed, too, and then said, "You know, I really didn't want anything from him other than my share of the house when it sold. I would prefer to be totally free of him, including his money. It has helped while I'm trying to decide which direction I'm to go, but after I'm settled and working, I don't want it anymore."

"Well, on that note, we are home, my friend," Karen said, wheeling into her gated community. "Suddenly, I can't think of anything more appealing than a shower…and there's plenty of water pressure, so we can both take one at the same time."

Grace couldn't help laughing in remembrance of their college days when a draw on the water from any other source in the building practically stopped the flow of the shower, usually when the one showering had a shampoo-lathered head.

"I am really glad to hear that," she said.

CHAPTER 7

"Whoa there, big guy! Frisky this morning, are you?" Zach patted the beautiful black horse that seemed so eager to leave the stall. "Can't blame you for that." He grinned as he thought of how he had awakened this morning with a new sense of hope himself. He hadn't felt this way since Sasha became ill nearly five years ago. He knew that getting things right with the Lord was at the root of it.

Still, he thought of how Grace and Karen had come to his aid and so smoothly had taken care of things as if they'd always been doing the tour with him. And how they had sung with him so beautifully. The Spirit of Christ was evident in Grace as she sang with true worship.

It was just as easy as it had been singing with Sasha at the cookouts. That surprised him. He had been so sure that there was no other woman he could share that with…maybe Jim was right. Thinking of Grace's sweet voice singing Amazing Grace, he began to hum it as he took care of the horses.

Jim Sheridan walked into the barn and stopped in surprise. He stood still and listened as Zach hummed that favorite old hymn. Tears moistened his eyes as he realized God was doing a work in his friend. He folded his arms and leaned against the barn door with his eyes closed, silently thanking the Lord for answered prayers.

Zach turned and saw Jim standing there. "Well, are you going to help with the horses or just stand there?"

Jim grinned. "I was enjoying the concert."

Zach nodded sheepishly, "Yeah, that's one you haven't heard for a while."

"For way too long, brother." Jim grabbed him in a hug.

"Whatever's happening, I'm glad to see it. 'Want to tell me what's going on ?"

Zach laid aside the curry brush and nodded his head. "I've got coffee made; let's go upstairs."

When they were settled on the patio with coffee in hand, Zach took a deep breath.

"First, I want to thank you for being a good enough friend to tell me the ugly truth when I needed it. You were absolutely right−I've been stuck in a horrible place, not helping myself or anyone else. 'Just want you to know I've repented of that, and though I don't have a clue where I'm going from here, things are good between me and God again."

"Man, you don't know how glad I am to hear that, Zach. We were all really getting concerned about you," Jim said.

"I've never in my life been in that mindset where nothing had any meaning or importance to me. I can see now that it's a dangerous place, one void of any sense that God cares. Without that, life has no meaning, no purpose. In that condition the enemy has such power. I believe it has been the prayers of all of you at the church that have kept me sane. All I can say is, thank you for hanging in there for me."

"We love you, Pastor, and as my friend I could hardly bear seeing you in that place. The least I could do was pray."

Zach seemed lost in thought for a minute, then smiled. "Remember that pretty blonde whose phone number I neglected to get?"

Jim cocked his head, "Yes…and…?"

Pulling the notebook from his shirt pocket he held it up to Jim and said, "Got it."

"No way!" Jim grabbed the pad and read, "Grace Morgan," and then the number. Surprised, he said. "But you told me you didn't know how to get in touch with her."

Zach reached out to take the pad and returned it to his pocket. "I didn't."

"Then how…?" Jim stuttered.

Zach chuckled. "You're not going to believe this; I'm still having a hard time believing it myself. I was standing there, taking tickets for the tour and I looked up. There she was —she and her friend, Karen. They were taking the tour."

"You have got to be kidding," Jim said, his eyes wide.

"And more than that, she and Karen saw that I was having a rough time trying to get the cookout going and they just pitched in and did all the things Sasha used to do. I honestly couldn't have done it without their help."

Jim leaned back in his chair, laughing. "This is hilarious! Wait 'til I tell Susan. She's going to freak out!"

"The best part, Bro, was the singing on the beach. Grace and her friend are obviously Christians. She sang with me just as naturally as Sasha did. There was a beautiful presence of the Lord as we worshipped. More people came to me and made comments in appreciation of that than ever before. I truly believe there were some who received the Lord."

Jim shook his head. "Wow, God is so awesome. I don't know what else to say."

"I know. That's what I've been thinking all morning. I know I'm not ready just yet to return to the church, but I'm headed in that direction. As far as Grace is concerned, there's something there, but I think it's just that I'm supposed to help her through whatever she's dealing with right now."

"And that's all? You're just supposed to *help her?"* He asked with an 'I-can't-believe-you're-saying-this' look on his face.

Zach patted his pocket with Grace's number in it. "I am. I'm going to call her this morning and ask her to work for me, helping me with the cookouts. If she agrees that will make it possible to find out more about her and what has made her so sad."

"Does she live in the area?"

"I don't know…guess I'll find out soon."

They stood and Jim high-fived him." Go for it, Bro. Just make sure you're not in self-denial. Grace Morgan is a very attractive woman."

* * * * *

Grace and Karen shared breakfast and then Karen went to her office to work on paperwork she would need for the business trip she was about to take. Grace tried to keep her attention on the book she was supposedly reading, but she couldn't remember what she had just read. Zach had said he'd call "in the morning," and what time that meant, she had no idea. With stock to attend his day probably started early. It was almost eleven and her phone still hadn't rung. Somehow, she didn't think he was one of those men who said they'd call and then didn't. Her insides were buzzing like hundreds of butterflies were trapped in there. She had never felt like this around a man, not even Damien, whom she had really loved.

Or had she genuinely loved him? The thought came out of nowhere. Grace laid aside the book and looked out the window. If she was going to rebuild her life, maybe it was time to do some soul searching. She thought back to when she met Damien at Bible college.

Everyone was attracted to him. He was a born leader that men followed gladly. Women adored him for his charm and his good looks. There was a quality about him that made whatever he did appear believable and acceptable.

When he asked her to go out, she was in shock that he wanted to date her. There were so many other striking young women he could have chosen. She'd been told she was pretty, but she was timid and would never do anything to make herself noticed.

As she thought back to that time, it dawned on her; Damien liked being the one everybody looked at, turned to, and admired. He knew she would never be competition to him. She was pretty enough to look good at his side, but she would never outshine him. She would always put his needs first and not dare to demand much from him.

And that's exactly what had happened. Her life centered around him, and she satisfied herself with the small amount of affection he offered. She felt needed for the ministry work she devoted herself to.

With this realization Grace felt something break away from her. What she and Damien shared had never been true love. He likely had chosen very carefully when he decided to ask her to marry him. She knew that most of the other young women surrounding him would not have settled for a lifetime of serving him with so little in return.

Remembering the bold redhead's saunter through his office, Grace knew that woman would not quietly take the backseat. She laughed and felt a release of the pain that had choked her heart. "Oh, Damien, what have you gotten yourself into?" She honestly felt sorry for him.

"What are you laughing about in here all alone, Gracie-Lou?" Karen asked as she appeared with her empty coffee cup in hand.

"I just realized I never really loved Damien, and he certainly never truly loved me," Grace told her.

Karen went to the coffee pot and filled her cup. Settling onto a barstool she sipped and looked at Grace. "Boy, did I miss that one. I thought were you were nuts about him, even though I could never understand why."

"I know, but it was more fascination with the way other people admired him. Honestly, when I think back to when we were dating there were times I felt his behavior was very self-centered. But I followed him anyway, like all the others did. He really is a con man."

Grace got up and went over to Karen and gave her an exuberant hug. "You have no idea how freeing this is, KK!"

"No, I don't think I do, but as long as it makes you happy, I'm happy. 'Want to go celebrate?"

"Umm…I can't…Zach said he'd call."

"Ohhh, yes! That long, tall, God-man. I'll have to come up with a nickname for him."

"No, you don't, Karen." Grace poked her friend, then jumped as her phone rang. She looked at the caller ID. "Oh, my, it's him."

She started to leave the room, but Karen waved her hand. "Don't bother, I'm going back to my work," she said,

Grace wanted to kick herself for the shaky, "Hello," as she answered the call. "Hi, Grace." Zach's smooth baritone made her weak in the knees and she sank onto the sofa.

"I meant to call earlier, but we had an issue with a cow giving birth."

Grace couldn't help but laugh. "You know, that's the first time I've been given that excuse for someone being late—not that you're late; you didn't say what time you'd call."

Zach chuckled, too. 'I'm guessing none of your other acquaintances help birth calves."

"No, but that's a noble profession. I'm sure the mama cows are quite appreciative."

Zach groaned. "Uh, do you mind if I start this conversation over?"

"Go ahead, Zach."

"Good morning, Grace. I hope you're having a nice day."

"And good morning to you, Zach. I'm glad your calf birthing has gone well."

Zach chuckled. "I'd like to talk to you about something, preferably over lunch. Are you free today?"

"Yes, at least I think I am. Karen hasn't said that she had anything planned to entertain me."

"In that case, will you go to lunch with me?"

"Yes, I'd like that."

"Shall I pick you up at Karen's?"

"I guess so, but it's a gated community. Let me ask Karen how to handle it. Maybe she should give you directions, herself."

"Okay, how much time do you need?"

"I'm dressed, so whenever you get here will be fine. I'll get Karen now." She was walking as she spoke and opened the office door.

.

"Karen, will you give Zach directions to get through the gate and to your place?" She handed her the phone.

"I will indeed. Hi, Zach! Are you kidnapping my roomie?"

He said something, and she laughed. "Just bring her home eventually." Then she gave him directions and information he needed.

Handing the phone back to Grace, she said, "He'll be here in thirty minutes…if there are no more calf-birthing issues to delay him. What's that about?"

Grace smiled, took the phone, and turned to go. 'You don't even want to know."

Karen shrugged and went back to her computer.

Grace stood before the full-length mirror and checked her image. She was wearing new skinny jeans, one of the blouses she had bought in Galveston, and a lacy, long vest.

The blue of the blouse was just a bit darker than her eyes and made them look more intense. Hair, lipstick, teeth, clothes, shoes…there wasn't anything else she could do to improve any of it, so she took a deep breath, picked up her purse and headed for the living room. It seemed downright surreal. After all these years she was going out with a man other than Damien, and she was definitely nervous.

Karen intercepted her in the hallway with a gate card and a house key in hand. "I meant to give these to you earlier, but we were always together, and you didn't need them. Now that you're entering a life of your own —take these. The key fits both front and back doors in case you ever need to know that."

"Thanks, KK…for everything. I always know that you're on my side, no matter what."

"You betcha, kiddo, and I know it works both ways."

She gave Grace a quick hug and a gentle push toward the living room. "You can pace in here until your handsome hunk arrives."

"Just be sure to lock the door behind you. I've got to finish these reports."

Holding her middle to quiet the butterflies, Grace muttered to herself. "Calm down, Grace! You just met the guy." This was new for her; she only hoped her excitement didn't show on the outside.

The doorbell rang and she waited a few moments before answering it.

"Hi, Zach," and one look at him threw caution to the wind. He was wearing his usual western wear, the Stetson and boots, and a look of admiration on his face that matched the one on Grace's.

"Down boy!" he thought to himself. *"She's beautiful."* He smiled down at her upturned face and blushed at his thoughts of what it would feel like to kiss her.

"That was way out of line! Remember, you're just here to help her!" He took off the Stetson, ran his hand through his hair, and said, "Good morning, Grace. You look lovely."

"'Not so bad yourself, Cowboy," she said with a mischievous glint in her eyes.

"Are we ready?" he asked.

"Yes, we are," Grace took the door key out.

Zach reached to take it. "Let me do the honors," he said and locked the door. Handing the single key back to her, he said, "We need to get you a key chain while we're out."

"I have one, "Grace said. "I just haven't needed any of the keys on it since I've been here. I'm not sure where it is."

"You need a Texas key chain, one of those big things women can find easily in their purses."

Grace laughed. "Okay, if you say so."

They walked over to Zach's deep blue Ford F150 club cab pickup truck which was parked in the driveway.

"Have you ridden in a pick-up truck in a while?"

Grace stopped to think. "Probably not in the last ten years or so…as a child I rode in my Dad's truck with him ."

Zach smiled. "Well, you're in Texas now, so you might as well get used to it."

He wasn't prepared for the fresh smell of Grace's hair as he bent toward her, or the desire to bury his face in it. The warmth of his breath on her neck sent feelings all the way to Graces' toes as a blush rose to her cheeks.

"O-okay," she managed to say.

Zach laughed out loud and opened the driver's side door. "There's a step here; let me help you,"

With a quick boost, Grace was on the seat, sliding under the wheel and over the seat.

Taking her hand, Zach said, "Don't go too far; there's a seat belt in the middle. Then his face reddened. 'Is that too forward? It's just that the seat is so wide…I didn't want you …uh…way over there."

Grace laughed at his confusion. "That's okay, Zach. I like the middle."

Zach got in, hooked his seatbelt, and checked to see that Grace's was buckled. He removed his hat and reached over the seat to place it in the back. This movement put him even closer to Grace as his arm was practically around her. He stopped and she looked up, her blue eyes wide. His lips were mere inches from hers as he held her gaze, then he sighed and placed both hands on the steering wheel.

"Get it together, Clayton! Remember—you're not looking for another woman in your life!"

He took a deep breath, then backed out of the driveway. Sneaking a look at Grace as he turned to view traffic from the right, he saw that she was sitting stiffly and appeared ill at ease. He didn't want that. Pausing before pulling out onto the main street he looked at her and smiled.

"All right, Miss Grace, do you have a preference of food?"

Grace was about to say she didn't when she remembered Karen's remark.

"Actually, I do. Karen's been telling me about your Gulf Coast shrimp and I'm dying to try it."

Zach smiled. "Aha, a lady after my own heart. I know just the place…a little mom and pop café near the water. Sash…" He stopped abruptly. "I'm sorry…I…I didn't mean to mention her. This is all so new to me."

"Zach, please don't apologize." She placed her hand on his arm. "We both have memories that are not going anywhere. If it feels awkward for you to take me the place where you and Sasha had special times, then let's go to another restaurant."

Zach was quiet for a moment. "You're a very special lady, Grace. I know that much about you already. You're gracious and kind. Sasha would have liked you a lot. I think she would like the idea of me taking you to a place we enjoyed. So, if you're still game…?

Grace gave his arm a sharp tap. "I'm all in, Cowboy."

They rode in comfortable silence for a while, then Grace spoke. "What was it you wanted to talk to me about?"

Oh, yeah, that…" Zach said and grinned.

"I guess I should know more about your situation before addressing that subject."

"Like what?"

"Like…are you living here, or just visiting Karen?"

Grace sighed. "Good question."

When she didn't continue, Zach asked, "Does it have an answer?"

Grace honestly didn't know what to say. "I'm sure there's an answer out there somewhere, but I truly don't know what it is at this moment."

"Should I have waited 'til we've done some 'get acquainted' talking before I asked that?" Zach questioned gently.

"Probably so. I think I'll need to give you a little background first."

CHAPTER 8

"Oh, my, that was delicious!' Grace said. "I can't believe I ate that whole platter of shrimp. My appetite has certainly increased since I've been in Texas."

Zach grinned. "I can't think of a single comment that would be safe."

"You are truly a Southern gentleman," Grace said smiling.

Sensing that she still wasn't ready to talk about her life when they first arrived, Zach had told stories about growing up on the coast—escapades he and his buddies had gotten into.

"Can I get you anything else?" the waitress asked as she took their empty platters. "Dessert…coffee?"

"I think I'd like a cup of coffee," Grace said. "Black."

"Make that two, Candace," Zach told the familiar waitress.

"I know…black for you, too, Pastor Zach." She smiled shyly. "It's really good to see you again."

Zach reached out and patted her arm. "It's good to see you, too, Hon." To Grace, he said, "Sasha and I always sat in Candace's station when we ate here."

Grace smiled at the waitress and nodded. "I'm sure you have missed them both."

"Candace, this is my friend, Grace," Zach said. "If her empty platter is any indication, I suspect you'll be seeing us again."

"Shame, Zach! But I'm afraid he's right, Candace. And we'll certainly sit in your station," Grace told her.

Candace smiled. "I'll be right back with your coffee."

"It's easy to see that you are loved in this community," Grace told Zach.

He started to speak, then stopped, as if choosing his words carefully.

"God truly has given me favor in the area, Grace. Sasha was also very loved by the people. I haven't been out in public much in the last three years, so when people see me, most of them want to express their condolences and their love for her. I hope that doesn't make you feel uncomfortable."

"Zach, our lives didn't begin when we met. Please don't apologize for people wishing to speak of your kind, loving wife. I only wish those things could be said about my ex-husband."

She hesitated a moment, then said, "I need to tell you my story, but can we go someplace a little more private?"

A few minutes later Grace stood before the mirror in the ladies' room and took a deep breath. She met her gaze in the mirror. Was she really about to tell all the ugly past to a man she hardly knew? Yes, she was, and she had peace about it. That had to be God.

Soon, they were driving over the causeway to the island. Grace recognized the turn-off as the road leading to the cookout spot for the tour. What a perfect place for them to talk.

Now that Zach had parked, he turned to her with a twinkle in his eyes.

"'Want to walk on the beach and get some sand between your toes?"

"That would be nice"

"Good. Let me slip my boots off."

Grace took off her sandals, too, and wriggled her toes in the sand. How long had it been since she'd done this? More years than she could remember.

Now barefoot, Zach called, "Ready?" He tossed her a bottle of water and took one for himself.

Grace caught the water and grinned. "Ready."

Side by side they walked down the beach. The breeze off the water was just enough to cool what could have been a warm afternoon.

Grace knew Zach was waiting for her to begin the conversation and she was trying to determine how to tell what needed to be told without them being there until midnight.

She sighed. "I don't know where to begin."

"Why not start at the beginning. Where were you born?"

That made it easier, not having to start with the ugliness. Once she began, Grace found it easy to tell Zach about her childhood, her loving parents, her one brother and their sibling rivalry that turned into friendship through the years. Just about the time she was getting to meeting Damien at Seminary, Zach motioned to an outcropping of rocks and they sat.

After taking a long drink of water, Grace began.

"Damien was the guy at the top of the list for girls to be seen with at school–handsome, charismatic, well-off, a great speaker, and sure to be successful in ministry. He was the talk of the dorm —among the beautiful, talented girls who were competing to be his wife. I wasn't one of his groupies, so I was really shocked when he started asking me out. We were married right after graduating and Damien got offered the pastorate of a mid-sized church right away. We were there for over two years when he was offered the position as pastor at a larger church. The church grew so fast, by hundreds, until it was one of the largest in the city."

Grace looked out at the waves of the Gulf for a few moments before turning to Zach and asking: "Do you recall seeing on the news…ten months ago, the story – the scandal —of the Los Angeles pastor who was discovered having an affair?"

Zach thought a minute. "Yes, I think so. His church shrunk to practically nothing…his wife divorced him." Zach continued to look at Grace as the truth dawned on him.

"Oh, no," he groaned. "Oh, Grace, I'm so sorry." He reached out and drew her to him. He held her gently, stroking her hair. "That must have been pure hell for you. I'm so sorry."

Grace had not wanted to cry, especially in front of Zach. She really thought she'd be able to get through this without falling apart. But Zach's genuine grief and sorrow over her ordeal broke through the last barrier and she wept until at last she felt at peace. Finally, she pulled back from him.

"I'm sorry, I got your shirt wet."

"Are you kidding?" Zach pulled her back close to him and rocked gently back and forth. "I thought I went through the worst hell ever losing Sasha. But she didn't willingly leave. She did everything in her power to stay with me. Just losing her was bad enough. I can't imagine going through media blasting our personal tragedy all over the news."

Grace broke down again at that. "Oh, Zach, it was so awful. They twisted everything, so it made me look like I'd done something wrong. Every day and evening on every station they broadcast their lies about me and any scoop they could get on Damien and that woman. The paparazzi waited outside my house twenty-four hours a day and bombarded me with obscene questions when I had to go out.

"I finally went to the home of friends and stayed in hiding for several weeks. My hairdresser came to the house, gave me a new hairstyle, and changed my hair color to blonde.

"Another friend is a dresser for stars in Hollywood and she replaced my entire wardrobe so that I have a totally different look."

As he held Grace, Zach thought back to some of the newscasts he'd seen of the Reverend Damien Vincent's scandal. He recalled pictures of a dark-haired Grace with her head bowed in shame, trying to escape the reporters. He brushed back her hair so he could look into her eyes.

"How did you learn of Damien's affair?" he asked.

She looked down and shook her head, the memory of the discovery bringing all the negative emotions to the surface.

"I had gone to southern California to spend a few days with my parents and was supposed to return to LA on Saturday. I was unaware of plans Mom and Dad had made for Friday with a senior group that they do things with from time to time. So rather than sitting there alone on Friday and driving back Saturday, I decided to dome home a day early. I got busy and didn't call Damien until I was almost home. Apparently, he was so involved with his lady friend that he didn't check his phone messages.

"When I neared our home, I clicked the garage door opener, but instead of an empty space, there was a small European sports car in the place where I normally park."

Grace shook her head. "I was so stupid. I didn't have a clue what was going on. I thought Damien had bought a new sports car for himself. I just left mine out on the drive and walked into the house with the usual, "Honey, I'm home!"

"I walked down the hall toward his office and as I passed the living room, I heard the romantic music and…and they didn't even hear me come in."

Grace pressed her hands to her eyes as though trying to remove the sight of her husband's infidelity from her memory.

Zach held her close. "Oh, Grace…Grace, I'm so sorry."

His own heart ached at the pain this beautiful woman was carrying. How could he possibly help alleviate it?

Silently, he prayed as he held her. *"Father, please help her. Mend her broken heart."*

As clearly as though someone had audibly spoken to Zach, he heard: *"Your love will heal her."*

Zach was stunned. He knew he was supposed to help Grace, but he wasn't prepared to love her or any other woman. How could he when Sasha still filled every part of his heart?

He admitted that he found her attractive, but physical attraction wasn't love. Unconsciously, he stiffened and pulled back from Grace.

Grace felt the rejection as though Zach had spoken the words aloud. She stood and began to walk toward his truck. She shouldn't have told him about her life. Whatever he was thinking had placed a wall between them that had destroyed any sense of togetherness.

"Grace, wait!" He didn't know what to say, but Zach didn't want their day to end this way.

With tears filling her beautiful eyes, Grace softly said, "Will you just take me home, Zach?"

He nodded and unlocked the truck door. They put their shoes back on in silence and he helped her up into the truck. They rode in silence, this time with Grace on the far side of the seat. Zach hated the separation that had come between them, ruining the beautiful day they'd been enjoying, but he didn't know how to change it.

Turning to look at her, he asked softly, "So you're here at Karen's just for some time out of the heat of the situation?"

Grace shrugged, "I guess that's one way of putting it. I'm trying to figure out my next step. I've realized that this chapter of my life is over. I just don't know where the next one begins. Karen is such a wonderful friend. Her home is open to me as long as I want to stay here. I'll need to find work because I intend to stop taking the alimony from Damien. I want to cut every tie to him."

Zach knew that what he could pay her to help him with the tours wouldn't come close to what she would need to support herself. It wasn't steady work, even in the summer, and was non-existent in the winter months. He and Sasha had started it more as a ministry than for income. He decided not to mention it to her; he'd just find someone else to help. But then he heard the Voice: *"Ask her to work with you."*

He ran his finger through his hair and winced.

"Grace, I almost hate to bring this up…but…well, the thing I wanted to talk to you about…I was going to ask if you'd consider working for me…helping me with the tours for the few weeks left in the summer months. I don't take bookings past the end of September. I know you could find better paying employment for sure…and I won't be offended if you say, 'No.'"

Something stirred in Grace's heart at Zach's offer. She had enjoyed her part in the cookout that day. And now that she had gone through the routine, she felt she'd have no problem doing it without Karen's help. She didn't even want any pay but was sure Zach would insist on paying her. Money wasn't an issue at the present since she had her half of the sale of their expensive home and Damien's hefty alimony payments.

She couldn't deny the attraction she felt for Zach. Could she take working that closely with him? At times she was sure he shared that same attraction, but just minutes ago at the beach, she could feel him pulling away. He was obviously not over his deceased wife.

Grace looked at Zach as he awaited her answer. "I enjoyed working with you the other evening, Zach. Let me think about it. How soon do you need to know?"

"I have tours coming up this weekend, so I'd need to know pretty soon."

Grace nodded. "Okay, I'll let you know in a couple of days."

They were at Karen's house now. Zach pulled into the drive but didn't kill the engine right away. He still wanted to make things right with Grace. He wanted to take away the sadness in her beautiful eyes. But he just couldn't give her what it would take to do that, and he didn't know if he'd ever be able to.

"You've got my phone number?" He asked.

Without looking at him, Grace said, "Yes, it's in my phone."

He opened the truck door. "I'd better get home. It's about time to feed the stock." He paused. "Grace…thank you for trusting me with your…your situation. I'll be praying for you."

"Thank you for lunch and for listening, Zach. "I'll be in touch."

She looked up at him as she spoke, and her heart did that funny flip thing. His dark eyes were filled with so much hurt and yet, with compassion, too. She couldn't allow him to leave feeling like he had added to her pain.

"Come here," she whispered, holding out her arms to him.

Zach stepped into them and wrapped his arms around her. They stood in this wordless embrace for a long moment, drawing strength from each other.

Then Grace pulled back, smiled at him, and said, "We're going to make it through all of this."

Zach couldn't speak for the lump in his throat, so he gave her a nod and turned and walked to his truck.

CHAPTER 9

Grace slipped inside, closed the door, and leaned against it with closed eyes as she listened to Zach's truck driving away. This day had been an emotional rollercoaster, leaving her exhausted.

The sound of soft footsteps on the carpet made her aware that Karen had entered the room. She opened her eyes but didn't move.

"Aaii, practically catatonic! Is that good or bad?" Karen asked with her eyes wide. "Do we need coffee?"

Grace pushed away from the door. "Hi, KK. Yes, we definitely need coffee."

"I'll do the honors. From the looks of you, I don't trust you to count the scoops."

Grace dropped her purse and seated herself at the bar.

"Zach wants me to work for him."

Placing a filter in the coffee maker, Karen smiled.

"Why am I not surprised? He obviously can't do those cookouts by himself."

Grace chuckled, remembering how flustered Zach had been before she and Karen went to help him.

"Yeah, I just don't know if I should be the one to help him."

Karen pushed the brew button and joined Grace at the bar. "Now why would you say that? The guy was practically drooling over you." She stopped and took Grace's arm.

"He didn't do…something…?"

Quickly, Grace shook her head. "No, no…he was great…sweet. I do believe he's attracted to me, but he's still very much in love with his deceased wife and there's no way I can compete with that."

"Umm," Karen nodded, "That's a tough one. Did he say anything to that effect?"

"No, he didn't have to. We were talking at the beach and I told him about all my mess. He was so caring and compassionate I…I just lost it. He took me in his arms and was comforting me, but I could tell the instant he realized he was holding another woman. The day had been really enjoyable until then, but changed after that."

Karen got up to pour the coffee that was now ready. "What did you tell him about working for him?"

"I said I'd let him know in a couple of days. I've got to pray about it. I really like him—whether I wanted to or not. And I guess I'm just afraid of getting hurt again. I'm not over the pain Damien caused; I don't need to invite more."

"But you don't want to miss God, either." Setting Grace's coffee in front of her, Karen looked at her friend.

"The very last thing I want is for you to be hurt, Gracie Lou, but I can't help feeling God has something for the two of you. And in spite of how you think he feels about his wife, I know what I saw in his eyes when he looked at you.

"I think it's very possible that your cowboy is quaking in his boots. As much as you don't want to relive the pain of divorce, he surely doesn't want to risk the pain of losing another woman he loves. Remember how he freaked out at the mansion when we went outside, and he thought he'd lost you?"

Grace smiled, remembering.

"Besides, I just can't believe God went to all that trouble to bring the two of you together the way He did for it all to be wasted."

"So, you think I should work for him?"

Karen spoke gently now. "My dear friend, I think you should do exactly what God tells you to do. I know you hear Him. I'll back you up, whatever that is."

Changing her tone and the subject, she asked, "Did you guys eat somewhere?"

"Yes, we did—at a little seafood place— 'Sam's. I took your advice and ordered the shrimp. You're right, it's the best shrimp I've ever had. I ate the whole platter."

Karen laughed. "I've eaten there several times. They do have really good food and it's a homey little place."

Patting Grace on the shoulder, she stood. "I've got to get back to my packing. What do you want to do for dinner?"

"I don't care to go out anywhere. You've got a ton of food here; shall I just whip up something?"

"That would be lov-er-ly," Karen sing-songed. "I haven't

had an in-house cook since we were college roommates. Did I ever tell you how glad I was that you liked to cook?"

"Not in so many words," Grace admitted. "You just ate up everything I made."

Karen left the room laughing, and Grace sat thinking back over her day with Zach. Just the thought of his cocky smile beneath that black Stetson gave her goosebumps. Sipping her coffee, she thought about what it would be like to work with him on the tours.

There probably wouldn't be too much work for her to do before the cookout, but she could mingle with the tour guests and be open to however the Lord might want to use her with them. Thinking of the tasks she and Karen had done at the beach, she felt she could handle it alone without problems. She still didn't know who prepared all that wonderful food but assumed they would continue to supply that.

Grace's heart warmed at the memory of singing with Zach at the campfire. That was a special time, something she had never experienced with Damien. It saddened her to think that as a couple in ministry they had never truly worshipped together.

Looking back at her marriage now Grace could see things more clearly. She realized that her husband had fooled, not only her, but a lot of people, even the godly men on the church board.

Damien had grown up under the tutelage of a successful pastor/father. He had learned how to run a church, to bring in newcomers, and how to influence people. He had used his God-given leadership skills to manipulate them to his advantage. Had he chosen to go into the business world he would likely have been the CEO of some large company. Maybe that's where he would end up now that he was no longer respected in the ministry.

Suddenly, Grace determined that she would never again settle for marriage without spiritual unity – spiritual honesty. Anything else was a sham. It hurt to think that as much as she had given in her marriage, that was all it was—artificial and so very empty.

Unwittingly, she had been part of the sham, refusing to see her husband as he truly was. Maybe she would never have recognized the truth while in that marriage, but now that she had, she would not spend one more day grieving the end of it. For the first time she could honestly say she was glad it was over.

Grace thought of the people of their congregation. She had tried to personally know as many of the thousands of parishioners as she could. Tears flowed as she sorrowed over their betrayal. Hopefully, those who were wounded over their spiritual leader's sin would somehow find healing for their broken hearts.

"Don't let them give up on You, God," she prayed and took her coffee cup to the dishwasher. She still had some free time before starting dinner, so she headed to her room. Karen turned in her office chair as Grace passed the doorway.

"I forgot to tell you, Gracie…remember the couple with the three little boys that practically attacked Zach at the beach? Well, the young lady – Lana—called and said she'd been thinking about us and wanted to remind us of her invitation to come to the Cowboy Church on Sunday."

"That was sweet of her," Grace said.

"I told her I'd be out of town, but maybe you'd like to go. She said you could ride with them if you'd like and they would be glad to pick you up."

"Handing Grace a post-it note, she added. "She left her number and asked for you to give her a call."

"I think I'd like that," Grace said, taking the number. It would be interesting to see what Zach's church was like, even if he wasn't there.

* * * * *

As Zach drove away after leaving Grace, he felt saddened and very much alone. He couldn't deny the fact that he really enjoyed having her with him. He also couldn't fool himself into thinking he didn't find her extremely attractive. He knew that he'd hurt her when he put up the wall between them and his heart ached for that.

When she'd looked up at him with those beautiful blue eyes and invited him into her arms, he thought his heart would melt. Just standing there in that embrace he knew they had imparted something to each other. Strength, healing – whatever it was, it comforted him.

Zach thought back to the word he had heard while on the beach. *"Your love will heal her."* What was he going to do about that? How was he supposed to stop loving Sasha and start loving Grace? If it had been possible to stop loving Sasha, he would already have done it because it was too painful.

A new thought came to his mind. *Love given must be received for it to bring joy to the giver.* He'd never considered that before, but he thought of how his heart felt when Sasha was alive and received his love. He didn't love her any less now, and he'd been trying to give that love to her in the same way for the past three years. But she wasn't here to receive it, so the cycle that brought joy to him couldn't be completed.

This reminded him of the situation with his college buddy, Aaron. There was a girl in one of his classes that captured his heart and Aaron couldn't think of anything but this girl. While she was pleasant to him, she didn't return his feelings, and for months Aaron lived with the pain of that unrequited love.

Zach felt he'd stumbled onto something important in his thinking, but he was still trying to sort it out. Had he been trying to prove to Sasha these past three years how much he had loved her? Or maybe he was trying to prove it to himself. Sasha was in Heaven, with God who was love personified. She had no need of Zach's love there.

For three years he had stubbornly been fighting to keep his relationship with Sasha in the forefront of his mind and his life. No wonder he felt angry and unhappy all the time. That had proven to be an absolutely futile battle. It might take some time to do a total "about face" in his thinking. It would certainly take the Holy Spirit's help.

"Who do you think brought this understanding to you?"

Zach laughed. "It certainly wasn't my brilliance, Lord! I would have recognized it long before now!"

"When a lie is broken, truth is revealed. Why continue to walk in the lie as though you didn't know its deceit? Didn't I say, 'Truth will make you free?"

Zach was stunned by the power of this statement. He had believed the lie that told him he had to stop living because Sasha was no longer alive here on earth with him. He had believed that he didn't have purpose without her.

If someone had asked him why he couldn't take back the leadership of his church, he really couldn't have given them a true answer. Now, as revelation came to him Zach understood that deep in his heart he had believed the lie that God was not faithful, so how could he stand in the pulpit and preach that He was?

Another thought hit him with its truth. He wasn't saying it from the pulpit , but his living for three years in that lie was a message to the people that if God couldn't bring Pastor Zach to victory, how could they expect Him to come to their rescue in times of trouble?

"Oh, God!" he groaned. "What have I done? Have I destroyed their faith in You in my doubt and unbelief?"

Zach's tears flowed as the faces of his congregation came before him. People who were in Cornerstone Cowboy Church because he had stood beside them in trials and encouraged their faith. What a hypocrite he'd been. Grief overwhelmed him as he pulled over to the side of the rural road and wept.

Being a leader meant that others followed you, Zach knew. Had some of his people followed him into unbelief and forsaken serving the Lord as he had? "God, forgive me. Help my people!"

"They are first my people. I love them more than you do. I sent them a protector, a guardian. Not one of the sheep has been lost."

Jim Sheridan's face came before Zach and gratitude flooded his heart again. It was Jim's faithfulness and obedience that had formed a wall of protection around the people of his church. How could he ever thank him enough?

"You can't, but I will bless him and his family."

The burden lifted from Zach's shoulders. Yes, he had failed, but God didn't fail him. He patiently waited for Zach to become willing to receive the restoration of his faith and everything else in his life.

Suddenly, Zach felt a longing to be with his people. He'd never been a parent, but surely those feelings were akin to a father missing his children when he was away from them. It was time to go back. Not to take up the leadership just yet, but to love them and receive the love they gave to him.

Zach had to laugh. He was free! Free, with no guilt, to have another woman stand beside him in the place Sasha had filled. Free to acknowledge his feelings for Grace that he had been denying. It had happened so quickly…could a person actually fall in love with someone in just a few days? What about a few minutes? He hadn't been able to stop thinking about Grace Morgan since he first laid eyes on her. Those thoughts had brought such conflict because he had stubbornly refused to let Sasha go.

Zach felt that Grace had feelings for him, too. Sometimes her eyes were so full of love it had frightened him because he was bound in that prison of his own making. He might need to take things a little more slowly than his heart was desiring for her sake. It had only been a matter of weeks since her divorce. He'd just let God determine how this played out.

Zach had given little thought to his ranch in a long time. When Sasha died, he couldn't bear to be in the place where everything reminded him of her. When Jim and Susan offered their apartment over the barn, he had gladly moved there to avoid the pain of the memories.

An older couple from his church, Jay, and Lillian Rogers, had moved to the ranch as caretakers. Zach had sold off much of his stock and brought most of the horses and cattle he still owned to Jim's ranch. The Roger's had been ranchers themselves and still enjoyed horseback riding, so Zach had left a couple of horses for them. Lillian loved her chickens and kept enough to provide eggs for her and Jay, Zach, and Jim and Susan's family. They came by about every two weeks to deliver eggs and give Zach an update on things at the ranch. Knowing it was in good hands, he'd had no desire to drive out there. But today, as he was nearing the county road that led to his ranch, he felt the impulse to go to the home and land that he'd once truly loved.

Zach could feel his heart rate increasing as he drove the once familiar road. Why was he doing this, and how would he feel when he got there? It would probably be a shock to the Rogers for him to show up like this.

Slowing his truck to turn onto the road which led to the ranch house Zach drove over the cattle guard and under the iron pipe canopy which held the sign: "Clayton Ranch." He was now on his land−the land that he and Sasha had worked for, sacrificed for. It had taken them a few years to accumulate enough money to pay a sizeable down payment on the property. They had wanted to keep the mortgage payments as small as possible so they could be free to pastor without the concerns of a large mortgage payment.

As he drove past the white wood fencing that lined the road Zach remembered the many church functions they'd hosted here.

As a cowboy church their people loved to hold their own small rodeos and roping events, sometimes inviting other churches to join them.

Zach and Sasha enjoyed nothing more than having the people there. The children ran freely as they played. Adults pulled out folding chairs from the storeroom and sat in groups and visited. The long tables that were filled with food at those times now sat bare under the tin-roofed, open sheds.

As Zach followed the curved driveway and parked in front of the ranch - style house, the door flew open and a petite, sun-tanned woman with gray hair that curled around her face came running out to meet him.

"Zach, I'm so glad to see you! My, what a wonderful surprise!" She threw her arms around him and hugged him with warmth that brought tears to his eyes.

Lillian pulled back to look at him, her sweet, round face alight with pleasure. "What are you doing here?" Then embarrassed at her question, she blushed. "I mean, it's your place…you can come anytime…but…"

"I know what you mean, Mama Lil. After all, I haven't been out here in three years, so you have the right to be surprised." He put his arm around her as they started for the door. "As to your question—I don't really know why I came. It just seemed like my truck headed this way on its own."

"Well, whatever the reason, I'm tickled pink you're here. Come on in. Jay's feeding the horses. He'll be here in a few minutes. He'll be as happy as I am to see you."

Zach felt dread rising within him as he held the door open for Lillian. She had told him once that she had left everything just as it was when she and Jay moved in. That meant that all the pictures of Zach and Sasha that she had artistically framed would be there. All the mementos of trips they had taken, all of Sasha's clothing and personal items.

Zach tried to ignore the sweat breaking out on his upper lip and instead, concentrated on whatever it was that Lillian was saying to him. His senses were bombarded with the aroma of sweet chocolate.

"Smells good in here. Is that chocolate cake I smell?"

"It certainly is—a Tunnel of Fudge cake. You're just in time for supper. I made chicken and dumplings, collard greens and cornbread, too." She patted his arm. "Have a seat there at the table. Would you like a cup of coffee?"

"You know I never refuse coffee, Mama Lil." He said with a grin, "But I can pour it. 'Smells like you might need to check the cake."

Lillian laughed as she picked up a potholder. "You're right, it was nearly done when I went running outside to greet you." She opened the oven, pulled the rack forward and gently tapped on the top of the chocolate Bundt cake.

"Perfect timing," she said as she removed it from the oven. Turning to Zach she just stood and looked at him. Her scrutiny made Zach blush.

"What?"

She simply smiled with a twinkle in her eyes. "You look…I don't know…better, son."

Zach knew that this precious woman and her husband were some of the people who had prayed faithfully for him. His voice husky, he returned her gaze. "I am, Mama Lil. I am."

Just then the back door opened, and a tall, gray-haired man stepped inside. His piercing blue eyes landed on Zach, but a broad smile lit his face.

"Who is this long-legged scoundrel sittin' at my table?" He asked loudly.

"Hey, Pops!" Zach stood and the two embraced warmly, Jay slapping him on his back.

"How are things going?" Zach asked him.

"Just fine now that you're here. It's good to see you, boy. You've been off galivantin' somewhere the last few times we brought eggs to Jim and Susan's. I missed you." He hugged Zach again.

"I've missed you guys, too "Zach told him, returning the hug. Lillian and Jay filled a special place in his heart.

"You're staying for supper, aren't you?"

"You bet. Wild horses couldn't drag me away after smelling all this good stuff Mama's Lil's got on that stove."

"And if you'll get in there and wash up, Papa, I'll put it on the table," Lily said firmly to Jay.

"Yes, Ma'am!" Jay said but stopped to place a kiss on her cheek. "I'll be right back," he said to Zach as he went down the hall.

"Can I help, Mama?" Zach asked.

"You can set the table if you like." She smiled gently at him. "Everything's still in the same place."

Zach stood and walked over to the sink to wash his hands.

"It's good to be back," he said softly, realizing it was true.

Wordlessly, Lillian turned and wrapped her arms around him for a long hug, then released him and went about her work.

As Zach removed three plates from the cabinet, he felt the small dart of pain as the memory of the day they bought that set of dishes flooded over him. Sasha had insisted he accompany her to choose the pattern.

He tried to tell her that dishes really didn't matter to him, but she insisted it was important that he like them, too. It had turned out to be a fun process and he was glad later that he had gone along. He smiled and tucked the memory away in his heart.

As Zach set the table he was confronted with more memories, but it became easier as he continued to face them, honoring them for the joy they had brought in their making.

The meal with Lillian and Jay was delicious, but it was the time spent with them here in his home that nurtured his soul. He and Jay discussed ranch business over cake and coffee as Lillian cleaned up afterward. When she saw that the men were finishing their business talk, she went over and put her arm around Zach's shoulder.

"Do you want to look through the house, Hon?" she asked.

Zach looked down at the table for a moment, then up at her. "Yeah, I think I'd like to do that."

With a knowing look at Jay she said, "Well, Papa and I are going to go sit a spell in the swing on the porch. We like to watch the sunset from there. "

Zach nodded as Jay stood, clapping Zach on the shoulder before following Lillian out the door.

Emptying his coffee cup, Zach sat for a few moments.

"Help me, Lord," he prayed. He didn't know what to expect of his emotions, but he couldn't hide from them forever. He stood and walked into the large, comfortable den. Instead of feeling pain as his eyes went from one photograph to another, there was sweet comfort as he recalled the good times that were captured on camera.

He hesitated before their bedroom door. Jay and Lil had chosen not to use the master bedroom. Lillian had kept it dusted and vacuumed, but otherwise, it was just as Zach had left it when he moved out.

He opened the closet where Sasha's clothes still hung. His eyes stung with tears as he smelled the lingering fragrance of her favorite perfume. He smiled at the quantity of shoes. How she had loved shoes! He looked at things on her dresser and placed a few items to one side along with her jewelry box.

Zach had avoided the bed, but now he faced it and the memories of so much love that had been shared there. He laid down on what had been his side and imagined Sasha being there with him. But it brought no comfort.

Again, he thought of the things that had gone through his mind earlier about love needing to be received to bring joy to the giver. It reinforced his understanding that the beauty of love between a man and woman was a gift from God meant for their time together on earth.

No wonder the scripture said that men and women would not marry in heaven. The only marriage it speaks of taking place there is the Marriage of the Lamb, Jesus Christ, to his Bride, the Church, which will include all believers, both men and women.

Joy rose in Zach. He had known this for years, but somehow this revelation filled his heart with deeper understanding today. We'll all be married to the Lamb! We will be so complete in His love that there will be no need for the love we had known on earth, as wonderful as it may have been.

Zach stood and lifted his hands in worship, rejoicing in this newfound freedom. He looked around the room. It was time to take the next step, to remove Sasha's things. She was no longer holding to them, why should he?

Walking back through the house he joined Jay and Lillian on the porch. They could see from the glow that lit his face that something good had transpired since they left him, but they'd wait for him to tell them about it.

He sat on the edge of a lawn chair in front of them trying to find words to begin.

"Jay…Mama Lil…I don't think I can share right now what the Lord was showing me in there. It's something I need to… I guess you'd say…process. I just want you to know, it's all good."

He paused a moment then looked to Lillian.

"I need you to do me a favor if you would, Mama. I'd like you to remove Sasha's things from our room. I'd like others to enjoy them, but I think it's best not to give them to ladies from the church. I wouldn't want there to be any hard feelings over them. And I don't think I'd want to look out over the congregation and see her things."

Jay elbowed Lil but looked straight at Zach.

"So that means you're going to be up there…in the pulpit again?"

Zach smiled at him. "Yeah, Pops, sometime soon."

"I'd be honored to take care of Sasha's things for you, son," Lil said. "We're preparing some barrels of clothing and useful items to take to our mission in Mexico. Those ladies will be thrilled to have her beautiful things."

Zach nodded. "That's good. I put a few items with her jewelry box at the end of the dresser. You can leave those, and I'll decide later what to do with them. Everything else can go."

"Is there anything more you'd like me to do?" Lil asked.

Zach took a deep breath and let it out. "I hate to put this on you, but if I don't get out here to take care of it, would you put away the pictures of us? "

Lillian looked at him for a few moments with her head cocked to the side. "Is there something you're not telling us, Zachary?"

Zach couldn't stop the flush rising upward to his face. He looked up at Jay and Lillian. "I'm not sure what will come of this, but I've met someone…a really sweet lady who has gone through a horrendous divorce from her pastor husband. She's totally different from Sasha in looks, but she really loves the Lord and ministry to people."

Jay and Lil looked at each other and smiled. "We've been praying God would send you someone to help heal your heart and get you back on track with your ministry," Jay said. "This is really good news."

"Well, like I said, I don't know if this will be something permanent…we're just getting acquainted. I started the tour business again and I've asked her to work with me."

He chuckled, remembering the last tour. "She and her friend were guests on the tour and had the insight to see that I really needed help. They pitched in and did all the things Sasha used to do."

He told them about the beautiful time of worship around the campfire and how unexpectedly comfortable it was for him.

"I'm hoping she'll take the job. That will give us time to get better acquainted." He stood to his feet.

"I'm running a little late feeding the horses, so they'll be looking for me. 'Sure enjoyed the supper, Mama Lil." He reached out to hug her and then Jay.

"Pops, I'll come out soon and we can take a look at those things we talked about. Don't work too hard."

"I've got leftovers ready to send with you, Hon," Lily told him as they headed back into the house.

"Will we see you Sunday at church?" Jay asked.

"I think there's a good chance of that," Zach said with a smile. He picked up his Stetson, put it on and took the bag of food Lillian handed him.

"I love you guys," He told them. They all walked out together, and Jay and Lillian stood arm in arm watching Zach until the taillights of his truck were out of sight.

Drawing his wife closer, Jay smiled and said, "Our preacher boy's gonna be all right, Mama."

Chapter 10

Grace had enjoyed her phone conversation with Lana Caldwell last evening and had a feeling of expectation as she waited for the call that would announce their arrival at the gated community. She was excited about going to church, and doubly so that it was Zach's church. There wasn't any church she could attend in the LA area where she would have felt free to simply worship.

Even with the change in her appearance, sooner or later someone would recognize her. She was extremely grateful for televised ministries that brought worship and preaching of the Word. That had sustained her, but she was hungry to be in the presence of the Lord with other believers and was grateful for Lana and Bruce's offer to bring her with them today.

Grace had never in her life gone to a new church alone. That thought made her wonder about people who had come by themselves to their church in LA. Both she and Damien had encouraged their people to be friendly. She had heard remarks that visitors returned and became members because of the kind, friendly way they were received when they first came. Now, she could truly understand how important it was to make people feel welcome—just one more entry added to the list of things she was learning through her nightmarish experience. There were so many things she would see and do differently if she was ever in a position of leadership again.

Zach's image came to mind and Grace blushed at the thought of standing by his side before his congregation. How hard would it be to try to fill the shoes of the perfect pastor's wife? Would the people receive her?

"Whoa, girl! You are getting way ahead of yourself!" she spoke aloud. "He doesn't want a replacement, remember?"

Fortunately, the phone rang and interrupted her line of thought...

"We're at the gate, Grace," Bruce Caldwell said.

"Okay, just stay to the left and you'll see me."

"Gotcha!"

Grace pushed the button on the phone, picked up her purse and Bible and stepped outside, locking the door behind her. The Caldwell's large SUV pulled into the drive and Bruce got out of the driver's seat and opened the rear door. With a smile he greeted Grace and shook her hand.

"Good morning," he said. "It's good to see you again."

"Hi, Bruce. Thanks for picking me up."

Lana leaned over from the far side of the rear seat. "Hi, Grace. Sit back here with me." She reached out and squeezed Grace's hand. "I'm so glad you could make it."

As Grace got settled in her seat and buckled her seat belt, Lana spoke to the children. "Boys, say hello to Ms. Grace."

In a trio of young voices in unison they did. "Hel-lo, Ms. Grace."

Grace laughed. "Hi, guys. How are you this morning?"

The youngest spoke up, "I had Lucky Stars for breakfast."

Lana groaned. "This is Carson He would tell on me. I don't allow them to have sugary cereals on weekdays. But on Sundays it's an incentive to get them out of bed, knowing they get their favorite treat."

Bruce looked back at them in the rear-view mirror with a grin. "Tell her the truth, Lan; on Sundays you know we're going to drop them off in children's church for the teachers to deal with the sugar high!"

Lana reached forward and lightly slapped husband on the shoulder. "Bru-uce." Then she smiled and in a loud whisper said to Grace, "There may be some truth to that."

She patted the shoulder of the eight-year old boy in the front passenger seat. "This is Robbie, our oldest son." He turned and gave Grace a shy smile.

Turning in her seat, Lana said, "And back here with Carson is Max, and that makes up our crew."

"Mom's the only girl," Max told Grace.

Grace laughed. "Yes, I can see she's outnumbered."

Lana shook her head. "Sometimes I just have to go do something girly to get away from the rough-housing. I never know what I'll be coming home to, though."

Bruce chimed in from the front again, "Now, Honey, it's not that bad."

"Now, who's not telling the truth, Bruce Caldwell?"

"Well, from a male point of view, the den covered with throw pillows is just not a problem."

Lana turn to Grace, who was enjoying their friendly banter. "See what I mean?"

"Dad…Mom?" Robbie spoke up. "Can we go to Chuckee Cheese for lunch? 'Member last week you said if we'd not complain about going to Olive Garden, you'd take us to Chuckee Cheese this Sunday?"

Looking into the mirror again, Bruce gave a sheepish smile. "Sorry, Ladies, I did say that. Grace have you ever been to Chuckee Cheese?"

Grace smiled. "No, but I've wanted to go there. I've heard it's a fun place."

The boys all began to chatter, telling Grace what they liked best about their favorite eating place.

"Okay, guys, rein it in. We're here at the church," Bruce said.

So interested in the conversation in the car, Grace hadn't noticed that they had driven out from town into a rural area. She looked up and saw the neat, blue, metal building, and the sign, "Cornerstone Cowboy Church." Her heart quickened in excitement.

On one side she could see the fencing of what appeared to be a large corral with roofed bleachers. A larger number of pick-up trucks than cars were already in the parking lot, and more were driving in behind them. Almost all the men and some of the ladies, too, were wearing jeans, boots, and western hats.

Grace smiled. The scene was so different from what she was used to seeing in California, but she found it very pleasing. Almost everyone was carrying a Bible and they greeted each other with hugs and smiles. There was something almost tangible in the air—expectation! She could get used to this.

Lana began introducing Grace as they greeted people on their way into the building. She tried to remember names, but quickly realized it would take hearing them more than once to recall so many.

"Can we go to children's church now, Mom?" Max asked.

"I'll see that they get there, Hon," Bruce said. "You and Grace find us seats."

He and the boys headed down a hallway and Lana directed Grace into a wide, open area with a coffee bar complete with an unbelievable number of large boxes of donuts. Small tables filled the area, and a few people were sitting there, visiting over coffee and the glazed treats.

"This area will be packed after church," Lana said. "Our people love to fellowship with each other. Would you like something? There are several kinds of coffee, bottled water, and of course, the necessary donuts."

"I had enough coffee this morning, but I would like a bottle of water," Grace told her. "I think I'd better skip the donut. I've been eating like a pig since I arrived here in Texas."

"Believe me, Grace," Lana said, indicating Grace's lithe figure, "Nobody's going to know." She smiled and pointed a direction. "Come on, I want to introduce you to Jim and Susan, our interim pastors."

Grace recognized the man that Lana indicated as the one who had met Zach at the airport the night they arrived.

His wife was a pretty brunette with a sweet smile. They were greeting the people as they came in and were obviously loved by them.

Jim looked up and was surprised to see the woman that had waved to Zach at the airport. Apparently, she and Lana had become friends. He wondered how that had happened.

"Jim and Susan, I want you to meet Grace Morgan. She's here in town visiting a friend. Grace, these are our pastors, Jim, and Susan Sheridan."

"Hello, Grace," Susan said, taking her hand in both of hers. "We're so glad to have you here today."

Grace felt the sincerity in Susan's words and immediately liked her.

"Grace…" Jim said, and lowering his voice asked…" You're Zach's friend?"

Grace could feel her face getting warm. "Yes…I guess you could say that."

"Does he know you're here today?"

"No…at least, I didn't tell him I was coming."

Lana spoke up. "Bruce and I took the kids to the beach and Grace was a guest on Zach's tour. We kind of hit it off and I asked her to come to church with us."

Jim shook her hand. "Well, we are delighted that you're here with us, Grace. I hope you're blessed by the service."

"I'm really looking forward to it," Grace said. Surprisingly, she could feel tears welling up in her eyes.

Susan reached out and took her in her arms. Grace could feel the love that radiated from this sweet woman and soaked it in. After a few moments, she pulled away and smiled at Susan.

"Thank you, Susan."

"Grace, any friend of Zach's is a friend of ours. We'd love to have him bring you to dinner one evening."

"I'd like that," Grace told her. "I'm free anytime, so just have Zach tell me when."

"We'll do that."

Lana led her into the sanctuary part of the building and Grace was delighted at the western décor. Some of it reminded her of the desert Southwest look popular in the western states, but the distinctive red, white, and blue starred flag made it exclusively Texan.

They found seats in the middle section, about halfway to the front. The music team was already in place, the band playing a lively song. There were several guitars, drums, a keyboardist, and a saxophone player. Their sound was invigorating, and Grace found herself wanting to clap her hands to the music.

Lana leaned over and said, "They're good, aren't they? And all of them are solid Christians who love the Lord and honor him with their talents."

Knowing that Lana was unaware of her past, Grace didn't say what she wanted to—that just being here with other Christians and hearing the beautiful music was the best thing that had happened to her in a very long time. She did reach over and squeeze Lana's hand saying, "Thank you so much for bringing me. It's wonderful already!"

Bruce joined them, having settled the boys in children's church.

"Boy, am I glad God hasn't called me to children's ministry! Our kids aren't the only ones wound up. It seems all the kiddos are coming in with sugar highs."

Lana laughed. "You'd be surprised, though how those children's workers can turn that hyperactivity into hyper praise and worship with those kids. Karla and Janice are amazing and actually enjoy the rowdiness as much as the kids do."

Bruce just shook his head. "To each his own."

Another jean-clad young man and a pretty young woman in a flowery cotton sundress stepped forward and began to clap to the music.

"Are you glad to be here in the house of the Lord this morning?" the young man asked with a big smile.

The crowd replied vigorously with responses from YeeHaw's, to Amen's, to ear -piercing whistles.

"That's Josh McAdams and his wife, Sibby," Lana told Grace. "They're our worship leaders."

The people had begun to stand, obviously ready to move with the music.

"All right, let's give Him praise!" Sibby told them.

Josh turned to the band. "Hit it, guys! Four strong beats later Josh and Sibby joined them:

"Worship the Lord.
Give Him praise with hearts full of gladness
Lift His name over all the earth
He is worthy of our praise."

The song went on through a couple of verses and repeated choruses. Grace loved it but she had never heard it before. She closed her eyes and just drank in the beautiful sound of believers worshipping their God. Tears of joy began to flow down her face as she lifted her hands in the most freedom of praise she had experienced in years. All the music moved her in the same way, though she wasn't familiar with most of it.

Lana explained later that Zach had recognized the gift of the psalmist in Josh several years ago and had given him liberty to use the music God gave him for this congregation. That was apparently a good decision, for the people entered into the praise and worship wholeheartedly.

Zach awoke knowing he was to go to church this morning. He really wanted to be there, yet the questions bombarding his mind had brought butterflies to his mid-section. What would it be like to be just one of the worshippers and not the pastor? How strange would it seem to be there without Sasha? He knew the people would receive him warmly, but what would they expect of him?

Finally, he stopped just before pulling on his boots and prayed.

"Father, I know I'm being ridiculous. You always have things under control and You always help me, so I'm not going to be paranoid any longer. I'm just going into that church and I'm going to concentrate on worshiping You. All right! That's settled."

He pulled his boots on, picked up his keys, Bible and Stetson and headed out to his truck. In spite of his prayer, it still felt strange to be going to church alone. He thought of Grace and what it might be like to have her there with him. He wondered what she was doing this morning. He knew Karen was out of town and doubted that Grace would go anywhere to church by herself in a strange town.

When he arrived at the church, he was thrilled to see the number of vehicles there. The church was still doing well.

Zach had intentionally arrived a little late so the service would be in progress and his coming in wouldn't be a distraction. Ushers surprised to see him greeted him quietly, but warmly as one of them walked in with him and located him a seat near the back. Several people around him greeted him quietly as well, all of them thrilled to see their pastor. Eventually, Zach was able to place his attention on the worship service and felt the peace of God flow over him. There was a depth to the level of worship that impressed him. He could sense the spiritual growth of the congregation, and he certainly could take no credit for it. Jim Sheridan was doing a far better job than he thought of pastoring Cornerstone Cowboy Church.

When the worship service was over, and the congregation was seated Zach looked around. Seeing so many of the people he'd known and loved still there, still faithful, touched him. There were also many faces he didn't recognize. As his eyes scanned the middle section, he saw Bruce and Lana and…was it Grace? He had no idea she would be there. It seemed she was with Bruce and Lana.

Zach remembered them meeting at the beach when he did his tour. He also remembered hearing Grace say something about coming to church with Lana, so here she was. And he had a perfect view and could watch her.

There was special music by a mixed trio, then Jim got up to preach. Zach knew the moment when Jim spotted him in the congregation and saw his eyes light up. Zach gave an almost imperceptible nod and Jim continued with his sermon. Zach had always felt that Jim did a good job of preaching, but now after three years' practice, he was even better.

His topic was on the importance of living our Christian lives with consistency. As he talked about the time we lost in our spiritual growth when we allowed inconsistency in our walk with the Lord, Zach could feel the sting of truth in his words. He could tell that the people had grown; Jim had. Only he had been stuck in his self -pity.

When Jim encouraged the people at the end of his sermon to repent if they'd been living a life less than full-out for God, Zach wholeheartedly did so.

It only took a few minutes after the last "Amen" for the word to spread that Pastor Zach was in the building, and he was swamped with handshakes and hugs. He tried to keep an eye out for Grace during all this and saw that she wasn't aware of his being there yet. Then someone spoke to Lana and they both turned and saw him. Zach had only a split-second connection with Grace before he was grabbed in a bear hug by one of the church brothers. It was only fair to give his attention to these people who loved him so. Surely, he'd be able to speak with Grace before she left.

Her heart skipped a beat when she saw Zach and knew he saw her. She was happy that he was so well received by his congregation. There were a few hundred people there and it seemed most of them personally greeted him.

"Shall we try to speak to Pastor Zach?" Bruce asked.

Lana looked to Grace. "Do you mind waiting?"

Grace smiled. "Not at all."

"Then I'll go collect the boys," Bruce said.

As they waited, Lana and Grace slowly made their way along with the crowd in Zach's direction. Several times Grace looked his way and caught his eye. Once they connected long enough to exchange a quick smile and Grace's heart did the little flip-flop again. She hadn't expected to see him today; she was still considering his job proposal.

"Grace!" Lana whispered, but Grace felt as though everyone around heard her. "Pastor keeps looking at you like he's afraid you'll leave before he can talk to you." She turned to look Grace full in the face and her eyes widened.

"There's something going on between you two! Oh, that is exciting. He needs someone like you."

Grace wished she could control the flush that rose to her face. She took Lana by the arm and drew her closer.

"Please, Lana. I don't know if it's anything. I'm asking you to not say anything to anybody. Rumors like this could be bad for either of us. If something does develop between us, I promise, I will let you know. Right now, we're just getting acquainted and I'm not sure he's over Sasha enough to move on to a relationship with someone else. Just pray that we'll know the will of God."

“All right, I promise. I won’t say a thing, but there’s something in his eyes when he looks at you.” She paused a moment, then said,

“Grace, Zach Clayton is one of the best men God put on this earth. He has been such a good example for men in our church. Sasha always said he was the best husband a woman could ever wish for. So, if God gives you the go-ahead, don’t hesitate–go for it!”

Grace couldn’t help but laugh at Lana’s exuberance and reached out to hug her. She caught Zach looking at her again and smiled at him over Lana’s shoulder. She was beginning to agree with her new friend’s advice.

Chapter 11

Across the church a tall, attractive woman with stylish frosted hair and designer clothes watched the crowd welcoming Zach. *It was about time he came back—way past time for him to be over Sasha.* Her insides churned as she thought of how many times she had tried to convince him to move on and allow another woman in his life. And she was determined that *she* would be that woman. That was the only reason she had stayed at this cowboy church.

It was evident by her clothing that she wasn't a cowgirl, and honestly, there was only one cowboy Alysse Stratton had any consideration for and he was in the middle of half a church of people now. There wasn't anything she could do but wait and fill her eyes with the sight of him until enough people left that she could have him to herself.

It had been almost a year since she'd seen him. He refused to meet her, even for a cup of coffee and strictly forbade her to come out to the Sheridan's ranch where he lived. She had to admit that he had never encouraged her interest in him, but still, she was determined to win his affections. Just the sight of him in the western clothing, boots, and most of all, that hat, made her blood boil. She wanted him, and she intended to have him. As she watched Zach's every move, she saw that his gaze repeatedly went to a woman that seemed to be with Bruce and Lana Caldwell. Alysse had to admit—she was attractive.

This must be the blonde's first time to attend church here. Alysse would have noticed her…any attractive woman could be a competitor. The woman smiled over Lana's shoulder—right at Zach, and he smiled back. Like they had a secret between them! Whatever it was, she intended to find out.

Alysse moved closer to Zach from her direction, even as that woman and the Caldwell's did from the other side. Finally, she was close enough to see the three little boys practically knock Zach down as they embraced his legs. Stupid kids!

But Zach didn't seem to mind. He bent down and hugged them warmly. Then it was Bruce and Lana 's turn. When he was done with them, he turned to the blonde and instead of hugging her immediately, he took both her hands and looked into her eyes. They exchanged a few words then smiled at each other and embraced. Alysse could see that Zach was talking right into the woman's ear, then positioned her right at his side as he turned to greet someone else! This was obviously not the first time he had met the woman.

Alysse was absolutely furious! Apparently, he had finally decided to allow a woman into his life, and he had not bothered to contact *her*. Well, she would let him know that she was still in the running and at the same time make it clear to the blonde that Alysse Stratton would be the next Mrs. Zach Clayton.

There had been many ladies who hugged Zach with genuine affection and no sense of impropriety. As she stood beside him, Grace saw only love for their pastor coming from these ladies.

Then she sensed the lustful spirit of the woman with the frosted hair who somehow suddenly managed to have her arms around Zach's neck. Grace recognized the same spirit that had emanated from Damien's lover, Cici Jacquess.

"Hello, Zach, darling," the woman said. "I see you finally came back to me."

Zach appeared stunned. He grasped the woman's hands and forcefully pulled them from his neck.

"Alysse," he said coldly. Then quietly, he hissed. "That was uncalled for."

Grace thought she'd be sick. It was like reliving the moment she walked in on Damien and that awful woman.

"Lana," she whispered. "Where is the ladies' room?"

Lana took one look at her white face and grabbed her by the arm. "I'll take you."

When Zach saw that Grace was leaving, he pushed Alysse out of his way and went to her, taking her arm.

"Grace, please…don't leave. I know how that must have looked, but I assure you, I want nothing to do with that woman."

Grace nodded. "I know, Zach. I just…I think I'm going to be sick."

"Lana, I still want to keep our plans," Zach said. "Don't leave without me…and take care of Grace, will you?"

"I will, Pastor. We'll be back in a few minutes." She guided Grace down the hallway as Zach looked after them, then took a deep breath and turned to face Alysse.

Quietly, so that only she could hear, he told her in a voice like steel, "Don't ever touch me again. Not even a handshake. I don't want you anywhere near me. I will never have anything to do with you. Is this clear?" His eyes flashed fire it seemed as he stood staring at her until she cowered, and he felt he had finally gotten through to her.

Some of the people who had witnessed the disturbing situation politely left and waved to Zach. Others still waited to speak with him, and he went to them as though nothing had happened. Jim and Susan had witnessed the entire scene and could see that Zach was doing his best not to let it ruin the day.

Thankfully, Alysse Stratton left after Zach had spoken privately to her. Jim had often wished the woman would leave the church altogether. There was always conflict around her. He kept hoping that she would repent of her ugly attitudes and allow God to change her. It didn't appear that she wanted to change, though.

She had relentlessly pursued Zach, even before Sasha was gone. It seems she had expected to walk right into Zach's life as soon as Sasha died. Hopefully, this wouldn't interfere with Zach's new relationship with Grace. It had obviously affected her.

Jim was relieved to see Grace and Lana returning to them. Grace looked better, but still a little pale. Zach saw her too, and now that all the other people were gone, he went to her.

"How are you doing? Are you okay now?"

"I'm fine, Zach. I'm sorry to worry you," Grace assured him.

"Are we still on for lunch?" His eyes were full of concern.

Bruce and Lana had invited him to come with them to Chuckee Cheese and he had agreed since Grace would be there. But if Grace really wasn't feeling well, that would be the last place she needed to be.

"I think I'm game for Chuckee Cheese for a while anyway. Will you take me home if I can't cope with the big mouse?"

Lana laughed and Zach grinned. "I promise," he said, "Scout's honor."

"Bruce took the boys to the car a while ago," Zach told Lana. "Would you mind if I stole Grace to ride with me? I'd like to talk to her for a few minutes and there will be no talking once we enter Chuckee Cheese."

"Sure, Pastor." Lana agreed. "We'll meet you there."

"Thanks, Lana…for everything," Grace gave her a quick hug.

Grace turned to Jim and Susan who had been standing by.

"Jim…Susan…Would you care to join us for lunch? We'd love to have you."

"Yeah, why don't you come, Bro?" Zach said.

"I heard where you're going," Jim said with a chuckle. "Fortunately, Jay and Lil invited us to the ranch for lunch. The kids rode out with them already."

"Ohhh, I'm envious," Zach said. "I dropped in and had supper with them last evening. Mama Lil had cooked up a feast."

Susan looked surprised. "You went out to the ranch?"

Zach looked a bit sheepish. "Yeah, I did."

Jim eyed him closely. "Things go okay?"

"Remarkably so," Zach told him then placed his hand at Grace's back and looking down at her asked, "Ready to go, pretty lady?"

Grace smiled up at him, "I am, Cowboy."

Jim and Susan looked at each other and held their comments until Zach and Grace had walked outside. Then Susan squealed and grabbed Jim around the neck.

"It's happening, Jimbo! Yes, yes, yes! Our prayers are being answered."

Returning her hug Jim grinned. "Yep, he's been a goner from day one." He snuggled her closer. "I kinda like how this is comin' down. Zach falls in love and I get hugs."

* * * * *

Since Zach had arrived late, he'd had to park his truck in the farthest area of the parking lot, so they had a bit of a walk. Grace looked up and found his brown eyes looking tenderly at her.

"I'm glad you came here to church this morning. I was pleasantly surprised to see you," he said.

"I'm really glad I came, too. You have a great church, Zach. I was truly blessed. Your people were thrilled to see you."

Zach smiled. "Yeah, that was special. I shouldn't have been away so long."

"Are you thinking of returning to senior pastor soon?"

He paused a moment, then cocked his head and nodded. "I'm headed that way."

"Jim Sheridan has certainly done a good job with the church and his sermon today was great," Grace said.

"Yes, it was. I needed it too–'had to do some repenting myself. I didn't get a chance to tell him what a good job he's done, but I will. I sure appreciate that guy. He's the best friend you could have."

They were at the truck now and Zach helped Grace step up into the cab. He removed his Stetson and reached over to put it on the back seat. As before, the action placed his face within inches of Grace's. Both froze. This time Zach ran his index finger down her face and along her jawline as he looked into her eyes. He held her gaze, trying to decide if it would be wrong to kiss her when Grace suddenly smiled and broke the moment.

"The big mouse is waiting," Grace said.

Zach chuckled and pulled back. "Yeah, Bruce and Lana are going to think we ran out on them."

He started the ignition and pulled out onto the road. "I doubt they'd be surprised if we did. Not many people without kids are brave enough to go there."

"Well, I want to see this famous rodent, and I've heard the pizza there is pretty good. I think the boys were excited about bringing me for the first time."

"I love those little guys. They're a riot."

"It's evident they really love you, too. I'm kind of impressed with the whole family. Lana has become a friend very quickly. It will be good for Karen not to feel that she has to be responsible for all my friendship needs."

They rode quietly for a few minutes, then Zach said, "Grace, about that woman there at the church."

Grace blew out a deep breath. "I was going to ask you about her."

"Her name is Alysse Stratton. She has had designs on me ever since she learned that Sasha was ill and might not live. Not once have I ever given her any encouragement, but it hasn't fazed her. I guess she's had success in seducing men in the past and thinks if she persists, she'll eventually have her way. I was horrified at the way she acted today in front of the church people, and especially in front of you."

He turned to look at Grace. "I think she saw the attention I gave you and was sending you a message. After you and Lana left, I told her in no uncertain terms to stay away from me. I think I finally got through to her. She's a trouble-maker, though, and I don't trust her."

"She has the same spirit as the woman who had the affair with my husband. I think that's what made me feel sick. It was like reliving that situation all over again."

Zach reached over and took her hand. "I am so sorry, Grace. I hadn't even thought about her…about how she'd react when I came back to the church. I can't stand to be around her. She makes me feel dirty, as though I had taken part in her vile behavior. Everything she's done in the hopes of enticing me has only made me more determined to stay away from her."

He looked down at Grace as he squeezed her hand. "Are you sure you're okay?"

"I'm fine, Zach. Thank you for being concerned about how I'd take all that."

They had arrived now at Chuckee Cheese and Zach killed the engine. He retrieved his hat and got out of the truck. Turning to take Grace's hand to help her down, he grinned.

"All right, let's go meet the big mouse."

Two hours later they were saying goodbye to the Caldwell family. "Thank you for the most fun I've had in ages," Grace said.

"You did good at the games, Ms. Grace," Max told her. "Will you and Pastor Zach come with us again?"

"How about it, Pastor Zach. Can we do this again," Grace asked him.

"You bet, Maxwell," he said, ruffling the boy's hair.

"Yea!" Carson and Robbie both yelled.

"All right, boys," Lana said, "I think it's time for a more mannerly tone."

Bruce agreed, telling them it was getting time for his Sunday afternoon nap.

"Do you mind if Zach takes me home? Grace asked. "You were so sweet to pick me up. I don't want to be rude."

Lana and Bruce smiled at each other and then at Grace. "We don't mind at all." They shook hands, gave hugs all around, and walked to the door, waving as they went their separate ways.

"That really was fun," Grace said, looking up at Zach. "I doubt that either of us has laughed that much in a long time."

"I know I haven't. See, you're good for me." When they reached his truck, Zach stopped before opening the door.

"All right, I'm dying to know…are you going to work for me?"

Grace looked up and saw hope in his eyes. Her fear had been of that wall between them, but she hadn't felt its presence even once today.

"Yes, I'll work through the rest of the season, and who knows what will happen after that. We'll re-evaluate things then."

"Whoo-hoo!" Zach yelled, picked her up and swung her around. "Thank you, thank you!"

Grace could feel her face reddening. "Zach, could you thank me a little less noticeably?"

Zach lowered her to her feet. "Sorry, I've just been afraid you'd tell me you couldn't do it."

"You'll need to tell me what I should be doing other than what Karen and I did the last time."

"Yeah, there are some things I need to go over with you, get your Social Security number, set your enormous salary, etc."

Grace smiled. "Come in when we get to Karen's place and we can discuss it. I'll make us some coffee."

When they were inside the house Grace led the way to the kitchen. "I'll get the coffee going, and then I'm going to change into something more comfortable."

"Why don't you show me where things are, and I'll do it. I make a mean pot of coffee," Zach said.

"Okay, there is the coffee maker," she pointed to the appliance on the counter, "and coffee and filters are in a canister just above it. I'll be back."

Grace turned to leave, but Zach drew her back to him. "I don't think I've told you how pretty you look in that dress. Well, actually, it's you that makes the dress look good."

Grace looked up into his eyes that were gentle and filled with admiration. Damien had never looked at her this way. A girl could get used to this.

"Thank you, Zach. I'm really glad you came to church; I wasn't expecting to see you today."

Zach nodded. "It was good to see everyone. It made me realize how much I've missed being part of their lives. But…about coming back…I don't think…, he stopped, "Grace, I don't know…"

Grace could see his frustration, feel his fear of trying to lead his church without a wife by his side. She reached out and placed her hand on his arm.

"Zach, you don't have to have all the answers just now. God's got this. Why don't you get the coffee going while I change clothes."

He grinned. "You're right…I can handle coffee."

When Grace returned to the kitchen a few minutes later in a pair of knit lounge pants and a tee shirt, the smell of fresh coffee filled the air.

"Hmm, smells good."

"Yeah, it does," Zach said. "That was a good idea."

"I guess I need pen and paper, don't I?" Grace asked. "To write down my new job duties? "

Zach chuckled. "Yes, that multitude of tasks. I'll have to admit though, it seemed they multiplied when I was trying to do all of them myself."

Grace remembered how panic-stricken he looked that day on the beach. "Well, the rescue team is here now, so you won't have to go through that again."

She pointed to the top right cabinet. "Since you're on coffee duty, the cups are on the lower shelf up there in case you'd like to pour it. I'm going to raid Karen's office for writing materials."

"Yes, Ma'am," Zach replied. "Uh, who's the boss here?"

Grace gave him a saucy grin. "Well, you are, of course. You get to pick the cups."

"She is just too cute," Zach thought as Grace walked away.

They had begun their discussion about things Grace would need to know on the tours when his phone rang. She noticed that he frowned when he saw the name on the caller ID.

"Grace, would you excuse me? I need to take this." He hurried outside as Grace said, "Sure."

Stepping out onto the porch Zach pushed the answer button.

"Yeah, Joe, this is Zach. Is my mother all right?" He knew there would be no reason for the owner of the Beachside Bar to call him unless there was a situation with his mother.

"Hey, Zach. I think she will be, but she fell going to the restroom and she's hurting in several places. I've called an ambulance just in case. They should be here any minute."

"Okay, Thanks, Joe. Do you know where they'll take her? I'll meet them there."

"I'm not sure, but I'll call you back as soon as I find out."

"Thanks, I appreciate it. I'm heading to Galveston now. Would you tell her I'm on my way?"

"Sure, Zach, I'll let her know." Joe replied kindly.

"Thanks, buddy." Zach tried to choke back the fear that rose in his chest. Was this the awful event he felt would inevitably come? His mother couldn't continue her current lifestyle without an unpleasant ending. He hurried back inside to get his hat and say goodbye to Grace. What would he tell her? He just wasn't ready to bring up the subject of his mother to her. Her parents were godly people. How could she possibly understand that his mother spent almost every waking hour drinking in a sleazy bar?

She was standing, waiting for him with concern on her face.

"Grace," he paused. "I have to go. I…I…"

Sensing his hesitation Grace, touched his arm. "It's all right, Zach. You needn't explain. Just go."

Relief flooded his face. "I'm really sorry. I'll be in touch." He gave her a quick hug and headed for the door.

Grace closed and locked the door behind him and returned to the table to gather up the unused writing materials and put them away. She took her coffee to a comfy chair and sat down. The house seemed so empty with Zach's sudden exit. Karen was gone to her conference. For the first time since arriving in Texas Grace felt loneliness settling over her like a gray cloud.

"This is ridiculous, Grace!" She said aloud. "You had a wonderful day with new friends, found a church where the presence of the Lord was so comforting, spent time with a very attractive, sweet man."

"But that man left," the thought came. Was that what was really bothering her? Zach was obviously concerned about someone or something to leave so suddenly, and she wasn't close enough to him to be included in whatever troubled him. She was used to being needed and at the moment there didn't seem to be anyone who needed her.

"So, you're going to have a pity party?" she scolded herself. She had counseled many women who were caught in that trap of feeling that life had no meaning without a man, and here she was on the brink of that herself.

"No, I refuse to go there," she said. Whatever new path the Lord was leading her to take, He would always be with her. She headed toward the kitchen for a coffee refill and her phone rang. The caller ID read Marla Sanders…the Hollywood stylist-friend who had given Grace her new look.

"Marla, hi! What a pleasant surprise."

"Hey, Grace! How's my friend doing in Texas?"

"I'm doing well…for the most part. It's so good to hear your voice. How are you?"

"I'm good. Actually, I'm in Texas, too."

"You are? Where?"

She laughed. "Really close, Grace… I'm in Houston."

Grace squealed. "Are you kidding? What are you doing here?"

"I'm attending an annual conference for people in my trade. My assistant booked my flight a day early by mistake, but I told her not to worry about it, that maybe I could spend a little time with you."

"That is wonderful, Marla. The timing couldn't be better."

"Is it okay if I come and spend the night with you? I'll just be sitting here bored in the hotel room. Our first meeting is tomorrow evening."

"Yes, you can spend the night! Karen has gone to an educational conference. I'll use her room and you can have mine."

"Great! I've already put Karen's address in the GPS of the rental car and it says I'm just a little over an hour away. I'll treat you to dinner when I get there."

"Why don't I just fix us something here and we can put our jammies on and talk half the night?"

"Even better! I'm so glad this is working out. I'll see you in about an hour and a half."

"I can't wait to see you. Oh, Marla, this a gated community…just punch in *322."

"All right, bye!"

Grace headed to the kitchen to decide what to prepare for dinner, but stopped and looked upward. "God, you are so amazing! Just when I was needing a friend, You send one!"

Marla called from the gate just as Grace had taken her favorite chicken casserole out of the oven .

"I'm here," Marla said.

"Okay, when you come through the gate take the fork to the left and you'll see me standing on the sidewalk. I'll open the garage and you can pull in next to Karen's car."

"All right."

Grace barely had time to push the garage door opener and step outside before Marla pulled up to Karen's home. Grace smiled at her friend and directed her into the garage as the door completely opened. It was too crowded between the cars for hugs so they waited until they stepped inside.

"You can't believe how glad I am to see you," Grace told Marla as they hugged.

"Me, too, Grace. I just wanted to see for myself that you're all right."

Marla was as chic as one would expect a stylist in Hollywood to be...a pretty brunette and as shapely as the models and actresses she clothed. She put her hands on Grace's shoulders and peered into her face. "You look good, Grace. Better than I've seen you in almost a year. Texas must be agreeing with you."

"It is," Grace assured her. "I've met some really nice people here. Hey, I've got dinner ready; let's eat before it gets cold."

"I'll agree with that. I had a pastry and coffee in the airport before leaving LAX this morning, and only pretzels on the plane since, so I'm famished. Whatever you've made smells wonderful!"

"It's one of my favorite 'go to' chicken casseroles with pasta and pesto, and of course, salad. Is iced tea okay?"

"It's not 'Texas style sweet tea,' is it?"

Grace laughed. "So you know about that elixir ? No, I still make it unsweetened." She pointed to the right hallway. "My bedroom is that direction if you'd like to freshen up while I put dinner on the table."

. "I'll just be a minute."

After dinner they were loading the dishwasher and putting left-overs away and Marla said, "Karen's home is lovely. It's charming and peaceful."

Grace nodded. "Yes, it's been just what I needed and Karen has been so gracious."

"I wish she'd been here so I could meet her,"

"I know; I'd love for her to meet you, too. Do they always hold these conventions in Houston ?"

"No, whoever is in charge chooses different cities, always large ones, of course, to host them."

"Is your work going well?" Grace asked.

"Yes, I'm staying busy…really busy. I've been tossing around the idea of starting my own business. Most of my work comes through several clients who are very loyal to me, so I'm thinking I could start with a solid customer base up front. At present I do all the work and my employers get half the income just for having me on their payroll. I've made them a lot of money in the past few years."

"I know you have," Grace agreed. "I think you should pray about starting your own company. It wouldn't surprise me at all if God's just been waiting for you to catch that idea He's been tossing out there."

Marla smiled. "Ya think?"

"I do," Grace replied. "Hey, how much time do you have tomorrow before you have to head back to your conference? We need to think of something fun to do."

"I won't have to leave here until about 3:30. That gives me time to get back to the hotel and dress for the evening. I wish you could be there just to see all the amazing clothes everyone will be wearing. Our work is dressing people to look their best, so you can imagine the time and money that goes into our showing off. It's like a style show for stylists! They're serving us dinner, so I don't have to worry about that. There IS something I was hoping to get to do while I'm here, though."

"Okay, what's that?' Grace asked.

"We're close to Galveston, aren't we?"

Grace laughed. "Yes, we certainly are. Karen and I were there just over a week ago."

"Well, would you mind going again? My grandparents took me to Galveston beach the summer I was ten and it was such a wonderful vacation. I've always wanted to go back. Could we just walk the beachfront, maybe peek in a few shops….have lunch?"

"Of course we can;. that would be fun. After all, Karen and I didn't have enough time to check out ALL the shops on the strand."

Marla yawned. "Oh Grace, I'm sorry. I was thinking we'd talk half the night, but I am suddenly jet - lagged big time. I got up at four this morning, so I guess I shouldn't be surprised."

"I know that feeling. I took a red-eye flight that was delayed, so it was the middle of the night when I got here. Poor Karen, she was really sweet about having to pick me up at that awful hour.. We just had a snack and crashed. By the way, that bed you'll be sleeping on is wonderful."

"Well, I'm ready for it. Thanks for giving up your room for me. Do you need to get anything from there"

"No, I've already gotten my things. We should plan on leaving here about 9:30 in the morning if we're going to fit in everything we want to do."

" Okay, I'll set my phone for 8:30." She reached out to give Grace a hug. "It's so good to be with you again. 'See you in the morning."

Grace returned her hug warmly. "It's wonderful to have you here. 'Sleep well." She found herself yawning, too as she made her way to Karen's room. Thinking back over her day as she dressed for bed she realized that it had been a busy one…church that morning, the disturbing encounter with that woman who was chasing after Zach, the very active time at Chuckee Cheese with three adorable, but rowdy little boys. Then she remembered Zach receiving a phone call that obviously disturbed him so much that he had to leave suddenly. She felt badly then that she hadn't prayed more about that, even if she didn't know what was going on. It slipped her mind after Marla called and she had to get busy preparing dinner.

"Lord, I'm sorry," she prayed as she settled into bed. "I pray that whatever was concerning Zach has worked out well. Please be with him."

CHAPTER 12

Zach headed for Galveston as soon as he left Grace. He felt guilty about not explaining why he was leaving so suddenly, but he just couldn't dump that on her without having the time to discuss it. He needed to get to his mom and learn her condition.

He pulled his phone out and pushed the speed dial number for Jim. His friend picked up on the second ring.

"So you survived Chuckee Cheese, I see," Jim said.

"Yeah, Buddy," Zach said and sighed.

"Hey, what's up?" When Zach didn't respond with a quick witted comment Jim realized something was wrong.

"It's Mom. Joe just called me and said she had a fall at the bar. He's waiting for the ambulance to get there and then he'll tell me which hospital they're taking her to."

"Do you have any idea how bad she's hurt?" Jim asked.

"Joe wasn't sure, 'said she's hurting in several places."

"How can I help, Bro?"

"Just pray at this point. I'll call you as soon as I know more."

"You got it. I'll tell Susan and we'll get the prayer going."

"Thanks, I'll keep in touch."

Zach put his phone down, thankful for a friend that he could turn to. Previously he would have called his Dad, but now that Dad was married to another woman Zach wasn't sure if that was appropriate At times he still had to battle the anger that made him want to strike out at his mother for choosing to live her life numbed by alcohol. Since childhood he had been embarrassed and ashamed of her behavior. Even now, knowing that when he discussed her situation with a doctor and nurses, they would know she had fallen because she was drunk. Tears filled his eyes.

"God, help me not to make this about me. Help my mother. I forgive her, Lord, and I know that You do, too. Give me the grace to overlook her faults and to love her like You love her. Please let her be all right. I'm just not ready to lose her."

Zach realized then that inside he was still that little boy who was holding onto the hope that his mother would become sober and the loving relationship they once had known would be possible again. It had to be her choice, but in all these years, she had not wanted to face life without the bottle. Maybe she simply couldn't. She not only still bore the pain of losing her precious baby girl, but now she had years of remorse for what she had done to her son and her husband.

More than once she had heard other children saying derogatory things to Zach about her and even through his tears he would defend her.. That had to break her heart because in spite of her behavior Zach knew that she loved him. The shame she had brought to her loving, faithful husband all those years...surely, in her mind there was just no making up for that, or forgetting it. At least the alcohol numbed the pain for a while.

"Lord, it seems so hopeless. I'm sure Mom feels that it is. But You have promised that Your grace and love have done away with hopelessness. I choose to believe Your Word. Help me to be strong enough for both of us."

His phone rang and Zach saw it was Joe again. "Yeah, Joe," he answered.

"The ambulance just left, Zach. They're taking your mom to John Sealy.. The EMT's initial examination here showed that nothing is broken. Of course, they'll check her more thoroughly at the hospital."

"Okay. I'm close to the turn-off , so I'll be there in a few minutes. Thanks, Joe."

"Uh...Zach, I want you to know that I don't just keep letting Amelia drink when I know she's had enough. I do cut her off. I hope you won't hold me responsible. I care about your mom."

"I appreciate that, Joe. I don't think every bar owner would do that."

"Would you call me when you find out what the doctors say? Lots of folks here are waiting to know ."

"I will, and thank all of them for caring, okay?"

Zach could tell that Joe was struggling with his emotions as he choked out. " Yeah...I'll tell 'em."

As usual, the hospital parking lot was full. Zach wanted to get inside as quickly as possible and this was frustrating. He drove slowly up and down each row until finally, a car drove out and he hurriedly pulled into the empty space. His long legs carried him quickly into the corridor that led to the front desk.

"Yes, sir; can I help you?" The mature woman at the desk looked kindly at him.

"My mother has just been brought in by ambulance in the past half hour or so. I'd like to know where she is, please. Her name is Amelia Clayton," Zach told her.

The woman clicked a few keys on her computer and gave him a smile. "Sir, your mother is being taken to room 242 as we speak. That's on the second floor. I wish her well."

"Thank you," Zach replied, touched by the clerk's kindness. The nursing staff would obviously be getting his mother settled into the room, so he decided to take the stairs rather than the elevator. Suddenly, he felt alone. Sasha had always been at his side when he had to make hospital visits for people in his church and he hadn't realized how much he depended on her strength. He thought of Grace and knew that she would be that way, too. But he hadn't told her about his mother and now wasn't the time to spring that on her.

When he reached the second floor he approached the nurses' station where a nurse was busy at the computer. She looked up at him when she became aware of his presence.

"Yes?"

"I am looking for Amelia Clayton. I understand she's been brought up to room 242. I'm her son, Zach Clayton."

"Yes, Mr. Clayton. We've just got her settled into her room and the doctor is with her. He probably doesn't have much to tell you until he has examined her. If you'll have a seat in the waiting area one of us will come and get you when he's done. Oh, and there's complimentary coffee in there as well," she said with a smile.

Thinking of the good coffee he had left at Grace's he smiled, too. "That is most appreciated." He went to the waiting room, poured himself a cup of coffee and found a seat. There were only a few people there and no one sat near him, so he closed his eyes and tried to make sense of the various thoughts racing through his mind. What if his mother was injured badly enough that she shouldn't be alone? He knew she wouldn't want to leave her apartment, but he also knew that the condition of her place would very likely be deemed unlivable if anyone else saw it. He hadn't been inside it for several years, but it could only have gotten worse through time. It was almost at the unlivable stage when he had last seen it. He just happened to come to check on her and the door was open. She had been on her way out and turned back to get something she'd forgotten or she would never have allowed him to see inside. She was very angry to find him there in the doorway and told him to never come there again. From that time on he had gone to the bar to check on her and give her money.

Zach had the feeling that his mother would fight any decision he suggested about her staying anyplace else, so he didn't know what he would do. He didn't want to be at war with her, but he felt responsible to see that she was taken care of. Would she be willing to stay at his ranch? He didn't think so, but he couldn't think of any other option. He knew that Lillian would be willing to help if she was needed.

"Mr. Clayton?" The voice startled him out of his reverie and he stood quickly. A young man dressed in a white doctor's coat stood a few feet away.

"Yes, I'm Zach Clayton."

The doctor reached to shake Zach's hand. "I'm Dr. Reginald Whitmore. I just examined your mother. I'd like to talk with you a few minutes. Let's sit."

Zach returned to his chair and the doctor found one nearby.

"How is my mother, Doctor?"

"If you're asking if she is in any immediate danger from the fall, no. There is bruising already beginning to appear and by tomorrow she will likely be experiencing severe soreness. Honestly, I am more concerned about her overall condition than the results of the fall."

Zach sighed. "Her drinking?"

The doctor nodded. "I'm sure this is no surprise to you. There are numerous symptoms that indicate that she's been drinking heavily for a long time. In fact, I'm surprised that we've not seen her here in the hospital before now."

Zach nodded. "Every time my phone rings with an unknown number I wonder if it's a call that something bad has happened to her," he said. "My father and I have tried for years to get help for her, but she doesn't want it. She has absolutely refused to go into any kind of program to help her stop drinking."

"Well, her body has reached the place now that she will either have to stop, or she will die. I hate to sound so negative but that is the medical truth. Do you think telling her that will make a difference? Does she want to live badly enough to try?"

Tears welled up in Zach's eyes. "Dr. Whitmore, I wish she did. Not once has she even considered trying to get off the poison. My dad put up with this for forty years and finally divorced her a couple of years ago. He found a loving, Christian woman, has recently remarried, and is happy for the first time in all those years. My mother is my responsibility now, but I've had no better luck. She doesn't want me to check on her because she knows it hurts me to see her like this. What can I do?"

The doctor's voice was kind as he leaned in toward Zach. "I wish I had an easy answer for you, Mr. Clayton. Alcoholic addiction is as varied and complicated as the individuals it torments. It might be helpful to discuss this with one of our counselors here at the hospital." He stood and crossed his arms. "Let me go back in there and talk to her. She wasn't completely sober when I examined her, but maybe by now she will allow me to reason with her. I think it might be better for me to speak to her without you being present. Is that all right with you?"

Zach nodded. "Yes, I'm sure she would prefer I not be there."

"I'll be back after I talk with her," the doctor said. Giving Zach a pat on the shoulder he left.

Zach walked to the windows and looked out over the crowded parking lot. Were there really that many people visiting loved ones here? How many of them faced situations that left them in the same turmoil he was feeling now? Surely many of the patients were facing life or death situations. There were likely people visiting mothers who had given birth to precious, newborn babies. They were probably the only ones who realized happiness from their time in the hospital.

"Oh, God, forgive me," he prayed silently. "I've been sitting here engrossed in my own situation and I'm surrounded by multitudes that are hurting as much as I am, and whose situations could be much worse. Help them, Father. Be their strength, their comfort. I don't know their needs, but You do. Please intervene and reveal Your love to them."

He sat quietly as peace filled his heart. He prayed that Amelia would listen and receive the advice of the doctor. That somehow her heart would change and she would be willing to attempt to lay aside the habit that was destroying her.

Zach drank the rest of his now-cold coffee and poured another cup. Again, thinking of the coffee he'd left at Grace's, he wondered what she had thought at his sudden departure with no explanation. The

Lord had been urging him to tell her about his mother. Now, it could be awkward to explain that he'd been keeping a part of his life from her. When would he ever learn that God is always right!

He heard footsteps and looked up to see Dr. Winthrop headed his way. Zach stood. "Well, did you have any luck?" he asked. They returned to their seats.

"I do believe that your mother is taking seriously what I had to say to her. I couldn't get her to commit to entering rehab, at least not just now. She did say she'd think about it. I didn't tell her I had spoken with you, but she said she didn't want anyone 'hounding her' to do this, and that I was supposed to tell you not to pressure her."

'Well, I guess that's a bit better than an outright 'No,'" Zach said. " I know it has to be her decision, so I'll just keep praying that she makes the right one. How long do you think she'll need to be hospitalized?"

"I'd like to keep her a couple of days, but I doubt that she'll stay. Her body is used to a continual intake of alcohol and it's going to demand it. If she refuses to go into rehab, she will need to either satisfy the need for the alcohol or she will go into withdrawals and in her condition that would not be good."

* * * * *

Grace had the coffee made and was buttering raisin bread toast when Marla entered the kitchen. She looked up and smiled at her friend. "Good morning. I sure am glad you took the time to fit me into your trip to Texas."

Marla poured herself a cup of coffee. "I've really missed you, Grace, and I wanted to see for myself that you were all right. I have to say that you are doing far better than I expected."

Grace nodded. "Texas has been good for me."

"Well, if I do start my own company I'd love for you to come and work for me. Do you think you'll ever come back to California?"

Grace thought for a few moments. "I know time will help ease the pain of this past year out there, but I have felt so much better since being away from all that happened. Honestly, I don't know how I'll feel in the future."

She motioned toward the living room. "Let's sit in here where we can put our feet up." They took their coffee and toast and made themselves comfortable on either ends of the sofa.

Marla took a deep breath and exhaled. "Grace, I ran into Damien and…and *HER*.."

Grace's eyes widened, but she didn't say anything.

"He looked terrible. He's lost weight; his face looked haggard. He's aged several years in just one. His hair is graying."

"Did he talk to you?" Grace asked, knowing that Damien was well aware that she and Marla had been the best of friends.

"I could tell that he wanted to, but SHE wasn't going to let that happen, 'practically pushed him out the door of the restaurant when she saw that we recognized each other. I got the feeling that she is definitely the one in charge now."

Grace shook her head. "Oh, Damien. You know, I have a much clearer picture of our relationship now that I'm out of it. I'd never want to go back to it, but I still hate to see him suffering the consequences of his actions."

"That's because you've got a heart of gold, my dear Grace. Your parents named you perfectly," Marla said. "And speaking of them, how are they?"

"Mom and Dad are doing well. They went through all of my heartache with me, but as I get better, so do they."

"And that handsome younger brother of yours?" Marla asked.

"I haven't spoken with Josh personally since a couple of weeks before I left LA. I could see that it was really hard for him to hear what Damien did to me. He wanted to go and punch him. I thought it was best to just not talk to him for a while and not keep upsetting him."

"Well, if he was about ten years older I'd be setting my cap for him. Not only is he one of the best looking guys I've ever seen, he's a real sweetheart and a true Christian to boot. And those are really hard to find."

"Yes, they are," Grace agreed, but couldn't help smiling as she thought of Zach.

Marla noticed the smile and kicked Grace's foot with hers. "Hey, what are you not telling me?" When Grace didn't answer she leaned toward her. "Don't tell me you've met someone."

Grace said, "Okay, I won't."

Marla just stared at her for a few moments. "What?...Really? Have you met a guy? Not that it should surprise me; you're gorgeous!

"It's kind of a long story," Grace said, "and we need to get to Galveston. "But I really think it's a God-thing. I'll tell you in the car."

Marla gave her a feigned fierce look. "All right, Grace Morgan. I'm holding you to that."

Chapter 13

After leaving the church Alysse Stratton paced the floor of her posh condominium, her emotions flip-flopping from anger to humiliation and back again to rage that threatened an unhealthy rise in blood pressure. She plopped down into a white leather chair and trembled as she recalled the fury in Zach Clayton's face when he told her to never touch him again. On numerous occasions over the past few years he had refused her advances. But he'd never spoken to her like that.

Maybe she did overdo the scene by putting her arms around his neck and saying the thinks she did with those people around. She just wasn't thinking straight when she saw him treating that blonde woman like something fragile. And the way he had pushed her aside when the woman was putting on her little, "I'm going to be sick" act. How was she supposed to react?

She stood and paced the living room again. There was no longer any doubt about Zach's lack of interest in her. But that didn't mean that she was through with him. And she definitely wasn't through with that blonde!

Alysse hadn't even started with her, but she needed to know her name. What was her story? Where did she come from, and where did Zach meet her? The way he interacted with her it was clear that he knew her. Alysse was positive it was the first time she had been to church there. She always watched for women that could be competition, but Zach hadn't been coming to church, so he couldn't have met her there. How was she going to find out about this woman?

Suddenly, it occurred to her that the blonde had likely filled out a visitor's card. If so, the young woman in the church office could easily be manipulated to give her the info
on the card. Yes, this would be easy!

Alysse picked up her phone and scrolled through names until she found the one she wanted.

"Hey, Rad," she said coyly when a man answered.

"Alysse? I can't believe it. You haven't been in touch for ages."

"Well, my design business is doing well and I've been busy. How's your P.I. business going?"

Radford Connally would never admit to Alysse that things were not going nearly as well as he would like, so he embellished the truth for his pride's sake.

"Going good…fine…staying busy."

"Well, I hope you're not too busy. I need you to do something for me."

"Hey, Babe, you know I've always got time for you. Whatcha need?"

"I want you to get me the scoop on a woman."

"Got a name?"

"Not yet, but I'm hoping to have one for you by tomorrow."

"Okay, just let me know when you get her name and I'll go to work on it. 'Want to give me any more info about why you're interested in this woman?"

"No, Sweetie, not just now…maybe later."

"Whatever you say. I'll be waiting to hear from you."

"I'll be in touch. Goodnight."

Radford pushed "End" on his phone and poured himself another Scotch. What was Alysse up to now? He didn't suppose for a minute that it was anything good…at least for the woman she was curious about.

Alysse and he went back a long way. So far back he remembered when she was still a nice girl. Even then, she had the drive to make something of herself. He couldn't blame her. Her parents were alcoholics, her brothers, drug addicts and thieves. It was no wonder she wanted free of them. He grew up across the street from her, his own family situation not a lot better. At least, it was only his father who drank every night.

Alysse was just a kid when her creative abilities became evident. She had a small bedroom to herself in the family's run-down house, and she was always re-decorating it with things other people tossed in the garbage. He remembered their almost nightly dumpster-dive outings. It really was amazing what people threw away. He'd help drag home all her treasures and was amazed at what she could produce from them.

At some point in all those years Radford had secretly come to love Alysse. He never told her of his feelings because he didn't think she'd ever see him as more than the boy next door. Still, those feelings had prevented his falling in love with any other woman.

When Alysse was struggling to get her Interior Design degree from the local junior college, he slipped her money as often as he could. It still irked him that her family had so little interest in helping her. She was tough, though. Too much so now. The interior design field could be a cut-throat business and he had watched her toughen with it. A brief marriage had at least given her a name free of her family's tainted reputation. From a distance Radford had kept an eye on Alysse, from her working for a large design firm to starting her own business.

He was really surprised when he learned she had begun attending a cowboy church, of all things! Once, when he'd convinced her to have coffee with him, he asked her about this. She had told him she was only attending there because she had a crush on the handsome pastor she had seen at some civic event. It didn't seem to matter to her that he already had a beautiful wife.

Radford had read in the local paper a few years ago that the preacher's wife had died. He didn't know if Alysse was still hot for the guy. He wondered if her interest in this unknown woman had anything to do with that pastor.

With a sigh, he also wondered if he'd regret helping her.

* * * * *

Alysse pulled into the parking lot of the Cornerstone Cowboy Church on Monday morning, glad to see there was only one car parked near the entrance of the building that housed the offices. The young woman at the reception desk looked up with a smile as Alysse entered.

"Good morning. How can I help you?"

Alysse assumed her most cordial smile and friendly attitude. "Hi! You're Brittany, aren't you? I'm Alysse Stratton. I'm hoping that you can help me get in touch with a young woman that was here in church yesterday. I'm almost certain that she is someone I met briefly at a design conference, but I didn't get her card, and you know how it is—when I'm busy names just go in one side and out the other!"

Brittany smiled and nodded. "I know. That happens to me, too. So how can I help you?"

"I was wondering," Alysse said slowly, tapping her chin with her long-nailed forefinger. "Do you think she may have filled out a visitor's card? I'd really like to know her name. I'm thinking of hiring another designer."

"That's very possible," Brittany said. "We could take a look."

She reached over to a shelf behind her and picked up the stack of visitor's cards from the Sunday morning service.

"Do you know if she had children, or was she alone?"

"I had the impression that she was alone…though it seemed she might have come with the Caldwell's."

Brittany went through the cards, setting aside any that might have been from a woman alone. There were three possibilities, and then she smiled.

"I think I found it — this lady is the only one who said she was a guest of the Caldwell's." She handed the card to Alysse who quickly read the limited information. The name was Grace Morgan, with an address in Friendswood which she quickly committed to memory. The phone number slot was left blank.

"Okay, Brittany. Thanks so much. She didn't give her number, but at least I can call her by name if she comes again.

Brittany agreed, taking back the card as Alysse handed it to her.

"You're a sweetheart," Alysse gushed, flashing a wide smile at the church employee. "Thank you, again."

Opening her car door, Alysse was mentally patting herself on the back, thinking how easy this was. As she drove out the church parking lot she punched in Rad's number.

"Hi, Babe," he answered. "Got something for me."

"A name and address," Alysse answered. "Got your pen ready?"

"Always…shoot," Radford replied.

Alysse gave him Grace's name and address.

"I'm pretty sure that's a gated community," he said.

"Is that a problem?" Alysse asked.

"Nothing I can't work around."

"Okay, let me know when you have some info for me. I'll treat you to dinner."

"That's a winner. 'Talk to you soon. Bye."

Alysse clicked the off button on her phone and took a deep breath. She couldn't wait to see what Rad came up with.

* * * * *

Zach woke up and immediately thought of his mother, wondering how she was doing this morning and knowing he would have to rearrange his day to go to the hospital. He couldn't skip taking the empty food containers to Georgia, though. She'd need them to get the food ready for the beach outing that was coming up.

A quick shower and two cups of coffee later he drove to her business, pulling up in front of a neat, white frame building trimmed in a soft aqua. The sign read, "Gulf Coast Catering."

He gathered up all the containers he could carry at one time and made his way through the front door. The bells hanging on the knob brought an apron-clad lady with a no-nonsense hairstyle from the back room. Her face broke into a smile when she saw Zach.

"Well, it must be ESP! I was just thinking you needed to get those containers back to me if I'm going to fill them for you this weekend." She came from behind the counter to wrap her arms around him in a warm hug.

"How did it go, Sweetie?" she asked, her eyes filled with concern.

Zach knew she was referring to his trying to handle the tour business alone for the first time. He hugged her back and smiled.

"Better than you would ever have believed, Georgia."

The caterer's eyes opened wide and she grinned. "I'm so glad, Hon. Have a seat; I just happened to have some goodies ready. I'll be right back.."

A few minutes later Georgia set a plate with two still-warm fried apple pies before Zach along with a large mug of coffee. "I'm giving you a head start on me 'cause I can hardly wait to find out what's put that spark in those baby brown's," she said. She returned shortly with her own cup of coffee and a single pie on her plate.

"Oh, Georgia," Zach mumbled around a mouthful of pie. "This is heavenly."

She smiled and forked off a bite of pie. "I have to say, there's something about eating desserts freshly made that makes them so good. That's why I try to get my products to the customers as close to their time of consumption as possible."

"I've not had a single complaint about your food. It's a

winner every time."

"Have you had any changes to the count you gave me for Friday and Saturday?"

"No, but as usual, you can give me enough for three or four extra people just in case. I have no qualms about eating it myself later if it's not used." He took his last bite of pie and swallow of coffee.

Watching him, Georgia smiled. "Okay, out with it!" She gave a little shudder. "I'm feeling this one in my bones."

Zach scooted back from the table and raised one booted foot to rest on his knee.

"You know that I went to California to attend my dad's wedding..." He went on to tell her about meeting Grace and the whirlwind that had transpired since then.

Georgia had tears in her eyes when Zach told her about finally coming to a place of releasing Sasha and feeling free to love again.

"Oh, Honey, I'm so glad. It broke my heart to see you so sad all the time and not moving on toward any happiness. I'd love to meet your Grace and I'll be praying that all things work out according to God's plan for the both of you."

"I'll bring her with me to pick up the food Friday if it works with her schedule and you can meet her then. I know you'll like her."

"I'm sure I will, and I look forward to Friday."

Zach stood. "Okay, I've got things to do. Thanks for the wonderful pie and the coffee."

"You're welcome. It was so good to get to talk with you."

They hugged and Zach headed for the door.

"See you Friday morning," he said.

"I love that smile," Georgia said.

Zach blushed and tipped his hat to her. He had to confess, he had caught himself several times, smiling from ear to ear as he thought about Grace. How thankful he was that the terrible weight that had burdened him was gone. He wondered how many people around him were living in that same emotional prison.

"Oh, Father, help me reach them," he prayed.

For the first time since Sasha's illness and death, hope for the future began to stir in Zach's heart. Thoughts of what could lie ahead for his church, his ranch, and the cattle business that involved were coming unbidden. Somehow, he sensed that there would be changes in a lot of areas.

He knew it was really premature, but he tried to imagine what it would look like to be married to Grace, what their life together would be like. She didn't even know he owned a ranch. Would she want to live there? The thought of never having another church picnic and rodeo there was painful.

Zach truly felt that God had made him aware that He had new things for Grace, too, that day he prayed for her. How was all this going to work together? Would his mother be in that picture, too? As all these things were tossing around in his head, he suddenly heard the Voice. *"Just trust me."*

Zach chuckled. "It still comes back to that, huh, Lord? Thanks for reminding me."

With that settled he headed for the hospital.

As Zach neared his mother's room he saw Dr. Winthrop coming from that direction. The doctor also saw him and waited to speak to him.

" Hello, Doctor, how's my mother today?"

"'Morning, Mr. Clayton. Your mother is doing all right. I hate to say she's doing well, because the bruises have all reached the height of their discoloration and she looks like she just survived a beating. Of course, she's pretty sore, as we expected, too." He sighed. "She's demanding to be released, and though I'd feel better about keeping her another day, there's not a good reason to do so."

"I'm sure she's really needing a drink by now," Zach said.

The doctor nodded. "Yes, she's becoming quite agitated."

"I've definitely seen that side before," Zach said.

"Are you prepared to take her home now?" the doctor asked.

"Yes, I am," Zach told him.

"Then I'll process her paperwork."

Zach walked on to room 242 and found Amelia with a frown on her face.

"Get me out of here," she said, "I want to go home."

"That's just what I'm here for, Mom. I saw Dr. Winthrop in the hall and he's starting your release papers now."

That seemed to pacify Amelia somewhat, but Zach could see that her body was trembling. His heart went out to her, knowing that the thing that would temporarily help her was also destroying her. He bent down and kissed her forehead.

"It's all right, Mom. Hang on just a little bit longer. I'm going to get you out of here. Are the clothes you wore when you were admitted still here?"

The nurse that had just walked in answered, "Yes, they're in that closet and I've come to help you get dressed, Mrs. Clayton. The doctor told me you are leaving us already." She gave Amelia a cheery smile.

"Okay, I'll leave you ladies to it," Zach said. "I'll be in the waiting room when you need me."

He'd had enough coffee for the morning, so he paced the floor, looking out the window and wondering what to do with his mother. He knew she didn't really want to go "home" to her apartment. She would want to go to the Beachside Bar. That was home to her. And as badly as he hated to do so, he would have to take her there and leave her in that smoke-filled, smelly place. He knew he may as well be prepared for the fact that she would refuse to go anywhere else with him. "Help me, Lord," he prayed. He wished that Grace was here with him. He felt that she would be supportive. He made the decision to tell her the truth about his family, even all the ugliness.

"Mr. Clayton," he heard the nurse call, "Your mother is ready to go now. They have finished her release paperwork and need you to sign it at the nurses' station. I'll bring her there in a wheelchair."

"Thank you, I'll take care of that." Zach headed for the desk, where he signed the paperwork.

The nurse appeared, pushing Amelia in a wheelchair. "It will take us a little while to get to the ground floor if you'd like to bring your vehicle up to the door, Mr. Clayton."

"All right, I'll meet you there." Zach hurried down the stairs rather than wait for the elevator.

Within minutes Amelia was in his truck and they were headed toward the beach area. Zach looked over at his mother and saw that the trembling had increased.

"Do you want me to take you to your apartment, Mom?"

"No!" she replied adamantly. "Take me to the bar."

"Could I treat you to a nice meal, first? It's almost lunchtime. How long has it been since you had a good seafood platter?"

Amelia shook her head. "No, I don't want anything to eat. Just take me to the bar."

"Okay, if you insist, but I sure hate leaving you."

Zach meant it. Somehow this couple of days' interaction with her had increased his desire to be with his mother. He wished he could talk to her about feeling better since losing Sasha, and tell her about meeting Grace. But none of it would matter to her in this condition. All she wanted was alcohol. So the little boy inside him went back into hiding and he drove her to the bar.

Zach parked as close to the building as he could and walked his mother inside. The few regular patrons that were there all came to welcome her back to their domain. Joe took her arm on the other side and guided Amelia to "Her" table. Zach felt somewhat better that at least there were people there who cared for her. She was obviously more comfortable with them than she was with her own son.

"Thank you, Son. You can leave me now," she said, her voice trembling. Zach opened his wallet and left money on the table. "I love you, Mom."

He looked to the bar owner, "Take care of her, Joe."

"I will, Preacher, I promise," Joe said.

Zach walked quickly to the door and out into the sunshine. He could actually feel the pain in his chest this time. Would things ever be better with his mother?

It seemed his truck found his favorite place on the beach all on its own. He needed to get himself back together before he could go on with his day. Sitting on the same rock where Grace had wept in his arms made him think of her. He couldn't believe that it had only been days since they met and yet his heart longed for her. It seemed that they had simply by-passed the getting acquainted process, and stepped directly into the sweetness of a long-time relationship. She seemed as comfortable with that as he was. He hadn't realized how much he needed her, but he was so thankful God had brought her into his life.

The sound of the gentle waves and the breeze blowing over the water of Galveston Bay soothed Zach's soul. Somehow, it strengthened him to face his newly-found future…with Grace, with pastoring again, and with whatever his mother's situation would bring. He remembered what the voice of the Lord had said, *"Trust me,"* and now he found that he could.

CHAPTER 14

"Turn right," Grace said as Marla drove her rental car through the property gate. A few minutes later they were out of the local area and headed towards Galveston.

"Okay," Marla said, looking toward Grace. "Tell me about this man you've met here in Texas."

Grace chuckled. "Well, I actually met him in LA."

"What?" Marla, exclaimed. "I thought you had a fellow here."

"I do," Grace said, enjoying her friend's confusion.

"Grace Morgan, you have some explaining to do."

"Okay. I actually met him while boarding the plane in LA the night I flew here." She proceeded then to tell the tale of the unusual way she and Zach reconnected in Texas, and how they instantly fell for each other.

"So, there's a really good chance that you'll be a pastor's wife again soon," Marla said, smiling.

"It looks that way," Grace said. "But Zach is so different to Damien. I can tell the way the people of his church love him even after being away from them for three years, that they had truly felt loved by him and Sasha."

"Has Zach talked about her much?"

"Enough for me to know that she was a very special woman, both to him and to the church members."

Marla turned to her, "How do you feel about following a 'class act?'"

Grace smiled. "Don't think I haven't thought about that, and when we first met I could tell that Zach was fighting letting go of his feelings for her. But lately, that seems to be settled for him. They apparently had a great marriage and worked together so well in building the church. I've heard nothing but wonderful things about her from a few of the people. I just have to believe that the Lord wouldn't have allowed us to come together in such an awesome way if it wasn't going to work out."

"Well, I am so happy for you. I never said anything to you, but I felt you were really being shortchanged in your marriage to Damien.

It was easy to see that you were the one doing all the giving," Marla said.

"You're right," Grace said. "I couldn't see that while I was in the marriage, but it's clear to me now. I don't understand how I was so blind to his selfishness."

Marla reached over and patted her hand. "Dear, dear, Grace, you were just so busy loving everybody and trying to meet people's needs. I do hope that this Zach guy puts you first."

"Well, I've been told that he was the best husband in the world to Sasha and a wonderful example to the men of his church." Grace pointed ahead, "Okay, we're here. Take a left at the next street and we can park there and walk the strand to visit all the shops."

"All right!" Marla exclaimed. "This is looking vaguely familiar to me now."

Soon they were parked and window shopping to choose which businesses they wanted to explore further. They'd made it through five of them when they both felt it was time for a break.

"Thank you so much for being willing to do this with me, Grace. It really does bring back the pleasant memories of being here with my grandparents," Marla said.

"I've enjoyed it, too," Grace told her. "The places we shopped today were not the ones that Karen and I went to the day we first came here."

"Good, now you have a better idea of which ones you like best. Hey, are you ready for lunch?"

"Yes, I am. That cinnamon toast is long gone. The restaurant where Karen and I ate is just a little way down the street. The food and service were both really good. Would you like to go there?" Grace asked.

"That sounds great," Marla said, "Lead the way."

A friendly hostess met them at the entrance and led them to a table.

"This is the same table where Karen and I sat when we were here," she told Marla.

The hostess heard her and asked, "Oh, would you like to sit somewhere else?"

"Oh, no, Grace," said. "This is fine."

"All right," the hostess said. "Your server will be right with you."

Marla looked around. "This is a really cute place. The decorator did a good job."

"Karen and I thought so," Grace agreed. "And since the food was excellent too, we decided it would be our go-to place when we have another get-a-way day."

Their server came and took their order and they settled in to comfortable conversation.

"What is a convention in your business like, Marla?" Grace asked.

Marla laughed, "Well, mostly there's a lot of 'posturing.' Some of these people act like they are on a runway and are continually striking a pose just in case someone is watching. There's a contest with different categories of our work, like outfitting actors for a movie, or some kind of big event." She blushed, "I entered one of those."

"You did?" Grace asked. "When will you know if you won?"

"The winners are informed beforehand so they can bring their garments, have models lined up, etc."

"And…" Grace waited.

Marla paused, grinned, and then said excitedly, " I won!"

Grace jumped up, moved around the table, and hugged her friend. "Were you even going to tell me?"

"Oh, I would have gotten around to it before I left."

"I am so proud of you!" Grace told her, taking her seat. "This is a BIG THING!"

"It's big enough that the other people who enter and don't win will hate the winner for a few years," Marla said, "So I have that to look forward to."

"It sure will look great on a resume' when you go to the bank for a business loan," Grace said.

"You're right," Marla agreed just as the server brought their food.

As they ate Marla shared more of her ideas for her dream business and Grace could see that much planning had already been taking place in her friend's mind.

"What's to stop you from taking that step to do this?"

"I guess it's fear. It's such a big step," Marla admitted.

"Well, I think you need to keep talking about it, start checking into a building, going over all your wonderful ideas until it becomes so real you just have to do it!" Grace told her.

"Maybe you're right, Grace. But I sure wish you were out there with me holding my hand."

"You know that I am supporting you 100 percent even if I'm miles away, my friend. You can call anytime and I'll give you a pep talk. You really do know what you're doing....remember, YOU won the contest everybody wanted to win!"

"I did, didn't I?" Marla said with a smile.

The server brought the check and Marla said, "This is on me." She pulled out a credit card and handed it to Grace. "I'm going to the restroom before we start back. Would you take care of this?"

"Sure." Grace signaled the server to pick up the folder with the ticket and credit card in it.

As the server left Grace looked up as she waited and her eyes wandered to the view of the strand through the restaurant window. Far down the street she was stunned to see Zach for an instant. He and a light-haired woman were going into that same bar that he had entered the day of their tour. She barely had a glimpse before a mail truck drove by and blocked her view, but it was long enough for her to see that Zach had his arm around the woman. There was no mistaking that tall figure with the black Stetson. By the time the truck passed he and the woman were inside the door of the bar. She was shaken to her core. Who was the woman, and why would "Pastor" Zach be going to that bar, not once, but twice that she knew of?

The server returned with the receipt and Marla's card and Grace was waiting near the door when Marla returned.

"Your card, Ma'-am, as Texans would say," she teased to Marla, trying to cover her shakiness as she handed the credit card back to her friend.

As they drove to Karen's house it was difficult for her to make conversation with Marla.

"Are you okay, Grace?" Marla asked. "You seem awfully quiet."

"I guess I'm just sorry to see you go," Grace said with a forced smile.

"Yeah, I do wish I had more time, but I have to fly back to LA after the conference. I have several jobs lined up that I have to get to work on."

"I understand. I was super busy all the time when I lived in LA, too. I have to admit, I miss it sometimes, but...

"Not enough to come back," Marla completed for her as they drove through the gate to Karen's gated community.

Grace laughed as she pushed the garage door opener she'd taken with them.

"I'll just park here on the drive since I've got to load my bags." Marla said. "I don't want to dent Karen's car."

Minutes later they were hugging goodbye and Grace watched as Marla drove out through the gate.

As she went back inside Grace allowed herself to drop the pretense of being all right. She kept seeing that quick picture of Zach and the woman heading into the bar. Did his sudden departure Sunday afternoon have anything to do with this woman? He certainly didn't seem to want to share any information about why he was leaving so quickly.

And he hadn't called. This was the first day since they met at the tour that he hadn't called her. They had only been acquainted for a few days, so she certainly couldn't know all about him, even though it felt like he'd always been in her life. She didn't have the right to question him about another woman; there was no commitment between them. Grace hadn't really seen the woman because Zach had his arm around her and his body was shielding her from Grace's view. She saw just enough to know that the woman had light-colored hair.

Tears flowed down her face. The relationship with Zach had seemed so real and so right. But then, she had thought everything was fine in her marriage, too. Was she so gullible that men could deceive her that easily?

Apparently Zach had his secrets, and Grace wasn't willing to be in a relationship without complete honesty. She'd have to cut this off before her heart became even more invested. It was incredibly disappointing and painful, but she'd made it through this same type of situation with Damien and she could do it again. The only good thing about this is that she wasn't married to Zach.

She would have to leave Friendswood. She couldn't bear the idea of running into Zach somewhere. But where would she go? She had run to Texas from California, and she didn't have friends anywhere else. But how could she possibly stay here? One look at Zach and she'd melt into his arms, and if he tried to sweet talk her into staying she knew she would.

Her phone rang and her heart pounded. If it was Zach what should she do? She looked at the caller ID and saw it was Karen. With relief she answered.

Immediately, Karen knew something was wrong, "Gracie-lou, you don't sound good…what's going on?"

"Oh, KK, it's Zach…I saw him going into that old bar again…and this time there was a woman with him. And he…he …had his arm around her," she said.

"Oh, Hon, there's got to be some explanation," she said. "I know it looks bad, just like before, but I think Zach really likes you, Grace."

"That's what I was feeling, too, KK., but I also thought Damien loved me all those months he was cheating on me. I can't go through this again. I've enjoyed being here with you, but I have to leave."

"Grace, NO! Don't leave until I get home, promise me! We'll see this through together. Anyway, where would you go?"

"I don't know, but I can't stay here and take a chance on running into Zach."

"How did it happen that you saw him? Why were you in Galveston?" Karen asked.

Grace told her about Marla's surprise visit and how they had ended up in the restaurant on the strand.

"Grace, I know it looks bad, but I have a feeling that it's not what you think. Will you please not leave until I get back? I would come right now, but it's just not possible. I'll be home tomorrow. Will you wait? And then I won't try to stop you if you still want to go," she pleaded.

Grace couldn't refuse her faithful friend who had been with her through so many difficult times. She sighed.

"All right, KK. I'll wait until you get here."

"Have you prayed about this, Grace?" Karen asked.

Grace was quiet before she answered, "No, I've just been so confused that all I can think of is to leave."

"Well, you know that prayer is always a good thing."

"You're right. I know better than to do anything without praying about it first. What would I do without you, KK?"

"Probably something not too smart, Gracie-lou, so stay put until I get there. Love you."

"'Love you, too." Grace laid aside the phone.

"Will you never learn, Grace Morgan?" she asked herself aloud. "You know better than to run with your emotions and not even pray about things! Forgive me, Lord."

She sat a few minutes in silence, gathering her thoughts and then began to pray. "Father, I think this situation makes it clear that I'm still in need of healing over what Damien did. I don't understand what is going on with Zach, but it's unfair of me to transfer Damien's sinful actions to him just because they may seem similar."

It was then that she heard the Voice:

What does your heart tell you?

Grace reflected on everything that had taken place between her and Zach in their short acquaintance. "My heart tells me that he is a godly man."

She acknowledged that what she had experienced with Zach was special and not something two people could make happen on their own. Even if what she had seen was questionable and might lessen her trust in Zach, she still believed that God had brought them together.

"I will trust You, Lord," she said. "If I get hurt, then You will heal me. Your bringing us together like You did was nothing short of a miracle. You must have an awesome plan for our future, so I am going to agree with that plan."

But she knew she would have to discuss this with Zach. She had to know why a Christian man who was so admired and trusted by the people he had pastored would be going to that bar. And did he have a relationship of some sort with another woman? She remembered the woman at the church, the one who definitely wanted Zach…Alysse Stratton. Had she managed to get him to meet her? But Grace couldn't imagine that woman going to the worn-down bar on the beach, and anyway, Zach had been adamant about disliking her.

Oh, well, it didn't matter **who** the woman was. It just mattered that there **was** one. Grace hated confrontation, but had to get this out in the open with Zach and see where their relationship went from that point.

Having made that decision she went to the kitchen and made herself a cup of hot tea. That was soothing, but she still felt restless and uneasy. She remembered that she needed to wash the bedding on both beds since having company, so she stripped the beds, got the sheets in the washer, and then her phone rang. It was Zach. Her heart pounded and part of her wanted to let it go to voicemail. But she had to talk to him if things were ever going to be right between them. She clicked the button.

"Hi, Zach."

"Hey, Beautiful. 'Seems like a month since I've talked to you."

"Yeah, I know." There was an uncomfortable pause.

"Grace…are you all right?"

"I'm not sure, Zach. I think we need to talk."

"Funny, I was going to tell you the same thing. Uh…is it all right if I drop by? I'm just a few blocks away."

"That's fine. Come on over. I'll put the coffee on."

"Thatta girl. I'll see you in a few minutes."

"Okay, bye." Grace went to her room and did a quick mirror check, then hurried to the kitchen to start the coffee.

"Oh, Lord, help me," she prayed. "Help us, whatever it is that Zach has to tell me, let me handle it well."

The coffee had just begun to drip when Zach called for her to open the gate. Moments later she heard the door of his truck close and went to meet him.

The sight of Zach made her heart do crazy things as it always had. She wondered if this would be the last time she'd have the opportunity for that to happen.

As Zach pulled into the drive he felt like a hundred butterflies were flying around inside him. What did Grace want to talk to him about? He knew what he had to reveal, but she sounded so serious. It wasn't usually a good thing when a woman told a man, "We need to talk." But whatever she had to say to him today wouldn't change his feelings for her. He only hoped that he left feeling more at ease than he did now.

As Zach approached the entryway Grace opened the door and looked up at him. That magnetic something that had always been between them drew them close. Without a word they were in each other's arms and didn't need anything else.

After a long moment Zach kissed the top of her head and said, "I've missed you."

Grace couldn't help admitting it, "I've missed you, too, Cowboy. Come on in; the coffee's ready."

Zach hated to let her go, wondering if what she had to say to him would mean he wouldn't get to hold her again. But she was pulling him toward the kitchen now.

"You look beautiful today."

Grace smiled at him. "Flattery will get you nowhere."

"You're making me nervous, you know," he replied.

She gave him a quick look, but continued to pour the coffee.

"Let's go to the living room," she said.

When they were seated on the couch Zach said, "All right, who goes first?"

Grace took a deep breath. "You can start."

"Okay." He paused as if not knowing where to begin. "First, I owe you an apology for not telling you this earlier. Our relationship is so new, and I didn't want it to end before we really had a chance to know if God has something more lasting for us."

He took a drink from his cup then sat it on the coffee table.

"The phone call I got the other evening when I left so suddenly without explanation was regarding my mother." He then went on, telling Grace the entire story.

"I can thank my father for having any semblance of home life after Mom began to drink. He was always there for me, and even when I was hurt by the ugly things people said about my mother, he comforted me. Not once did he ever say anything negative about her to anyone. So many times he tried to convince her that she could get help, and that he would do anything in his power to help her get free of the alcohol. She always refused. It seemed as though she felt she deserved to stay in that bondage for all the hurt she had inflicted on us.

"When we left the hospital and I had her in the truck, it was the first time she had been with me outside that bar in almost ten years. I was hoping she would allow me to take her to eat a decent meal. I wanted to talk to her, to tell her about my relationship with you, and about how I'm not living in that angry darkness anymore."

Zach shook his head. "But she wouldn't have it. She only wanted to get back to that bar and her beer. Nothing means anything to her but the beer!"

As she listened without comment Grace was both relieved and ashamed. Relieved that the "other woman" in Zach's life was in truth, his mother, and ashamed that she had so quickly thought the worst of his actions. The pain that filled his heart from the years of dealing with his alcoholic mother was so evident that it broke her heart for him.

She understood now why having Sasha's love had meant so much to him, and why it had taken him so long to let go of that relationship.

She reached out to take him in her arms. "Oh, Zach, I'm so sorry. I do wish you had told me. I would have been there for you…with you."

"I was wishing you were with me, but I had been so afraid that you wouldn't want to continue our relationship if you knew the truth about my family. Then when I got that call, I couldn't just drag you into all this without any prior knowledge of the situation."

"Well, that's behind us now. If I can be of help to your mother or to you, in any way, just let me know."

"I should have known you would be this accepting, Grace. But I found myself dealing with the same old feelings that I experienced for years as other children made fun of me because of my mother's actions. I hadn't realized that those feelings were still there."

Grace moved back to look into his face. "Zach, that makes two of us. "This situation has brought to light my need for healing of past hurts, too." She went on to tell him about seeing him going into the bar both times, and how it caused her to relate his actions to Damien's.

Zach put his hands on his head and groaned. "I had no idea that you'd seen me going there. It's no wonder God kept saying to me, 'Tell her; tell her about your mother.' I'm so sorry, Grace. If I had been obedient I could have spared you all the questions and doubts about me. There's no way you could have known why I would be going to that awful place. I absolutely hate walking in there, but my mother is ashamed of the condition of her apartment and won't allow me to visit her there. I just keep hoping and praying that someday this will change. This incident with her ending up in the hospital has really brought it home to me that if she doesn't stop drinking she is going to die in this condition. The doctor actually told her that himself."

"What was her response?"

"He was trying to persuade her to go into a rehab program from the hospital. She wouldn't do it now, but said she would think about it."

"Then we'll pray that she'll decide to get help."

"Thank you so much, Grace. My mother was the kindest, sweet woman before my baby sister died. She just couldn't get over losing her little girl. Even though she knew the Lord, somehow she couldn't allow him to heal that terrible hurt. And since it was too much to bear, she had to find a way to dull the pain. She hates seeing me in that bar as much as I hate being there, and has told me so many times not to come back. I admit, I have been concerned about how it could affect my church if it got out publicly that I go there periodically. That would mean more shame for her, too, so I just pray that the Lord keeps it covered."

"I want to meet her, Zach."

"I'd like you to meet her, but I'm afraid she won't agree to that. Sasha tried to have a relationship with her, but I think she's so ashamed that she just can't. I did tell her I had met someone and she told me to go on about my life, be happy, and forget about her."

He breathed out a deep breath and took Grace's hand. "Whew, I'm glad that's all out. Now, what did you need to talk to me about?"

Grace smiled. "I was going to ask what secrets you were keeping about why you were going into that bar, and who the woman was that you hadn't told me about. But since you've already explained that I have no further questions…well, maybe one. Are there any more secrets you have to 'fess up to?"

"Well, there's one pretty important thing I just haven't gotten around to telling you, though I wasn't trying to keep it from you."

"So spill it, Cowboy."

Zach laughed. "Well, it kind of has to do with me being a cowboy."

"And…..?"

"I own a ranch."

"Oh," Grace's eyes lit up. "Well, it doesn't surprise me that a cowboy would live on a ranch."

Zach picked up his coffee and took a drink. " That's not exactly true at the present…I mean, my living there." Seeing her confused expression, he laughed. Then he went on telling her about his reluctance to live on the ranch after Sasha's death and how Mama Lil and Jay were caretakers there now.

"Jim and Susan Sheridan have not only stepped up to take the place as interim pastors at the church, they provided me a comfortable place to live these past few years. I'll show it to you sometime."

"I'd like that," Grace said. "So that's all the secrets?"

"Absolutely. And Grace, I promise you, I will keep nothing from you in the future. Well, maybe I should re-phrase that…is it okay to surprise you with secret gifts and such?"

Grace moved into his arms with a coquettish smile. "Those types of secrets are not only permissible…they're expedient."

"Grace," he said softly.

"Yes, Zach?" she replied.

"Will you go steady with me?"

Grace burst out laughing. "I haven't heard that phrase since I was in high school!"

Zach laughed, too. "Neither have I, but it seemed to fit. So what do you say; will you be my girl?"

Loving the look in his brown eyes, Grace nodded. "Yes, Zach Clayton, I will be your girl and go steady with you."

And of course, that called for a kiss.

* * * * *

When Zach pulled into the drive at Jim's ranch, Susan was just ahead of him. When she stopped at the house she got out of her SUV and walked toward him. He met her halfway.

"Hey, Sue, how are ya?"

"Well, I survived the afternoon rush at the grocery store, so I guess I'm all right."

Zach grinned and nodded. He had become familiar with that rush when Sasha was ill and the grocery shopping fell to him.

"I just wanted to see if tomorrow evening would work for you to bring Grace for dinner." Susan said. "I know it's short notice, but she said she didn't have any commitments."

"Well, I'm meeting with her tomorrow afternoon to go over the things I need to tell her about the tour this weekend…oh, I don't suppose you would know…she's going to work with me, doing the part that Sasha did."

Susan's eyes widened and she smiled at Zach for a moment before saying anything.

"I can't tell you how glad I am, Zach. She has such a sweet spirit. I believe she's good for you."

Zach smiled sheepishly and nodded. "She is."

"Anyway," Susan said, "You're going to be with her in the early afternoon…hey, why not bring her out when you finish your business there. You can show her around the ranch, and I'd love to have her visit with me while I prepare dinner."

The thought pleased Zach. " That's a good idea, Susan. I'll ask her if she'd like that."

"Does she ride?" Susan asked. "It might be fun for all of us to take a ride as it's cooling down after dinner."

"Well, if she doesn't, she can ride with me. I certainly won't complain." Zach grinned mischievously.

"Oh, it sounds like so much fun. We haven't been on a family ride in months. I'm sure the kids would like that and Jim, too."

"Jim would always prefer to be on a horse than on the ground," Zach said with a chuckle.

"Speaking of the devil..." Susan said and they both turned at the sound of Jim's pick-up truck pulling into the drive.

He smiled at them as the truck came to a stop, shut off the engine and opened the door.

"What are you two cooking up? I can see it all over your faces." He grinned as he put his arm around Susan. They shared a kiss and then Jim and Zach bumped fists.

"Hey, Bro. I do believe it's Susan doing the cooking, but I'm in total agreement, "Zach admitted.

"Hmm, must have something to do with that pretty blonde you've been hangin' out with."

Susan gave him a light slap on the arm. "You always figure it out!"

Jim grabbed her and said, "Just admit it – you married a smart man...say it!"

Susan looked coyly at him. "I did indeed. You're smart enough to come home just in time to carry in a car full of groceries." She then turned promptly and went into the house.

Jim just stood and looked after her.

"What do you say to that, Jimbo?" Zach teased.

Jim blew out a long breath. "I say that after you tell me what you two were planning when I pulled up I will gladly carry in groceries for my beautiful wife."

"If it works for Grace I'm going to bring her over tomorrow afternoon. I could show her my penthouse there. "

Zach nodded toward the barn, " and Sue wants to visit with her while she prepares dinner for us all."

Susan had walked back to her car for a package she'd left there and joined the conversation "Then I thought it would be really fun for us all to go for a horseback ride as it cools down. I think the kids might like that, too."

"You know I'm always in for a ride," Jim said. "Want to build a fire and make s'mores, too?"

"Oh my, you're tickling my sweet tooth," Zach said. "I haven't had s'mores in years. Can I bring anything?"

"No," Susan said, "I have it all."

"There in the car..." Jim said.

Zach grinned. "Well, since you're providing everything the least I can do is help carry it inside."

"I knew you'd catch the hint." Jim said.

"Yeah, cause I'm a smart man, too, "Zach said, dodging the punch he knew would be coming his way.

* * * * *

Zach woke with excitement at the prospect of spending much of the day with Grace. By ten o'clock he couldn't resist calling her.

"Hey, Beautiful."

Grace heard Zach's voice as she answered her phone. "Hi, there."

"Am I interrupting anything?"

"No, 'just doing some reading. What are you up to?"

"I'm jotting down some notes about what I should tell you this afternoon , so I won't forget anything. Something happens to my brain when I get around you, so I don't think I should rely on it to remember everything."

"We really do need to make sure we get this done today. How many times have we put it on the back burner for some other reason?"

"I've lost count. I took the containers back to Georgia earlier this morning. She had to hear our story, and she's eager to meet you. I told her I'd bring you with me when I pick up the food Friday."

"Good, I look forward to meeting her. I may need some cooking tips from her someday."

"She fed me freshly made fried apple pies today. I'm still drooling."

"That does sound good…the pie…not the drool."

Zach burst out laughing. "Grace, Grace. Hey, I ran into Susan yesterday afternoon. She wants us to come for dinner this evening. Does that work for you?"

"Sure."

"Next question. Would you like to come here with me when we get finished with our tour stuff? I can show you where I live and Susan would like you to visit with her while she gets dinner ready."

"Yes, I'd like that."

"Okay, question number three…"

"Hey, is this some kind of test?"

"I don't know, but if it is, you're passing with flying colors."

"All right, I'm waiting…question number three, please."

"Would you like to join us for a horseback ride after dinner when it cools down?"

"A horseback ride? Uh, I've never been on a horse."

"You wouldn't have to ride by yourself. You can ride with me. Their family likes to ride together when they can. The kids will probably be with us, too. They've been riding since they were babies."

Grace laughed. "I have never even thought about riding a horse, but it sounds like fun. Yes, I want to go. What should I wear?"

"Tee shirt and jeans will be fine. You might ought to wear closed toe shoes rather than sandals. I think we're going to build a fire and make s'mores, too."

"Oh, my, this gets better by the minute."

"'Got a cap with a visor?" Zach asked.

"No, not with me."

"That's okay; I've got dozens. You can wear one of mine."

"Do you have a pink one?"

There was silence on Zach's end of the conversation, and then, "You're kidding me, right?"

Grace laughed. "Yes, I'm kidding, Zach."

"Whew!"

"You know, these western hats are growing on me. I think I'd like to try one on sometime soon."

"You'd look great in a hat. They've got a lot of pretty ones for ladies at the western stores, pretty boots for women, too. We'll have to go there." Then he stopped. "Grace, I'd love to see you dressed as a cowgirl, but only if you want to. I am completely happy with you just as you are."

"That's so sweet, Zach," she paused a moment. "I look forward to our time together."

She could hear Zach take a deep breath.

"I do, too, Sweet Lady. I'll see you in four -and -a -half hours."

"Bye now."

CHAPTER 15

Radford Connally sighed as he looked at the information he had gathered on the woman, Grace Morgan. Looks like she got a raw deal with that preacher husband of hers. It was plain to see she was no match for the woman who stole the guy from her. "Wicked Woman," was written all over that creature's face.

In comparison, the sweet little wife could have been an angel. From everything he'd read about her, she was a truly good person who was always helping others.

Of course, Rad saw the smut in the trashy papers, but a person would have to be an idiot to believe it when everything else about the lady was without fault. Probably the only mistake she ever made was to marry that cheating husband.

Pouring the last of the coffee in the pot, Radford wished he knew why Alysse wanted the information on Grace. He wondered if she would be Miss Wicked #2 in the poor lady's life. Radford tried to remember when his childhood friend still had some semblance of softness, any kindness, about her. It had to have been a really long time ago.

Something about this situation didn't sit right with his gut. He was certainly no goody-two-shoes, but he was beginning to wish he'd told Alysse he was too busy to look up the Morgan woman.

Stubbing out his cigarette and taking the last swallow of coffee, Rad picked up the bag that held his sleuthing equipment and headed to his car. Twenty minutes later he pulled into the entrance of the gated community which held the address Alysse had given him.

Driving slowly up to the gate he was glad to see that the attendant on duty was a young woman. Flashing what he thought was his most attractive smile, he greeted her.

"Hello there. How are you this beautiful morning?"

The young woman responded with a shy smile. "I'm okay."

"Well, I'm glad of that because I have a problem and I'm hoping you can help me."

Radford leaned toward the attendant almost out the car window. "You see, I'm an insurance agent and I have an appointment with the lady who lives at this address."

He held the paper for her to see. "The problem is that when I called this morning to get her gate code I jotted it down, but I left it lying on my desk."

Trying to see her name badge, Radford leaned even further toward her. "What is your name, sweetheart?"

"It's Carissa."

"Carissa," Radford repeated slowly. "What a beautiful name…well, my dear Carissa, I would appreciate it more than you know if I could get your help in reaching my client. You see, I am supposed to be there in two minutes, and if we take the time to look her up, then call her to open the gate, I'm going to be late. And my boss is a booger about us being late to an appointment."

Acquiring his best pleading look, he continued. "If you could just push your little button there…just this once…that gate will open and give me enough time to get to that address before I'm late. You could call it your good deed for the day, Carissa!"

Carissa only hesitated a moment and then did as he asked. The gate began to move slowly open.

Radford again flashed his best smile to the attendant as he shook his head. "Carissa, you are indeed a darling. Thanks for making my day, sweetie!" He wasted no time driving through the gate as soon as there was room enough for his car to do so, blowing a kiss to Carissa as he passed.

"Okay, now to find the address," he muttered. He'd only driven a few yards when he saw that the street split. He'd have to go either right or left.

"Aha, so it's left," he said, seeing the name of the street on the sign ahead in that direction. Only a few numbers down he could see the address he sought. Driving slowly by, he saw no activity. He continued down the street, looking for a place he could park and keep an eye on the house.

Where the street had split near the entrance of the community a large oval of land accommodated an Olympic-sized swimming pool, a shallow children's pool, and bath houses. Several metal picnic tables and chairs were placed around the pool area for use by the residents

. Radford parked his car at the farthest end of this oval and situated himself at a picnic table almost hidden from view opposite the home he was watching.

The pool was practically empty. Undoubtedly, a community as large as this would have several pools, and this one being situated so close to the entrance, it might not get as much use. The only swimmers were a teen couple who were more interested in each other than in swimming. They didn't seem to be aware of Radford's presence at all.

Out of his bag he pulled what had once been the cover of a hard-backed book, but which now hid a slender digital camera firmly attached where the lens lined up with a hole cut in the spine of the cover. He arranged it on the tabletop so that from a distance he appeared to be reading a book.

The camera was already set to zoom once he punched the button. He did so now to check that it was positioned correctly to record any activity at the front of the condo. It was indeed, so Redford turned it off to save the batteries.

Now came every PI's least favorite part of this occupation – the wait. Digging into his pocket, Radford pulled out change and walked to the vending machines near the bath houses.

He dropped coins into the drink machine, which with a resounding thump dropped his bottled water into the retrieval slot. He resisted the impulse to purchase a sweet soda knowing he'd need the water sitting out here in open sun. Again, reaching into his bag he pulled out a ball cap and popped it on his head, then he rummaged around until he came up with a package of peanut butter crackers and a large, delicious apple. Maybe it was weird, but he liked to eat those together.

He checked his cell phone for messages, glad there was no hurry - up request from Alysse. He knew if he didn't get back with her soon though, he would certainly find a few of those. There were no calls that he needed to return — unfortunately. He really could use more business but couldn't afford advertising. There were a few people making payments for services he had performed for them and that was keeping things going at the present. And here he was working for Alysse for free!

She could afford to pay him, but he never charged her. Having a history together meant that was a given.

Radford looked up at the sound of a vehicle approaching the area he was observing. His heart rate picked up when he saw the dark blue Ford F 150 slow and then pull into the driveway his camera was focused on.

"Bingo!" He muttered and flipped the switch on. The truck partially hid the tall cowboy wearing a black Stetson, but as he walked up the steps he was in dead center of the camera. The cowboy rang the doorbell and stood back, turning so that the camera got a full- on view of his face.

"Well, well. If it isn't Alysse's pastor friend! I knew it!

"She's still chasing the guy. But ... Oh, my ... He seems to be admiring someone else...Grace Morgan, maybe."

The woman who answered the door didn't give a first impression as being the jilted wife from California. Her hair was different, long, and blonde. Both those things were easy to achieve with wigs, hair extensions and a bleach job, though. She seemed quite happy to see the preacher.

Rad tried to zoom in more, to get a close - up of her face, but the preacher blocked the camera's view as he bent to hug her. Then they walked inside and closed the door.

Rad jotted down the time in his notebook and ran back the footage to see if he got the license plate number clearly on camera. Not that it was a real issue. He knew who the guy was. He turned the camera off and leaned back in the metal chair. He pulled out a cigarette and lit it, taking in a long draw to feed his nicotine habit. Then he started trying to put together the pieces.

Obviously, the jilted pastor's wife was no longer in California. He'd need better photos to prove it was Grace Morgan though, close-up shots to compare to all the paparazzi's pictures. How in the world did she end up in Friendswood, Texas? He wondered if she'd been here long. And how did she and the cowboy preacher get hooked up? Maybe Alysse knew more about that.

Alysse... She was not going to like what he captured on camera today. It was just a few seconds, really, but it was obvious there was some level of relationship between those two. Rad wondered if Alysse had ever managed to get her claws into him. If so, she obviously didn't keep him.

"Should I tell her what I found, or keep watching to see what more I can learn?" Rad asked himself. Somehow the thought of tailing the preacher and Grace Morgan made him sick inside.

As far as he knew, the pastor was as loved and admired as Grace was. From his point of view, it seemed that two nice, deserving people had found each other.

Radford was unprepared for the way this thinking unleased the loneliness that he tried to keep stuffed and hidden away. What would it be like to have a beautiful woman be as glad to see him as Grace Morgan was to open the door to that preacher? He'd likely never know that feeling, but even if it meant being disloyal to Alysse, he hoped things worked out for those two.

* * * * *

Grace brought a spiral notebook and pen to the table. Finally, she and Zach were getting to the tour business paperwork.

The thought of working with Zach excited her, and not just because she would be spending time with him. She looked forward to meeting new people and felt that the Lord would provide opportunities for her to share the love of Jesus with some of them. The sing-along time at the beach had been so awesome. It would be exciting to repeat that.

The coffee maker sputtered its last bit of water through the grounds as the doorbell rang. Grace's heart skipped a beat at the thought of Zach waiting on the other side of that door.

There was no holding back the smile as she saw him. Those dark eyes she was beginning to love spoke the things they'd not yet put into words.

Grace put her arms about him and squeezed him, laughing. "You feel so go-od!"

Zach grinned and looked at her with his eyes twinkling.

"Did you just say, 'Go-od?'"

Grace blushed. "I think I did."

He laughed and pulled her close. "We're gonna make a Texan out of you yet!

Since she had already gone through the cook-out procedures once, Grace didn't have any questions about that part of the tour. Zach wanted her to be aware of a few things that could happen when non-cooperative tourists don't obey the rules or stay with the crowd. Other than the food part, her job would basically be to mingle with guests.

She'd stand at the bus door and greet them after they give Zach their tickets or money.

Grace chuckled. "I've been standing at doors greeting people for years. I don't think I'll have a problem with that."

Zach insisted on paying her as she knew he would. Oh, well, she'd just sow it back into ministry as the Lord led her. Zach filled in her personal information, snapped his notebook shut, and reached over to take her hand.

"Now…are you ready for fun, Beautiful?"

Grace squeezed her shoulders together like a cute little girl and said, "I can't believe I'm going to ride a horse!"

Zach couldn't help but smile at her excitement about something that was so commonplace to him.

"If you enjoy it, I'll teach you to ride on your own." Then his eyes got that mischievous twinkle in them. "But until then, I have no problem at all with you riding close…uh…riding with me."

"Won't the horse object to carrying both of us?"

Zach threw his head back and laughed heartily. "He'll probably tell me to get off so he can have the beautiful lady to himself."

Grace blushed. "You know what I mean."

"I do appreciate your concern for Midnight, but he's a big, strong horse, and we won't be riding long enough for our riding double to be a problem for him."

"Okay, if you're sure." Grace said, still unconvinced.

Zach walked over to her and put his arms around her. Looking down into her eyes, he smiled. "I am absolutely sure of that and a few other things."

Grace looked up at him flirtatiously. "Oh…such as…?

"Such as, I think you're absolutely wonderful, and absolutely gorgeous, and I absolutely love spending time with you."

He drew her to him for a long moment.

Grace could feel his heart beating as he held her close. After all those months of feeling unprotected, afraid to walk out of her house, here in Zach's arms she felt safe.

"I never expected to have this in my life," she whispered. "What a gift from God."

"Yes, it is. I don't know why I fought it…but your blue eyes just wouldn't go away. He looked at her face as though loving every part of it.

"I'm getting tired of not being able to say, 'I love you,' and telling you how you have stolen my heart. I am in love with you, Grace Morgan. You're my first thought when I wake up in the morning, and the last one before I go to sleep at night. I only think of anything else when I'm forced to do so during the day. I know this has happened so quickly, but I'm hoping that you feel…"

Grace placed her fingers gently on his lips. "I never liked long-winded preachers. I love you, too, Zach, now kiss me."

And kiss her he did—gently, tenderly, passionately.

So lost in each other, they didn't hear Karen until she called, "You-hoo, I'm ho-ome!" As she walked into the kitchen, a blushing Grace, and a sheepish-looking Zach separated. Karen looked at them just a moment, then threw her hands up with a smile.

"I'm not even going to ask…" She turned and started for the hallway.

"Karen, wait," Zach said. "You may as well be the first to know." He slipped his arms around Grace from behind. "I've just told Grace that I love her."

"And I just told Zach I love him, too," Grace said.

Karen stood with her hands on her hips. "And this is supposed to be a surprise to whom?" Then she walked over to them and threw her arms around both at once."

"I'm so happy for you…both of you. I can't think of any two people who deserve each other more. Zach, Grace and I are like sisters, so welcome to the family."

"Thanks, Karen, your approval means a lot. Grace would likely boot me out of her life without your approval."

Karen and Grace looked at each other and laughed, knowing how Karen had never liked Damien.

"I wouldn't go that far," Karen said, "But you're welcome."

Suddenly, Zach's stomach growled loudly. Embarrassed, he looked to Grace. "I was just going to ask if you'd like to get something to eat. It will be several hours before we have dinner at Jim and Susan's and as you just heard…" He patted his middle… "I'm ready for food now."

"I could fix us something quick here," Grace offered.

"That's sweet of you, but I don't want you having to do anything. Let me take you out. There's a diner on the way to the ranch that has great, down-home, Southern cooking."

"Okay, I'll get my things," Grace said and headed toward her room.

"'Want to come and have lunch with us, Karen?" Zach asked.

"Thanks, Zach, but I have things to tie up from the conference."

Grace returned with her purse and tote bag. " Did everything go well, KK?"

"Yes, I'd say that it was a total success."

Grace gave her a hug. "Are you sure you won't come with us? We'd really like to have you join us."

"I appreciate your asking, but I really do have a little more work to do, and then I'm going to crash."

"Okay, I probably won't see you again this evening. We're going to dinner and then on an evening horse ride afterward at the Sheridan's."

Karen's eyes were wide. "*YOU* are going on a horseback ride? Go, Gracie-Lou!"

Grace laughed. "I know. You never expected to hear that from me."

"We're determined to make her into a real Texan," Zach said, as his stomach growled loudly again.

"Okay, I've got to feed this guy. Get some rest, KK. We'll catch up tomorrow," Grace said. "Ready, Cowboy?"

"I am," Zach said, picking up his Stetson.

"Have fun," Karen called, and together Zach and Grace chimed, "We will!"

CHAPTER 16

At exactly nine o'clock Alysse Stratton walked into the restaurant where she had agreed to meet Radford Connally. There was an excitement inside her that made her both eager to hear what he had to tell her and dread of hearing it at the same time.

"I'm meeting someone," she told the hostess and walked into the dining room where she saw Connally at a table near the back of the room.

He stood and gave her a quick hug. "Hey, Babe, you're looking good."

"Hi, Rad." She took a deep breath and let it out. "So, you have something for me?"

The server appeared and greeted them cordially. "Good evening. Would you care to hear the chef's specials for tonight?"

Both declined. Since Alysse was paying, Radford took the opportunity to order the best cut of steak with all its trimmings. Alysse ordered her favorite fish entre'. As soon as the server had left the table Radford laid a Manilla envelope in front of Alysse.

"Okay, this is what I've found. Do you recall all the hullabaloo on the news about ten months ago about the pastor of a big church in LA having an affair? He was popular in the area and well-known in the religious circles all over the country. Apparently, the wife walked in on him and his French lover."

"I vaguely remember it. His name was ...Victor...no..."

"Vincent," Radford filled in for her. "Damien Vincent. I'm assuming you saw pictures of his wife on those newscasts, too."

"Yes, I think so."

Rad took a drink from his glass. "Well, her maiden name was Grace Morgan." He watched Alysse as she absorbed that info. She was thoughtful for a long moment.

"I don't recall that woman on the news — the wife — looking like the woman that was at my church. Are you sure it's the same person?"

"Ninety-nine percent sure. I got some good close-up shots of Her today and the face is the same. She apparently went through a pretty intense make-over, though…changed her hair style and color, and the way she dresses."

"What would she be doing in Friendswood? I don't get it."

"My question, too. I don't have an answer to that without digging deeper. The place she's living is not in her name; I'm guessing she's staying with a friend or family member. I ran the plate of a woman that drove in there."

He checked his note pad. "A 'Karen Scott.' She's a professor at U of H, a department head, it seems."

Alysse waved her hand. "I don't care about her. I'm more interested in how Grace Morgan, from Los Angeles, California managed to get to know Zach Clayton."

"I don't know that yet, but she's apparently been here long enough for them to develop a relationship."

Alysse was obviously furious. Radford feared an outburst of rage was eminent, but the server appeared with their food just in time. Alysse pushed hers aside.

"I'm guessing you have pictures."

Radford handed the packet to her, then tackled his steak. Alysse was trembling with anger as she went through the photos, starting with Zach getting out of his truck, waiting on the porch, hugging Grace, them walking to the truck arm- in - arm, then leaving together in his truck. There were numerous shots of them eating at a restaurant, expressing affection, leaving the restaurant, then exiting Zach's truck at a ranch.

There was a closeup of the mailbox, the name reading, "James A. Sheridan."

"Jim and Susan Sheridan's place!" Alysse exclaimed in disgust, throwing the pictures down. "He refused to let *me* go there."

"That's where I called it quits," Radford said. "I had to get home and print the photos for you, and quite honestly, I'd had enough of the heat."

"I know, thanks, Rad," Alysse said quietly, placing the photos back in the envelope.

Connally swallowed the bite of steak he'd been chewing then quietly said, "So you've still got the hots for the cowboy preacher."

Alysse's lack of denial was her only answer, then she looked at Radford with such pain in her eyes that he got a glimpse of the girl he'd helped make it through design school. He saw the same pain and discouragement that she'd battled when her family did nothing to assist her. Their need for alcohol superseded anything Alysse might need for her education.

But this was an even more personal rejection — that of the heart. Rad understood that very well. He reached over the table and took her hand.

"I know it hurts, hon, but why not just let it go and move on? You've wasted three years waiting on the guy. A person can't make someone love them. It's either there, or it's not."

Alysse looked up, her eyes blazing. "But he didn't even give me a chance. He wasn't dating anyone — not for three years! And then when he decided to, he didn't even let me know."

Radford didn't know what to say, and Alysse was quiet for a few moments, then straightened her shoulders, and the needy girl was gone. The hard, angry woman was back with such vengeance Rad let go of her hand and instinctively pulled away from her. She caught the eye of the server, asked for the check and for a to-go carton for her untouched meal.

"It's not over, Rad. They are going to wish they'd never met."

"What are you planning, Alysse?"

"I'm not completely sure at the moment, but you can bet I'll come up with something."

Radford knew there wasn't anything else to say, so he walked silently with her out of the restaurant. When they reached her car, he gave her a quick hug.

"Thanks for dinner, Babe."

She just nodded, then said, "Rad, I need you to keep at this a little longer."

It was his turn to nod as he told her goodnight and walked to his car, wishing he'd never started this.

* * * * *

Zach knocked loudly on the back door of the Sheridan's house, then opened the door and motioned Grace in ahead of him.

"Knock, knock! We're here," he announced.

"Come on in; I'm in the kitchen," Susan called back.

Zach grinned at Grace. "Your ranch education begins now." He spread his hands toward the room they'd entered. There were benches along two walls, numerous pairs of boots of all kinds and sizes placed beneath them, and rain gear in the same variation of sizes on hooks above the benches. "This is the 'Mud Room,'" he announced, "though a more proper description would be, 'Rain and Mud' room. Susan says all dirt and water must stop here. Jim says, 'Wishful thinking, Susan!'"

Grace laughed. She noticed there was a big rug in front of the door that led from the room into the rest of the house. Another attempt at stopping the dirt and water, she supposed.

Zach took her hand and led her into the hallway that opened into the kitchen where Susan was bagging up the ingredients for S'mores.

She stopped and turned to them with an open smile. "Hi, I'm so glad you're here. Grace, I've been looking forward all afternoon to having this time with you."

She walked over and gave Grace a hug that warmed her to her toes.

"I've been feeling the same, Susan. It's so good to meet new Christian friends," Grace told her.

"I assure you that Jim and Susan are the best," Zach said. "I don't know what I would have done without them these past few years."

Susan just looked up at him and smiled. "We love our Zach," she said fondly.

Zach put his arm around Grace's shoulder and said,

"Hey, would you like to see my place? I've got chores to do so I'll be free this evening for our ride, but I'd like to show you the neat living quarters Susan designed for wayfarer's like me. Then I'll leave you girls to visit."

"I'd like that." Grace agreed.

"Okay, Sue, I'll have her back in a few minutes."

Zach took her hand as they walked across the property to the barn.

"A few months before Sasha died, Susan and Jim felt led to convert the area over their barn to living quarters in case someone came along who needed a temporary place to stay. They offered it to me when I just couldn't stay at the ranch.

He took out his key and unlocked the door when they reached the top of the stairs.

"Well, this is it—my home away from home."

It only took a couple of minutes to see the whole of the open, half-walled room which was divided into different living spaces. Grace was impressed with the peaceful atmosphere and could see how this had been a haven for Zach in his time of sorrow.

"This is my favorite spot, though," he said, opening the patio doors to reveal the peaceful view of the pasture.

"Oh, how beautiful!" Grace exclaimed.

Zach slipped his arms around her from behind. "Yeah, this is where I have my morning coffee and do my Bible reading and talking to the Lord. Sometimes, I just strum my guitar and worship. I know that Jim and Susan's commitment to the Lord has brought a precious spirit to this place. I'll be forever grateful for them allowing me to find rest here."

Zach chuckled and Grace turned in his arms to see what he had found humorous.

"I never told you, but Jim gave me a hard time all the way home from the airport for not getting your phone number. He saw us wave at each other and could not believe that I let you get away without any way to reach you. Honestly, I couldn't believe it, either."

"Then God delivered me right to your bus step," Grace said, smiling.

"We do have a story, don't we, my beautiful Grace?" He placed a quick kiss on her forehead. "And the best part is that it's just beginning."

Closing the patio doors, he said, "I promised to get you back to Susan, so we'd better get going."

As they walked back to the house, he squeezed her hand. "Are you sure you're okay with the ranch thing?"

"With you owning a ranch?" Grace asked in surprise.

"Well, I know you're a city girl…I just wondered…"

"You know, Zach," she said, "I am a child of God. Beyond that, everything else is up for change—and I'm finding that I am totally okay with it!"

"Grace Morgan, you really are amazing," he said as they entered the house.

CHAPTER 17

"Okay, is everybody ready?" Jim Sheridan asked.

A varied response of positive answers rang out as the Sheridan family, Zach and Grace answered.

"Then ride'em out!" he said with a grin and gave the slightest pressure to his own horse's flanks.

As Zach's horse, Midnight, began to move, Grace held tighter to Zach's waist. As excited as she was to be doing this, it was a completely new and unfamiliar experience. She felt that she was much farther from the ground than those few feet.

They'd ridden just a short distance when ten -year- old David held his horse back to ride beside Zach and Grace. With a shy smile he asked Grace if she was doing okay.

Grace smiled at him in return. "I'm still processing this, David, but so far I'm enjoying it. I'm quite impressed with how well you ride. You seem so comfortable on your horse."

David blushed slightly. "I can't even remember when I was on a horse for the first time. Mom and Dad started us out as babies." He motioned toward his sister. "Danette' started barrel racing when she was five, I think."

Just the thought of a small girl alone on the back of one of these large animals was unbelievable to Grace. "Oh my! I'd love to see her perform."

"I'll take you to see her," Zach told Grace, turning his head toward her. "She'll be competing in the big Houston rodeo in a few months. And you should see this little guy, too," Zach said proudly, nodding his head toward David. "He'll be in the calf roping competition."

"Really?" Grace looked at David. "You do that thing where you twirl a rope in a big circle over your head?"

David grinned at Zach. "Yes, ma'am."

Danette rode over to join them on the other side.

"Hi, Kiddo," Zach said to her. The love between Zach and the Sheridan children was evident to Grace as she had watched their interaction during dinner earlier.

"Hi, Uncle Zach," Danette replied. "Ms. Grace, are you getting the hang of riding?"

Grace laughed. "I don't know that I could say that just yet, but I'm enjoying it. David was telling me that you barrel race. I look forward to watching you. Your Uncle Zach said he'll take me to the rodeo."

"Oh, yeah. If you really want to see our western way of life you have to go to the rodeo. We look forward to it all year."

Jim and Susan looked back and saw both their children talking with Grace.

"Our kids like Grace," Jim said.

"I can see that." Susan agreed. "But what's not to like about her? I'm so thankful God brought her to Zach."

Jim nodded. "He's been happier these past few weeks than I've seen him since Sasha became ill. He's even mentioned coming back to the pulpit soon."

"That's awesome." Susan looked at her husband with admiration in her eyes. "But you know, Jim Sheridan, I'll miss hearing you. You've done a good job of feeding our people the Word. I hope Zach will call on you to preach sometime."

"Thank you for all your support, Babe. You're the best, you know."

They both leaned over from their horses to meet for a kiss.

"Let's see if Grace is comfortable enough to pick up the speed," Jim said. They turned their horses and rode back to join Zach and Grace and their kiddos.

"Hey, you guys tired of lolly-gagging along? Grace, are you ready to speed things up a little?"

"I guess so," Grace answered, "if Zach doesn't mind me squeezing him to death."

"Squeeze on, Babe," he said.

"All right," Jim said. "Let's go!"

Grace held on as they all began to ride faster. It seemed the horses had been waiting for this. It was scary to Grace at first, but as she relaxed in confidence that both Zach and his horse knew what they were doing, she began to feel the freedom and exhilaration that horsemen for generations have loved.

With her hair blowing behind her Grace felt like all burdens and cares were being left behind as well.

Zach could feel Grace relaxing as she stopped holding onto him so tightly. He really hoped she would enjoy riding. It had been one of his and Sasha's favorite pastimes and was such a part of his life he would love for his city girl to embrace it, too.

He turned his head toward her. "Having fun?"

"Yessss!" she called back. "I love it!"

Zach replied by allowing Midnight to go even faster. They soon reached their destination, a pond on the Sheridan property. The sun was beginning its ascent for the day and various shades of gold, pink and blue painted the sky in a myriad of designs.

Zach swung down from Midnight first, patting the horse's neck. "You did good, boy," he told him. Then he reached up to help Grace dismount. "You did good, too, Beautiful."

It felt good to Grace to have both feet on solid ground again, but she had to admit that she had truly enjoyed the ride.

A couple of hours and more S'mores than they wanted to count, Grace and Zach said their goodbyes to the Sheridan's and were driving back to her place.

"What a special evening," Grace said; "Thank you so much."

"I believe the thanks should go to the Sheridan's but, yes, it was a very special evening," Zach said, taking her hand.

They drove back to Karen's home in contented quiet. After pulling into the drive Zach turned off the truck engine and took Grace into his arms. He kissed her tenderly then drew back so he could see her eyes. "I know we've only known each other for a few weeks, but I can't imagine living without you, Grace. I'm not officially asking you to marry me tonight, but I want you to pray about us and ask the Lord if this is His plan. I feel I know the answer, but you have to know it, too. Be thinking about any questions you have about me and my life. I can't say I have all the answers right now about what's ahead, but I feel God moving things into place."

"I'll pray for all of this, Zach, our future." She smiled at him. "I sure hope He says 'yes'.

CHAPTER 18

Zach backed out of the drive and headed his truck toward the gate. He could see in the rear-view mirror that it wasn't until then that Grace stopped waving and closed the door. A sweet, yet somewhat painful feeling darted through his heart. It was becoming harder to leave her every time they were together. He began to think what he would need to do in order to ask her to marry him.

There was the situation with the ranch. It had been Jay and Lil's home for three years now. Where would they go? It wasn't that they couldn't find another house to live in, but would they be able to find one where they could continue to live the ranch life they loved? Would they have to move if he married Grace? It wouldn't be fair to ask her to marry him with another couple living there.

His current living quarters were certainly not the answer He had to laugh out loud at that thought.

"Sure thing, Gracie-Lou, as Karen calls you. You can leave your million-dollar home in California, marry a Texas cowboy, and he'll set you up just fine in one big room right over the barn!"

God certainly had a better plan for their living situation!
What about his ability to support her? He could easily increase income from the cattle business by moving the stock he had at Jim's back to his ranch and enlarging the herd. That was simple enough.

The church had insisted on paying him a stipend while he was out, but Zach felt so unworthy of it that he put it into an account and let it sit there. Maybe God had a special use for that money now.

When he came back as senior pastor his salary would be fully reinstated, so there was really no reason he'd have to do the cattle ranching if he didn't want to.

He was feeling the pull in his spirit to be back in place as senior pastor, but he just couldn't do it until he and Grace were married. He was seeing that in his mind often now— her standing beside him before his people.

"I need to go shopping for a ring," he said, thinking out loud.

The tour business would be the next consideration. Should he keep that going? It had never made a large profit, but it was such a wonderful avenue for meeting people and sharing Jesus. This season would be over in a couple more months, then he and Grace could pray about its future when summer came again.

So all this didn't seem so overwhelming. The first thing he needed to do was take Grace out to see the ranch and meet Jay and Lil. On impulse, he reached for his phone and punched in her number just as he pulled into the Sheridan's drive.

"Hey, Beautiful," he said when her heard her voice.

"Hi, are you home?" she asked.

"Just this minute. I'm already missing you."

"Oh, Zach. That's sweet."

"It's absolutely the truth, but that's not the reason I called. Would you like to go out to the ranch tomorrow? I want you to see it."

"I would love to see your ranch, Zach. Will I get to meet your friends there?"

"I haven't spoken with them yet, but they're almost always there. I'll call them in the morning; they're asleep now."

"What time should I be ready?"

"Ten-ish. Wear comfortable clothes. We may even ride the horses around the ranch. I still have a couple there."

"I didn't expect to get to ride again so soon. This is great."

Zach chuckled. "We'll see if you still feel that way when you get up in the morning. A hot shower relaxes sore muscles—just in case you feel the need."

"Ooo-kay, thanks."

Zach's voice softened to the tone that made shivers go up Grace's spine. "I sure enjoyed being with you this evening. And I really did start missing you as soon as I drove away. I'm trying to figure out how we can change that—my leaving you behind."

"Well, I heard that you told Jim the other day that you're a smart man. I'm just betting that you can come up with a solution to my having to stand here and watch your taillights go out that gate. Sleep on it, Cowboy. 'Nite."

Zach grinned and clicked off his phone. He could picture Grace's cocky little smile as she hung up and he totally loved that image.

* * * * *

Radford Connally dialed Alysse's number and waited for her to pick up, wondering what emotional state she'd be in.

"Yes, Rad." Her icy tone indicated she blamed him for the report he'd given her.

"Are you okay?"

"What do you think? You know how I hate being up against a wall!"

"I wish you could let this go. It's not healthy; I bet your blood pressure is sky high."

"I can't help it. It's all I can think about. I know I could have made him love me. He just would not give me a chance."

"Alysse…"

"Who does that blonde bimbo think she is? She couldn't hang onto her husband in California; what makes her think she can keep Zach happy?"

Radford could see he would get nowhere with this line of conversation, so he went another direction.

"What do you know about this tour business the preacher and his wife had before she died? Looks like it's called Sunshine Tours. Do you know if it's still in operation? Never mind, I just found the site. It hasn't been changed since the wife died, but it looks like he's still doing the tours—two of them this weekend. I'll book one and see what it's about. That should give me plenty opportunities to take pictures."

"Just don't give them your real name."

"I'd have to do that if I pay with my credit card online. It says on the site that they accept walk-up's, so I'll just show up at the last minute and pay cash."

"I'll pay you back for your expenses. Let me know what you find out as soon as you have it ready."

"Don't worry, doll; I will. 'Call you soon."

* * * * *

Zach woke early, pushed the brew button on the coffee maker and took his Bible with him onto the patio. As always, he loved the peaceful view of the pasture and the stock grazing. He'd gotten used to watching the colors in the sky unfold as the sun rose.

He'd miss this view when he moved back to the ranch. That thought brought him back to his questions of the night before. How would his marrying Grace affect Jay and Lil?

It was still not light enough to read his Bible, so Zach got a cup of coffee, returned to his chair, and began to pray.

"Father, I know that there is no confusion in Your plans. I truly believe that You brought Grace into my life, and You certainly gave me Jay and Lil. I know that You have answers to all situations that can benefit everyone involved, so I'm asking You to show me Your plan."

He thought about showing the ranch to Grace. "And Lord, if we're to live at the ranch, please let Grace like it. I know it's so different to living in a big city but cause her to feel at home there if this is Your plan. And the same thing for my church. Please give her love for the people of the church and let them love and accept her, too."

The faces of the people of his church began to come to Zach's mind and his heart was filled with love for them. He was eager to get his personal life in order so he could truly be the pastor to them that he once was. He loved receiving direction from the Lord for his sermons and then having so many of the congregation tell him it was just what they needed at that time.

He'd be forever grateful to Jim Sheridan for loving and ministering to his people for these past three years. Some men would have felt they deserved to stay the senior pastor after giving so much of themselves for that long, but Jim was eager for Zach to return to the pulpit.

"Lord, I hope you have a really special reward for Jim and Susan for this," he prayed.

Zach reached for his Bible and opened it to the book of Isaiah where he had been reading every morning that week. He began with the forty-third chapter and when he came to verse nineteen, he felt a quickening in his spirit. There was the sense that "This verse is mine." He backed up and read it again:

"Behold, I will do a new thing, now it shall spring forth; Shall you not know it? I will even make a road in the wilderness and rivers in the desert."

Excitement continued to grow as Zach slowly read the verse again. He didn't know exactly what this new thing was, but he could feel in his heart that there was indeed something new on the horizon that was going to bring good change into his life. The fact that Grace would be part of it was a given. He couldn't wait to talk to her about what he was feeling.

He glanced at his watch and knew that Jay and Lil would be up by now. Picking up his phone he called and on the second ring Lil answered. He could hear the smile in her voice. "Is this really my Zach boy calling so early? Are you coming for breakfast?"

"No, but if it's okay I'd like to come for lunch."

"If it's okay? Of course it is!"

"'Morning, Mama Lil. How're you doing?"

"Fit as a fiddle and tickled pink that you're coming out, son. Are you bringing company with you?"

"I can never put anything past you, can I? Yes, I'm bringing Grace out to see the ranch and to meet you and Jay. You weren't planning on going anywhere this morning?"

"No, we did our town errands yesterday, so come on out. What time can we expect you?"

"Probably, close to ten-thirty. That should give us time to ride around the ranch a bit before lunch." He chuckled.

"Grace had her first ride last evening. I don't want to keep her on a horse too long today. Could you ask Jay to saddle up the horses for me to save some time?"

"I'm sure he'll be glad to do that. And we've both been looking forward to meeting Grace. 'See you when you get here, hon."

"Thanks, Mama. We'll be there in a few hours."

* * * * *

Grace tossed and turned, hating to leave the comfortable bed, but finding it brought no relief to her racing mind. She knew that visiting Zach's ranch today was a milestone in their relationship. And so was meeting the couple that lived at Zach's ranch. She wasn't afraid that they wouldn't approve of her, but she knew their opinion of her would carry weight with Zach. They had known and loved Sasha as well as Zach. Could they love her the same way?

Suddenly, she had the image of the young girl, Mary, who faced a probably glowing, intimidating angel. His first words to her were,

"Fear not." He proceeded to tell her that she would give birth to a Savior who would change the world.

Grace knew that she wasn't another Mary. The world didn't need another Savior, but it did need people who would not be afraid to carry the vision for ministries to make that Savior known to the world.

With all her heart Grace wanted to be one of those people. Each day she was more confident that it was God's plan for her and Zach to do this together. She and Damien had physically worked in ministry together, but they had never shared the heart of ministry that Grace felt with Zach.

This feeling was what she had longed for when she was single and hoping for a godly husband. She still found it hard to believe that she had not seen the truth when she was with Damien, but what deliverance from the sorrow of that failed marriage the truth had brought.

Her phone ringing startled her but seeing that the call was from her mother brought joy. She'd been intending to call her parents, but Zach had kept her busy.

"Hi, Mom! I'm so glad you called."

"I've just been concerned, Sweetheart, since I hadn't heard from you. Are you doing all right?"

"Oh, Mom, so much has happened since I got here. I don't even know where to start."

"Well, you sound happier than you've been in a long time. Tell me what's going on."

Grace took a deep breath. "Mom, you won't believe this—I've met someone…"

CHAPTER 19

Zack hung up from talking with Grace and felt that this was the time to do something that just weeks ago he would have thought he would never do…say goodbye to Sasha. He couldn't quite describe his feelings. There was a sense of weightiness in what he was about to do and yet it wasn't sorrowful.

He stopped and purchased some of her favorite roses, more for himself than her. As he drove to her graveside he tried to think of what he would say, but the words wouldn't come. He parked his truck and took the roses and laid them at the base of the beautiful granite headstone that read, Sasha Marie Clayton, Beloved wife and Friend.

Always before when he came here his heart ached with sorrow, but today that sorrow was softened with a sweetness he hadn't felt before. As he knelt there he was reminded of a conversation they had held not long before her life ended. He hadn't remembered it until now.

"My dearest Zach," she'd said, her brown eyes large and full of love in her gaunt face. "We have been blessed beyond measure with the love God has given us. I have cherished every moment with you. But my dearest, I have been talking with the Lord about you and your future. I believe with all my heart that he has another love for you, Zach."

Zach remembered how he had so adamantly protested her statement, so sure that he could never give his heart to another woman.

"Listen to me, Zach," Sasha had said. "Our wonderful love was a gift from God…do you not agree? And do you think that was the only gift of love in God's possession? No, my darling, He has another woman for you, another love as precious as ours has been. Your love will be a gift to her, and hers a gift to you. But you must receive her, Zach. You must be willing to open your heart and allow her love to fill you as mine has. You will need her in your ministry, but more than anything, you will need her for the healing of your heart. Receive her, Zach. Receive her love."

He could hear her sweet voice as though she was still there in person with him. She had been right. God had brought another love that filled his heart and remembering that conversation was the last bit of reassurance he needed to move ahead with Grace and the new life that lay before them.

Tears flowed down his face as he placed his hand on the gravestone. "Thank you, my precious Sasha. Thank you for loving me, for working beside me as we gave our lives to the Lord's work. I wish I could know what awesome thing He has you doing in Heaven, but we'll catch up on all that one of these days. You will never be forgotten, my love. I will see you on the other side!"

Zach stood, taking one last look at the earthly place that held the body of the woman he had loved with all his heart. Peace covered him like he had never expected to feel. It was almost as though he could see Sasha, beautiful in a flowing robe of white, smiling and lifting her hand to wave as she slowly faded into memory.

"This is where my land begins," Zach said, pointing Grace to where the fencing changed from barbed wire to white painted wood. He slowed and made the left turn off the county road onto the gravel drive that led to the ranch house and outbuildings.

"The wood fencing makes it look really nice, Zach," Grace said.

"Funny you'd comment on that first," he said, smiling. "That was the one thing Sasha insisted on."

Grace nodded. "A woman thing." She tucked her hand under his arm and squeezed a little closer.

"Are you feeling nervous about meeting Jay and Lil?" Zach asked, noting that she seemed unusually tense.

"A little," Grace admitted. "They're just so important to you."

Zach slipped his arm around her and drew her to him. "I know that you haven't met them, but I can assure you that in the next few minutes all that anxiety will be gone. Jay and Lil are the most loving people you could ever meet. And even if you weren't the most loveable lady in the world, they would love you because I do."

He slowed the truck to a stop and gave her a sweet kiss. "Feel better?"

"Yes, I do."

"You know, I'm a little nervous, too."

Grace looked up at him in surprise. "Whatever for?"

"I don't know if you'll like my ranch."

"Why Zach Clayton! How silly of you. Don't you know that even if your place wasn't the greatest little ranch in Texas, I'd still love it because you do?" She gave him a slap on the arm.

Zach laughed and hugged her again. "Okay, fair enough." He put the truck in gear and drove the remaining distance to the house.

By the time they were out of the truck, Jay and Lil were standing in the doorway.

Zach was right. Within moments of meeting this elderly couple, Grace not only felt at home, but loved. They embraced her as though she had always been part of their relationship with Zach.

"Come on in the kitchen. I've got a fresh pot of coffee and cinnamon rolls just out of the oven."

"Oh my, it smells delicious in here," Grace said as Zach pulled out a chair for her.

"That's the second best thing about coming here," Zach said. "Smelling all the good stuff Mama Lil is cooking up. The best thing is eating it!"

Lil came over and slipped her arm around Zach. Looking at him with love, she said, "And he's a delight to cook for—he eats anything!"

Zach smiled at Grace, "See, I told you."

Jay set cups of coffee before each of them. "Grace, do you use anything in your coffee?"

"No, but thank you, Jay. I drink it black."

Jay smiled at her, his blue eyes twinkling. "So Zach's gonna show you around the ranch today?"

"Yes, I'm excited about it. I'm new at this ranching, horse riding, etc."

"You didn't complain about any aches and pains from riding yesterday," Zach commented.

"Well, I'll just say I appreciated your tip about the hot shower when I got up," Grace told him.

Lil brought the small plates of cinnamon rolls and passed them around. "So how do you like riding?"

"I loved it. I want to learn to ride solo, although that may be a little scary for me."

"Nah, you'll catch onto it. Jay and I still ride together. It's one of our favorite things to do. We've been so blessed to live here at Zach's ranch after Jay retired from the spread he was managing. I don't think we could have handled living in an apartment in town without horses and my chickens."

"Mama Lil keeps all of us in fresh eggs," Zach told Grace.

"You'll have to take some home with you. I think Zach told us you are staying with a friend?" Lil asked.

"Yes, Karen has been my best friend since we were college roommates."

"This cinnamon roll is excellent, as always, Mama Lil," Zach commented as he stood to bring the coffee pot to the table for refills.

"I'll have to come watch you make them sometime, Lil. I haven't had much luck with anything using yeast. I think this is the best cinnamon roll I've eaten," Grace said.

Lil gave her a sweet smile. "You should have seen some of my first attempts at sweet breads years ago. You can ask Jay."

Her husband chuckled. "Now that you brought it up, Lil."

He looked at Grace. "I remember the time she couldn't get the dough to rise. We tried everything to get those rolls to double in size. Finally, she baked them as they were," he laughed again, "but there was no eating those things. They were hard as bricks."

Lil chimed in, "The dog wouldn't even eat them. I think the chickens finally pecked them to pieces."

"Well, you certainly improved somewhere along the way," Zach said.

"Thank goodness, there was a sweet, elderly lady in our church whose specialty was yeast breads. She took me under her wing, and Jay has been eternally grateful."

"Well, now you can pass that information on to me," Grace told her.

"That's only fair, isn't it? I certainly will, Grace. We'll have to set up a time."

There was a moment's silence as everyone ate and drank, then Jay scooted his chair back and crossed one leg over the other. He looked at Lil, then to Zach.

"Son, there's something Lil and I need to talk to you about."

Zach looked at both of them, then said, "Okay."

"You remember our daughter, Crystal, and her husband, Tom."

"Sure. They were trying to go somewhere as missionaries, weren't they?" Zach asked.

"Yes, and they've been approved to go to Romania in a couple of months."

"That's great," Zach said.

"Well, this is the situation," Jay continued. "They bought a double-wide mobile home a couple of years ago when it looked like they weren't going to be approved for the mission field due to some health issues Tom had. That has all been taken care of now, and they are thrilled to be going to do the work of the Lord.

"The problem is that they need a place to leave their mobile home while they're gone. They'll be living on a very tight budget and can't afford much space rent. They're also concerned about the home being vandalized, or just going into decline with no one living in it."

Lil cut in here, "What we're asking, Zach, is if they could park the home here on the ranch, and if it's not too costly to get things set up for electricity and sewer, they'd like us to live in it."

"We'd still be here to keep an eye on things for you, Zach, but your home would be available for you to move back into anytime you feel you're ready," Jay said.

Zach could hardly speak. He was so moved at the goodness of God to so quickly take care of the thing that had concerned him most when he and Grace married—knowing that Jay and Lil would have a place to live the life they loved.

"I would be thrilled to have them bring their home here. Jay, there's electricity they can hook into easily, and the septic tank is large enough to accommodate two homes. Just choose the site you want. I wouldn't think of charging them anything. It will probably cost them quite a bit to have it moved."

"They've been looking into that, and it seems there's a fellow in that business who's a Christian and does this sort of thing for missionaries and ministers as his own ministry. He's already agreed to to move it for them at just the cost of the permit," Jay told them.

"That's wonderful," Grace said. "Would you find out what they'll need for the permit? I'd like to pay that for them."

"Oh, Grace," Lil murmured and reached out to squeeze her hand. "That is so kind of you."

"I remember what it was like when…when my ex-husband and I started out in ministry. Every time God used someone to meet a need that we had, it encouraged us to believe that we really were doing what He wanted us to do. We are all together in the work of the Lord."

Zach looked at Grace and felt so blessed that God had brought this special woman to him and had finally opened his heart to receive her.

"Jim Sheridan's brother, Greg, does that kind of work— setting up mobile homes. I'll give him a call and get him to come out and take a look at things. We'll probably need a pole and a meter. Just tell him where you want it. I think he can handle running a line to the septic tank, too. We'll need to bring in some shell for a driveway."

"I was thinking it might be wise to pour a concrete slab for stability. With the gully washers we get here in South Texas, it could be a problem to keep it level," Jay said.

Zach nodded. "That's a good idea, Pop. When Greg comes out ask him if he does that, too. Have him do whatever it takes to get it set up right. I'll take care of the bill."

Jay's eyes were misty. "Thank you, son. I know Crystal and Tom will be very appreciative."

"I'm glad to do it, Pop." He took a deep breath and stood. "Now I have a lady to take gallivantin' about a ranch."

"I left the horses inside the barn for the shade, but they're ready to go," Jay said.

"Thanks, I appreciate that." Zach gave Jay an affectionate slap on the back.

"The rolls and coffee hit the spot, Mama Lil. We'll be back for lunch," Zach said, hugging her.

"Yes, thank you, Lil," Grace said. "I'm looking forward to my lessons to make those myself."

"That will be fun, Grace. Don't let him tire you. Zach and Jay can both talk ranch talk 'til the cows come home."

"Well, we do have lunch to come back for, so I don't think he'll keep me out there too long."

Lil laughed. "You're right. He's not going to forget lunch."

"Well, I saw a section of fence that looks like it's rusted through, so I'm going to go fix that. I'll see you at lunchtime."

Jay gave Lil a peck on the cheek. "Later, Mama."

Zach took Grace's hand and led her to the barn where the saddled horses stood.

"Are you sure you want to ride solo?" Zach grinned. "I don't mind you riding with me."

Grace smiled back at him. "I loved riding with you, but don't you think this would be a good time for me to start learning to ride by myself? There are no other people around to see me mess up and we don't have to ride fast."

Zach cocked his head to the side. "Lady, your logic wins. Remember how to get up there?"

"Don't you think you should introduce us first?" Grace asked.

Zach laughed and looked a little sheepish. "You're right, I should." He patted the chestnut colored horse on the neck.

"Buttercup, this is Ms. Grace. She's going to be riding you today. Grace, meet Buttercup. She's a nice gentle mare."

"Hi, Buttercup." Grace gently spoke to the horse and stroked her neck. "You can probably tell I'm new at this, so I'd appreciate it if you bear with me until I get the hang of it. Okay, girl?"

To their amusement, Buttercup nodded her head and nickered as if agreeing to Grace's request.

"This guy is Rex," Zach said, patting the haunches of a dappled gray horse. "Rex, this is Grace, and we're all going to be buddies. Rex is a good horse, but he can cop an attitude sometimes. He likes to think he's boss."

Grace smiled. "Well, I'm glad I'm riding Buttercup, then."

"Ready for a hand up?" Zach asked her.

"Yep, here goes."

Zach placed his hands together and stooped to be at the level she needed. Grace placed her foot in his hands and hoisted herself up into the saddle. For a minute she felt uneasy as she saw how far from the ground she was, but Buttercup was steady beneath her and she began to relax. Zach handed her the reins and showed her how to hold them correctly.

He gave her tips on staying balanced in the saddle and how to communicate with the horse for it to know where she wanted it to go.

"And I'm to do all this without falling off, right?" Grace said nervously.

Zach grinned and patted her leg. "You'll do fine. I'll ride close. Are you ready?"

"I think so," Grace said none too confidently.

Zach mounted Rex and moved up beside her.

"Okay, put the pressure on her sides like I told you and click your reins."

Grace's heart was beating rapidly as Buttercup began to move forward. At first, she felt a little dizzy, but began to relax and enjoy the ride.

"I'll let you get used to riding for a while before I start pointing out things to you," Zach said. "You're really doing well."

She kept her eyes straight ahead, afraid if she looked away she'd do something wrong. She couldn't help smiling, though. She, city girl Grace Morgan, was actually riding a horse!

CHAPTER 20

Zach rode Rex closer to Grace and Buttercup, then indicated a group of trees to their right.

"I want to show you something over there."

He smiled as Grace comfortably reined Buttercup to head that direction. She really had taken to riding quickly. She would be a good horsewoman in no time. His smile widened into a grin. She was going to make a great rancher's wife.

Grace happened to look at him before he could change his expression,

"What? Are you laughing at me?"

"Why on earth would I do that? Can't a man just be happy doing his favorite thing with a beautiful woman? By the way, you're doing great; I'm proud of you."

Grace blushed at his compliment. "At least, I haven't fallen off—not yet anyway. We haven't actually gone very fast, though."

"There's plenty of time for that. Let's stop there under those trees and walk for a bit."

When they reached the area Zach dismounted first and looped the reins over a tree branch. Rex snorted his approval of the shade and being free of his rider.

"Hold still; I'll help you down." Zach said then took Buttercup's reins from Grace and looped them on another limb.

When she slid down into his arms Zach pulled her close and kissed her. "I've gone too long without this."

"I agree." Grace smiled at him and hugged him closer.

"Was this what you wanted to show me?" she asked.

Zach chuckled. "That wouldn't be a bad idea, but no, I do actually have something I want you to see—this way."

He released her to take her hand and began walking through a stand of trees, the only real group of trees Grace had seen on the property. While the major portion of the ranch they had ridden was flat land, there was now a rise to the acreage and more bushes and growth along with trees. As they reached the peak of the rise, Zach stopped.

"This is what I wanted you to see."

Ahead of them was a meadow surrounded by a fringe of trees as though they had been planted in an oval to guard the beautiful, grassy area. A natural pond was almost perfectly situated in the center. Wildflowers of numerous kinds and colors bloomed, some gently moving with the breeze.

"Oh, Zach, what a beautiful place—a special place."

"That's what Sasha and I always said about it—it's special. I feel that God has a specific plan for this little spot of Texas."

"It's as though He made it a refuge of peace and rest."

"I know. I've just never been sure how He plans to use it for that…or what I'm supposed to do to bring that about. I do believe there's something I need to do right away, though."

Grace looked up, waiting for him to continue. She watched curiously as he removed his Stetson and laid it gently on the grass. Then he took both her hands in his.

"Grace, I know that we haven't known each other long, maybe folks would say not long enough to be sure of our feelings. All I know is that you entered my very dark life and brought me back to the light. I know that you are God's gift to me."

He chuckled. "We can hardly talk about the future without it including us together, but we haven't solidified anything, so it's kind of awkward. I think we need to get that out of the way so we can wholeheartedly proceed on the path God has for us.

"We've both found out the hard way that there are no guarantees in marriage, but I can't imagine spending the rest of my life without you. If you'll take a chance on me, I promise to do my best to make you the happiest woman in Texas—and it's a big state."

He dropped to one knee. Pulling the ring box from his pocket, he opened it and looked up at her.

"Grace Morgan, I love you. Will you marry me and make me the happiest cowboy in the big state of Texas?"

"Oh, Zach!" Grace brought both hands to her face in excitement. "Yes, I'll marry you. I can't wait to marry you!"

She threw both arms around his neck and bent to kiss him. He stood, drawing her with him and into his arms. The possessiveness of his kiss left no room for doubt that she was his.

"Oh, Zach, I love you," she said when she could finally speak.

He drew her even closer. "Grace, there's something I want you to know. "He paused a moment. "I never believed that I could love another woman as much as I loved Sasha. But when you came into my life, that love for her found it's place in my past. I don't know that I can really explain it. I just want you to know that my love for you is in no way less than my love was for her."

He drew back from Grace so he could look into her blue eyes that he loved.

"You fill my heart, Grace…only you. I am so excited about a future with you by my side. I guess I should ask you about that—you know I'm a pastor—can you handle being a pastor's wife again?"

Grace smiled up at him. "I've told you, Zach, all I ever wanted to be was a pastor's wife. I just hope that your people will accept me."

"How could they not love you, my sweet, precious Grace? Sasha has been gone now for three years. Susan has been the interim pastor's wife that they've looked to. When they see how happy you make me, I know they will welcome you with open arms."

The fleeting image of a tall woman with her arms around Zach's neck made Grace unsure of Zach's statement, but she refused to allow it to mar her happiness.

"And now that you've seen the ranch, do you think you'll be okay with living here? We don't have to, you know. We can live in town if you'd rather."

"Zach, I love the ranch. I wouldn't want to live anywhere else. This is your home and wherever you are, that's home for me. It's wonderful that Jay and Lil will be close. I know they'll teach me anything I need to know if you're not around."

Suddenly, Zach became aware of the ring box still in his hand behind her back. "Oh, don't you want your ring?"

Grace blushed deeply. "Oh Zach, I'm sorry. All I could think of was you."

Zach grinned. "Well, I guess that proves you're not into this for what I have to give you."

"It's beautiful, Zach," Grace said as he slipped the sparkling solitaire onto her finger.

"With this ring I engage you," he said gallantly, bringing her hand to his lips just as his stomach growled loudly.

They both burst out in laughter.

When Grace could speak, she said, "That was so romantic." She glanced at her watch. "Well, your alarm is working well, it's about five minutes until noon."

"Hmm," Zach said, "Do you think you can ride a little faster going back?"

"I think so; we can try it."

Zach put his Stetson back on his head and took her hand.

"All right, fiancée. We have a lunch date waiting."

Jay walked out of the barn when he heard them riding up. "Hey, young'uns. Go on in and freshen up. I'll take care of the horses. Lil's got lunch about ready."

"Thanks, Pop."

Zach helped Grace dismount and turned to give Jay a slap on the back. "You're the best."

Jay couldn't help but notice the light in Zach's eyes and the possessive way he put his arm around Grace and drew her close as they walked to the house.

He chuckled as he led the horses into the barn. "I told Mama they'd come back engaged."

"I'm hungry, Mama Lil," Zach said as they entered the kitchen.

"As if I'm surprised," Lil retorted. "Hi, Grace, how was the ride?"

"I think I did pretty well—at least Zach told me I did."

"She did. She'll be riding like a pro in no time."

Grace laughed. "Now that's an exaggeration!"

She turned to Zach. "Where can I wash up?"

Zach extended his arm with a flourish. "This way, my lady." Down the hall he indicated the next doorway.

"Is it okay if I tell Jay and Lil our news at lunch? I mean, you might want to tell Karen…or your folks first."

"From the smiles on their faces as they looked at us, I don't think it will be any surprise to them, so go ahead and tell them."

"Okay." Zach walked into the bedroom that had once been so familiar. The furniture was the same, but all Sasha's belongings had now been removed. There was no life in the room. It was as bare emotionally as it was physically.

As he washed up at the sink Zach had a thought that he hadn't considered … about Grace's parents. He felt guilty realizing that he'd not given any thought to them. Here he was about to marry their only daughter and it hadn't even occurred to him to meet them first and speak to her father, asking him for her hand. Even if she had been married before, they had the right to at least meet the new guy, and hopefully, give their approval. He'd have to do something about this—and soon.

Lil had the table set when they returned to the kitchen. Grace couldn't help exclaiming when she saw the tableful of food. Golden baked chicken was surrounded by several vegetables in season locally—all of them cooked to perfection.

"Oh, my! This is what you're used to." Grace looked up to Zach with a defeated look on her face.

"Don't get me wrong," he said, "I enjoy Mama Lil's cooking, but what are you worried about? Everything you've fed me has been delicious."

Lil came over and put her arm around Grace's waist. "Grace, honey, don't you be intimidated by my cooking. I've been at it over fifty years. If I didn't do a good job of it by now, there would be something wrong. Besides, if there's ever anything you want to know about cooking, just ask. I love to share my knowledge."

"I'm really glad to know that. I'm sure I'll be calling you," Grace replied.

Jay entered the kitchen. "Give me just a minute to wash up, Mama." He whispered to Zach as he passed by him, "Don't ya tell any secrets 'til I get back."

Zach grinned. He never could keep anything from Lil and Jay.

"Y'all go ahead and sit and we can eat as soon as Papa gets back," Lil said. She approached the table with tea pitchers in both hands. "Grace, have we converted you to sweet tea yet or do you prefer yours unsweetened?"

"I'm tempted, Lil, but since I'm already used to drinking it without sugar I think I'll stick with unsweetened."

Lil filled her glass and looked fondly over at Zach. "I don't have to ask this guy. I doubt he'd drink it without the sugar." She filled Zach's glass from the opposite pitcher.

Jay returned and settled in his chair. "Well, why mess with a good thing? Sweet tea and Texas are a great combination, eh, son?"

"You bet, Pops." Zach said with a grin.

Lil joined them now and Jay extended his hand to her and to Zach as they connected with Grace. He bowed his head and prayed:

"Father, we are thankful for the food on this table and for the many ways You provide for us. I thank you for bringing Grace and Zach to join us today. May your blessings rest upon all of us. Amen."

The others echoed, "Amen."

Dishes were passed until everyone had helpings of each. After a few bites Grace couldn't help complimenting Lil.

"Everything is absolutely delicious, Lil. I will definitely be spending some time in the kitchen with you."

Lil laughed. "It's all in the spices, hon."

"But you have to know which ones and how much," Grace said. "and I look forward to learning that."

"Well, I'm here most of the time. Would you like me to choose something to cook or would you like to do that?"

Grace looked at Zach, blushing slightly. "Well, you know what Zach likes best, so why don't you choose."

"All right, I will." Lil held the platter with the remains of the chicken toward Zach. "More chicken, hon?"

Zach shook his head negatively. "I would, Mama, but I know that you've got some kind of dessert stashed away over there and I've got just enough room for that."

Jay smiled and nodded. "That's a smart move. I saw her makin' that dessert."

"And you're gonna tell me what it is, right?"

"And ruin the surprise?" Jay's blue eyes twinkled.

Lil stood and began taking their dishes. "Oh, you two, stop being silly. It's pineapple upside down cake."

Zach practically groaned. "Grace, you can make sure that's included in your cooking lessons. It's probably number one on my list of favorite desserts."

"It's another southern favorite," Lil said, returning to the table with the cake. "I think it's the visual effect that everyone likes as much as the taste."

Pineapple rings with red cherries in each of them were perfectly arranged on the square cake. Crushed pineapple cooked with butter and brown sugar filled the spaces between the rings and the sides of the cake.

"I think you're right; it's beautiful," Grace said.

"Would you all like coffee?" Lil asked.

Everyone voted in favor and Grace offered to get it.

"The cups are in that first cabinet," Lil told her and the coffee's at the end of the counter."

Zach smiled as he watched Grace in his kitchen. She seemed perfectly at home there. He wanted to blurt out their news but waited until they had finished the delicious cake. As they sipped on the coffee, he reached over to take Grace's hand. Clearing his throat, he spoke.

"I doubt that this will come as any surprise to you, Mama, and Pop, but Grace and I are getting married. I think we are more surprised than anyone else. Neither of us was looking for a mate, but we love each other and more importantly, we believe it's the will of God."

Mama Lil squealed in delight. "No, honey, it's not a surprise, but it sure makes us happy. We've been praying for the Lord to send you the right young woman and I believe He has."

Jay nodded. "We knew that you wouldn't go forward in your ministry without a wife, so we've been asking the Lord to bring her—quickly, since no amount of naggin' on our parts was getting' you movin'."

They all laughed, and Jay rose and walked around the table to hug Grace warmly. "Welcome to the family, darlin.'"

Lil hugged her, too. "We're so glad you're here for our boy, Grace. And just so you know, he's as good as they come."

Then she hugged Zach. "God had everything planned, didn't He? He knew you'd be concerned about us old folks having a place to live, so He already had it in the works to provide the kids' mobile home for us."

"And the best part is that we still get to have you close to us."

Jay was waiting to hug Zach when Lil released him.

"Grace is a jewel, son. God did good by you."

"I believe that Pops. I know He has something special for us. I'm just trying to figure out what it is."

"First things first. Get married, take the steps He places in front of you and you'll find yourself right where you're supposed to be."

Zach nodded and hugged Jay again. "I can't tell you how much I appreciate you and Mama Lil for being here for me. I always knew you were praying for me, even when I wasn't praying myself."

Jay gave him a firm slap on the back. "I'm sure glad that's changed."

CHAPTER 21

"It was all wonderful, Lil," Grace said. "Can I help clean up?"

Lil waved her aside. "I was thinking Zach might like to give you a tour of the house since you're going to be living here soon."

"That was the next thing on my mental list, Mama Lil," Zach said. "How about it, Grace? 'Want to see your new digs?"

"Of course, I do." She reached out to take Zach's outreached hand. "Lead the way, Cowboy."

Almost an hour later they were saying their goodbyes to Lil and Jay and heading back to town. Zach put his arm around Grace as he drove. He placed a quick kiss on her temple.

"I love your house, Zach. "Thank you for today. It was beautiful," Grace said.

Zach drew her closer. "I owe you an apology, Grace."

Grace looked up at him. "Whatever for?"

"It dawned on me a couple of hours ago that I have not given any thought to your parents in regard to us. I should have met them and talked to your dad about wanting to marry you before proposing to you. After all they've seen you go through with Damien I just want them to know that I will do my best to never hurt you."

"That is really sweet and thoughtful of you, Zach. I know my parents would appreciate that. When I told my mother I'd met you I could feel her reserve over the phone. My parents have never tried to run my life, but I know they are concerned. I also know they'll love you when they meet you in person., but I think it would relieve their fears."

"So, do we need to make a trip to California? I'd love to introduce you to my dad and his new wife while we're there. I don't think they live that far from your folks."

Zach could feel the tension that came over Grace. "Oh, Babe, I'm sorry. The reason you're here is because of your problems in California. Is there another way to deal with this? Would your parents come and visit us here?"

"Maybe I'm just being a wimp, but the idea of going back there makes me feel sick. As for them coming here —my parents don't do a lot of long distance traveling. They always drive because my dad refuses to fly. If we get married soon that would mean two long trips in a short length of time and that just won't work for them."

Zach raked his hand through his hair. "We need to start a list of things we have to do before we get married."

They were just pulling into Karen's driveway.

"I think you're right. Let's go inside. We can sit at the dining table and hash it all out."

A few minutes later the coffee was brewing and they both had paper and pens.

"Okay," Zach said, "I've already been thinking about some things I need to do before getting married, but it seems there are a few more." He began to list them:

"1. I need to meet and talk with your parents.

2. The mobile home has to be set up at the ranch so Jay and Lil can move into it.

3. I need to move back to the ranch.

4. We need to set a wedding date."

Grace chimed in:

"5. We need to decide where the wedding will be.

6. We need to decide what kind of wedding we'll have—small or large."

"Well, my vote for number six is 'small'," Zach said.

"I agree. I don't know that many people here, and I'd really prefer to have just close friends and family," Grace said.

Jovially Zach announced, "Cross number six from the list. The wedding will be *small*! Do you have any suggestions for number five—*where* this is to take place?"

"Yes, I do."

"Would you care to share your suggestion since I'll have to meet you there?" he asked.

Grace gave him a teasing look. "I suppose so, since I can't get married without you." She waited a moment then said, "The meadow—by the pond. I see a gazebo there."

Zach smiled. "You want to get married at the ranch?" He looked up. "My city girl wants an outdoor wedding at the ranch, Lord. Could it get any better than this? Number five settled! The wedding will take place in the meadow. I'll have to work on the gazebo part, though. Hey, we're doing good working backward. What was number four?"

"The wedding date," Grace said. "I don't think we can take care of that at the moment, though."

"Right. Number four tabled for further consideration. Next, number three…"

"Your moving back to the ranch."

"I can do that anytime. I don't have a problem living there with Jay and Lil until they move to the mobile home. In fact, it's all good for me. Lil will feed me much better than I've been eating in my over-the-barn apartment."

Grace poked him. "Remember, all that good cooking is temporary."

"Hey, I can't wait until you're the one cooking for me." He reached over and gave her a kiss. "Oh, this might be number three and a half, but I'll need to move my cattle back to the ranch. That's more trouble than moving me and my stuff. I can do that in the next couple of weeks though. That leaves what?"

"Number two, the mobile home, and number one, meeting my parents."

"This is making my head hurt," Zach complained. "I'll call tomorrow about the mobile home, but I don't know how we're going to work number one. I think we need to pray on it."

Grace gave him a pointed look. "You haven't mentioned the wedding details…reception, cake, decorations, even a small wedding requires all those things."

Zach groaned. "Would it hurt your feelings if I left all that to you?" he asked. "Just tell me how much money you need, and I'll be there when it's time to say, 'I do.' Oh, I'll take care of getting the gazebo built. Will that get me off the hook?"

Grace faked despair, " My disinterested groom."

Zach gave her that crooked grin and pulled her into his arms. "I am most definitely not disinterested in *you*," he said in that tone of voice that always made her feel like putty.

Grace sighed. "I am absolutely loving my new life."

CHAPTER 22

"Do I have to tell you every single thing to do?" Alysse practically screamed into the phone at her assistant. "What do you think I pay you for? Make a decision and don't call me again today!"

The stunned employee on the other end of the phone just looked at it in surprise. Since when did Alysse Stratton ever let her make a decision when it came to a design job? The past two days had been pure torment at work. She didn't have a clue what had gotten into her boss, but there was definitely something going on and everyone around her was paying for it.

Alysse continued to pace the carpet in her upscale apartment. She was so full of anger she felt she could explode if something didn't give, and she couldn't imagine any relief until Zachary Clayton and his blonde bimbo paid for her misery. She just hadn't been able to come up with a plan to make that happen.

As she paused by the wet bar she kept supplied with all varieties of alcoholic beverages for guests she suddenly had the desire to pour a glass of the amber liquid for herself. Not once had she ever wanted to partake of the poison that had ruined her childhood and brought so much pain. At that moment though, she felt as though everything she had worked so hard to attain, the image of success she portrayed to the world, all of it had slipped between her fingers and all that was left was the lost little girl with no self- esteem and her alcoholic parents that had given her little but shame.

With trembling hands she reached for a glass and opened the decanter. One whiff of the whiskey and she was back in the dilapidated house filled with garbage and empty liquor bottles. Still lonely, still aching for someone to love her, still taking a back seat to someone more deserving. Is that what her parents felt? Is that why they drank…to dull the pain of their own failure to gain success in life? For the first time she felt something akin to understanding. So here she was., their daughter with whiskey in her hand.

"I thought I had escaped," she sobbed and tossed down the drink before she could think anymore. She gasped as the strong liquor burned her throat, yet still reached for the decanter and poured another drink. This one she took to her easy chair and drank more slowly, still wincing at its bitterness. Soon she felt the warmth as her body responded to the unfamiliar substance. She was still angry, but at least she could think. The sense of being in her childhood home made her remember her two brothers whom she had forgotten even existed. Did they still live there in the old house?

She went back to the bar and poured another drink as a thought came to mind. Surely her siblings were still the low-life's they'd always been. She could easily entice them with a few bucks to do a little dirty work for her. There would be no connection between them and Zach or Blondie. The only person who knew she was related to "the boys" was Radford and he was in this with her, so he wasn't going to tell.

There really wasn't any use in making plans until she found out if her brothers were available and willing, so that would be her first task in the morning. Swallowing the last of the drink in her hand she settled into the chair, yawned, and slept for the first time in days.

* * * * *

Before Grace opened her eyes she had the sense that something good was taking place today. As the brain fog cleared she remembered — this was Saturday, the day she got to spend with Zach as they conducted their first tour together, well at least the first one she'd work as his employee and his fiancée.

She held up her left hand and admired the sparkle of the beautiful diamond in the morning sunlight. Who could possibly have imagined how quickly her troubled life would turn around? "God, You really are good. Please forgive me for wasting those months thinking that You had let me down. All that time you were working things for my good. Bless Zach today and help us keep things going smoothly on the tour, and more than anything, help us to point lost souls to You."

A glance at her bedside clock let her know the alarm would be sounding in a few minutes so she turned it off and headed for the shower."

She was ready and waiting when Zach arrived to pick her up. Grace could see the excitement in his eyes when she opened the door for him and knew he was as happy as she was that they were beginning this new adventure together.

"Good morning, Beautiful," he said, taking her in his arms and giving her a sweet kiss. "Are you ready for this?"

"Yes, I am, my handsome cowboy. Oops, let me get my sunscreen!" She darted back into her room to retrieve it.

"That's a good idea," Zach told her as she came back. "We'll be in and out of the sun all day."

Soon they were at the Sheridan ranch where they left Zach's truck and switched to the lime green tour bus. She had swept the floor and dusted the seats in it yesterday as Zach washed the outside, so everything looked fresh and clean. Grace settled into the seat behind Zach as he slipped into the driver's seat.

"Are we ready to pick up the food, Ms. Assistant?" he asked, meeting her eyes in the rear view mirror.

"Ready, Captain!"

Grace wanted to remember every single thing about this first excursion with Zach. It felt like a new beginning of something good.

"Would you like to pray for our day, Love? Things have a way of getting really busy from the time we get the food, and I don't want to forget prayer."

"I'd love to," Grace said, thrilled that he would ask her to do this. She reached over and laid her hand on his shoulder and he placed his hand over hers.

"Heavenly Father," she began. "We are so thankful for this day and the multitude of blessings that you have bestowed upon us. We ask that you protect us and every person who comes to take the tour today. Let the Light of Jesus shine through us into the hearts of those who may be in need of You. Give me the wisdom I need to be the helper that Zach needs. Amen."

Zach echoed her "Amen" with his own and squeezed her hand before releasing it. When she met his eyes in the mirror she saw that they were misty and filled with love. Softly, he said, "You're something else, Grace Morgan.

She returned his smile and sat back, enjoying the moment. Thinking of where they were headed she said, "I'm looking forward to meeting Georgia. I'm hoping she'll let me spend a day with her when she's making those wonderful little pies. Goodness, between her and Lil I just might learn to be a good cook."

Zach gave her his crooked smile. "I've already told you what I think of your cooking, but I won't object to you learning anything either of those sweet ladies want to teach you."

Grace laughed. "You and Karen! She doesn't really cook so she ate up everything I made when we were college roommates. I loved it though, and I love feeding you, too."

"What more could a man ask for? Beauty and good food, too! I am a lucky man."

The catering business was just ahead so Zach slowed and pulled into the portico where they would load the food.

Georgia stepped out of the door when she heard them arrive, her face already beaming with welcome.

"Hello, hello! You must be Grace," she said opening her arms to give her a hug. "I'm so glad to meet you and happier than I can tell you that Zach has someone to help him."

"Grace, meet Georgia, another gift of God to me and the world."

"Oh you," Georgia waved him away with a blush. "Come on in. Everything's ready to go."

The larger coolers were arranged to the side and smaller containers neatly stacked as well.

"I get the big ones, Babe," Zach said to Grace.

"Okay, I'll get the smaller ones. I'm sure you have a system for loading these so just tell me where to put them."

In minutes, the food was neatly packed into the cargo area of the bus and Georgia appeared with two bags in hand. "I know you're always in a hurry, so I packed you some peach fried pies and coffee for the road."

"Oh, my, I can smell them already," Grace groaned. "Thank you so much."

"You're the best, Georgia," Zach said with a hug. "We have another tour tomorrow, so I'll get these containers back this evening."

" Okay, I'll have them ready for you in the morning again."

"Georgia, I'm so glad to have met you and look forward to time to visit." Grace said.

"Stop by anytime, Grace. I would love it."

A few minutes later Grace bit into the peach hand pie and groaned with pleasure. "Oh my goodness! This is heavenly. What have I been missing living in California all my life?"

Eyes twinkling, Zach swallowed his bite of peach pie and grinned at her. "Do I need to make a list? Life with a handsome cowboy…horse rides in the meadow… the best food ever…did I say life with a handsome cowboy?

Grace simply rolled her eyes and continued eating her pie.

* * * * *

Radford Connally downed the last of his coffee and pushed his empty breakfast plate away just as Alysse plopped into the seat across from him. The first thing he noticed was that she looked terrible. He had never seen her in public without every hair in place and make-up perfectly done in more years than he could remember. And he'd certainly never seen her with dark circles under her eyes.

"Hey. Rad," she said, and looking to the waitress who had appeared with a menu that she pushed away, "Just coffee."

"You don't look so good, Kiddo," Rad said softly. "Are you okay?"

Anger flared in her eyes so quickly that it startled Radford. "I won't be okay until Grace Morgan is…." The waitress sat a cup of coffee and creamers in front of her and her sentence remained unfinished.

As unpleasant as Radford had found this "job" for Alysse, the venom in her voice and attitude sent chills down his back. What was she actually capable of? At the moment he feared the worst. As much as he wanted to get out of this, maybe he should stay involved to know what she was planning. There might come a time when he could keep her from doing something they would regret.

"I'm all set to take the tour. Just passing time so I can show up a little late and don't have to interact with people any more than necessary."

Leaning forward, Alysse said with intensity, "I want you to learn every single thing you can about that woman today and get pictures of anything I might could use against her."

"Got it," Radford said, rising and shouldering his camera bag.

"And call me as soon as you get home!" Alysse called after him.

Radford nodded in her direction, eager to get away. He paid his check and drove the few miles to the point where the tour began. Normally he wasn't nervous doing undercover work, but Alysse had freaked him out. He feared she might actually do real harm to Grace Morgan or the preacher, and he was aiding and abetting. Maybe he could manage to pass on trivial information without giving her more real fuel for this vendetta.

Radford parked his car and headed for the ticket area where Zach Clayton was taking money from a couple. Handing them tickets, he gave them a warm smile. "Enjoy the tour; we're glad you came."

Looking to Radford, Zach said, "Hello, Sir, what is your name? He had a clipboard in his hand and was obviously going to look for Radford's name on it. Panic hit Rad, as he realized he'd forgotten to decide on a fake name in advance.

" Uh, George… Williams…and I didn't book ahead of time. Is there still room?" he asked, knowing his face had reddened in his confusion.

"That's fine, Mr. Williams. We have several empty spots still. Would you mind signing this waiver for me?" He handed the clipboard to Radford. Minutes later Radford was headed for the bus and the pretty blonde lady that smiled so sweetly at him. Another pang of regret hit him as she welcomed him and told him to choose any empty seat he'd like.

Finding a seat toward the back of the bus Radford wished he could be anyplace else right then. As a private investigator it wasn't illegal to gain information about people, and he couldn't help what his clients did with that knowledge. But if he knew they planned to use the info he gave them to do harm… that fell into a whole different category. He'd simply have to try to prevent that from happening.

CHAPTER 23

As Zach began charming the tourists with his pleasant rhetoric about Galveston, Grace settled into the seat behind him. He had handed the money box and clipboard to her as he entered the bus and she had placed it safely under the seat. On a whim she picked up the clipboard and looked for the name of the last man who had joined the tour.

Maybe it was the camera bag that made her nervous about him. Months of dodging paparazzi with those same type bags had probably made her leery of innocent photographers as well. He had signed his name in a rather messy way, but she could make out "George Williams."

As the day wore on things went well with the tour. The people seemed to really enjoy exploring the beautiful historic homes and learning things from Zach that the brochures didn't tell. Grace's uneasiness about George Williams continued throughout the day until she began to understand that the feelings weren't in her head, but in her spirit. Could the Holy Spirit be trying to make her aware of something?

She noticed that when she and Zach stood together he would somehow meander close enough to be within hearing distance. He took a lot of pictures and it seemed that most of them included her and Zach. Should she tell Zach what she was feeling? She didn't want to ruin the day for him. Unless she felt more strongly that she was supposed to say something she'd just keep it to herself and pray.

Zach debated about whether he should go to the bar and visit his mother. It didn't seem right to leave Grace, but he certainly wasn't going to take her into that bar. His mother wouldn't be glad to see him anyway.

But what if she needed money? Even if she did spend most of it on alcohol she still had rent, utilities, and food to pay for. As much as he hated going in that bar he couldn't take a chance on her not having her needs met.

Only he and Grace were left on the bus now that all the tourists had headed for the shopping and dining areas. He stepped down and turned to give her his hand then pulled her into his arms when she joined him on the sidewalk.

He pulled back and looked into her eyes. "I want to take you to lunch, but then I have to leave you for a bit. As much as I dread this I have to go check on my mom."

" I understand, Zach. You're a good son." She hooked her arm through his and smiling up at him, said, "Let's go eat, Cowboy!"

Arm in arm they walked to a small deli that Zach knew served good food and enjoyed their time alone. Too soon, Zach knew he'd have to leave if he was going to see his mother. Outside the deli Zach gave Grace a hug.

"I really hate to leave you. Will you be okay?"

Grace looked up at him condescendingly. "You do know I'm a big girl, don't you, Zachary?"

"Uh-oh, the full-name treatment. I'm in trouble now."

" Just go and check on your mom. There's a street full of shops to keep me busy," Grace assured him with a smile.

Radford Connally had been watching the doorway of the deli for the preacher and the Morgan woman to exit. His heart rate quickened when he finally saw them pause on the sidewalk in conversation. What he hadn't planned on was them going two different directions. He had to make a quick decision…which one would he follow? It was easier for him to exit his hiding place without being seen to go after the preacher, but he had to hurry. His target had long legs and was walking fast.

To Radford's surprise Zach Clayton strode right up to a seedy looking bar, then paused, pulled out his wallet and removed what seemed to be several bills. Radford lifted his camera and got the perfect shot of Clayton walking into the bar. What would his admirers think of this? True, he wasn't the pastor of the cowboy church at present, but this didn't look good for him.

Connally found a spot where he could get a close-up when the preacher came out. He knew it wouldn't be a long wait because the tour group had to be picked up. He'd was barely situated when the reverend opened the bar door and quickly walked to his bus.

Radford circled around and headed back toward the tourist businesses. He'd been too busy tailing the preacher and Grace to get lunch, so he grabbed a premade sandwich from one of the vendors and found a bench where he could sit and eat.

Grace ambled through several shops passing the time until Zach returned with the bus. There wasn't anything she needed, and she wasn't one to spend money without reason. It was a pleasant day, but really no fun to be there alone. As she looked ahead she saw the man, George Williams, sitting on a bench. For some reason she felt she'd rather stay out of his sight, so she crossed the street and paused in front of several shop windows to kill time.

With a honk of the horn Zach pulled the green bus up to the curb at the assigned meeting place. He stepped down with a big smile on his face and the tourist roster under his arm.

"Hey, everybody! Is anyone ready for the beach?"

Cries of positive replies answered him.

"Okay, let's see if we've got everyone. Give me a 'here' when I call your name and then board the bus, please."

Grace had made her way to stand beside him, so he handed her the clipboard and pen.

"Would you like to check off the names, Love?"

"I would," she said, smiling.

Within minutes, the only tourist left was George Williams. He seemed preoccupied and didn't respond when Zach called his name.

"Mr. Williams, are you coming with us?" Zach asked good naturedly. He took a step in the man's direction and the man started and then realized he needed to board the bus. His face reddened and he fumbled with his camera bag as he hurried forward.

"I'm sorry…I…" he ducked his head and stepped up into the bus, heading to the back.

Zach and Grace exchanged a look and shrugged.

"That leaves us, Beautiful."

A few minutes later they were coming to a stop at the beach location where they would have the cookout and finish up with singing around the campfire. Before allowing the tourists to leave the bus Zach gave a few instructions.

"Okay, folks, we want you to enjoy Galveston beach, but we also want you to stay safe. We'll be eating in a couple of hours and until then you can choose how you want to spend your time.

" If you want to swim we're encouraging you to stay fairly close to shore since we don't have a lifeguard on duty, and I don't swim well in cowboy boots. If you need to change into swimwear feel free to use our spacious restroom in the rear."

Chuckles spread throughout the bus since most of the people were aware of the size of that facility.

"If you just want to sit and watch the waves I'll have chairs out for you in just a few minutes. We'll also have the coolers out with cold bottled water." He reached down and grabbed a handful of bags and held them up.

"There are always a few folks who would like to stroll on the beach and pick up a pretty shell or two but don't have a pocket, so feel free to take a bag." He handed them to Grace. "My lovely assistant will be happy to give you one. Okay, I think that's about it. What time did I say dinner would be served?"

The group answered together, "In two hours."

Looking at his watch Zach said, "Which will make it…?

"Five-thirty," they replied.

"All right, don't forget the bottled water, we want everyone to stay hydrated. There are sodas in the coolers, too if that's your preference. Use your sunblock and have fun. "

Zach hurried to open the cargo area and start unloading coolers, tables, and chairs. A few of the men offered to help and it was all out quickly. He set up the grill and got it to heating. Knowing that Grace was here to take care of the rest of the food was such a relief. He looked for her to be sure she was handling things and found her telling a couple of ladies where to place the various supplies they'd be using. Most of the dishes wouldn't be taken from the coolers until close to serving time.

As he watched Grace interacting with the other ladies his heart swelled with pride. Her friendliness and ability to simply step into the place where she was needed made her a perfect assistant for the tours and a perfect mate for him. He realized he was just standing there admiring her and grinned and went to work.

Grace came to a stopping point when everything was out that she could put in place this early. She looked at Zach and saw that he was sweating over the grill as he placed foil-wrapped potatoes into the coals. Taking two bottles of cold water she walked over to him.

"Time for a water break, Cowboy?"

"How about a water and Grace break?" he replied.

Grace handed him the water as he fit the grill back in place.

" How's everything going? Are we on schedule?"

"We are exactly on schedule, " he said. "Thanks to you."

"I had ladies that insisted on helping me. Does that usually happen?"

"Not all the time, but it's not uncommon either. There were times that women helped Sasha and as they talked it turned into a time of ministry to them."

Grace nodded. "I can see how that happens. It's surprising how much I learned about those two ladies in just a half hour."

Zach pushed his hat back and wiped his brow. "You know, it's almost as each tour group has its own personality. A couple of times we've had a mix of people that just didn't click as a group and it was a little uncomfortable. Other times it was as though it was one big family and I'd see the folks exchanging phone numbers so they could stay in touch when they left.

"The time around the campfire is the same way. I wish I could say that all of them were as great as the night you and Karen came. Sometimes it's really hard to bring the Lord into the time and others, the anointing just flows. I have to be sensitive to what the people want and need from this time and pray that the Lord uses it to bless them."

"I hadn't thought about that, but I can understand. It's similar to how church services differ," Grace said.

Zach nodded. "It sure helps when the majority of the people…whatever venue it is…are open to the things of God."

Radford Connally pretended to be watching the beach and people but was always aware of Zach Clayton and Grace Morgan. They appeared to be in serious conversation close to the grill at the time. He couldn't help thinking how well they worked together and again he felt the loneliness of his solitary life. He also tried to imagine Alysse being there in Grace's place and it was impossible to do so. Alysse would only have wanted to be hanging on the preacher, not helping in any way. Whatever made her think any man who lived a life of service to people could find her suitable as a mate?

If only he could go back to the night Alysse had called. He should have let the phone ring...not answered it. She never called unless she wanted a favor from him. A free meal or two was all it ever netted him and that certainly wasn't worth the misery this job was causing him.

He was curious about that. Why was this assignment different from any other he'd worked? Somehow he'd gotten emotionally involved in this situation, and in his business that was a big negative. There was just something so nice about Grace Morgan. He didn't think she had a mean or deceptive bone in her. And all he'd seen of Zach Clayton had been above board. He had probably been a really caring pastor before he stepped down when his wife died. Maybe now that he had Grace in his life he would take over his church again.

Funny, but Radford thought he might even show up there sometime if that happened.

CHAPTER 24

Alysse seethed, feeling that Radford was not as interested in getting the scoop on Zach and the Morgan woman as she'd like. Oh well, she knew how to work him. She wasn't as ignorant of his feelings for her as he thought. No man jumps at a woman's every whim unless he's harboring some kind of crazy emotions for her. As she drove home she tried to think of ways she might use any information Rad gave her to make things unpleasant for the targets of her anger. She still didn't know just how she was going to do this, but she was determined to make it happen.

She stood in front of the mirror in her bathroom and couldn't believe she'd gone out in public looking like this. See what Grace Morgan was doing to her? But power accompanies appearance and she needed to be careful that she didn't lose that. She'd have to try to find her brothers that she hadn't seen in years and if she was successful she wanted them to know she was the one in control — that she had the prestige and the money.

Less than two hours later Alysse was driving toward the older part of town where she grew up. Looking at the rows of houses that were still familiar it was evident that the neighborhood had deteriorated even more.

Some houses were actually sagging and looked like they might collapse under a strong wind. Garbage was everywhere; junk was piled around most of the buildings as if nothing ever got taken away.

Strangely, Alysse felt her heartbeat quicken as she neared her former address. She slowed and saw the house she'd grown up in. It was really in need of repairs.

Grass and weeds were at least a foot high in the yard, but someone had cleared them on either side of the broken concrete sidewalk. A battered older model car sat in the cracked driveway that was covered in oil stains.

Alysse walked slowly to the doorway, careful not to get her stiletto heels wedged in the cracks of the sidewalk. Gingerly she knocked on the door and waited. Moments later she heard someone unlatching a chain lock and the door opened as far as the chain would allow. Wide green eyes partially covered by light brown hair looked curiously back at her.

"Yes, Ma'am?" the young woman said.

"I'm looking for Carl and Richard Milton. Do they still live here? I'm their sister."

The green eyes widened even more. "You're Alysse?"

Alysse said wryly, "I see you've heard of me."

The girl blushed.

"That's okay, I wouldn't expect my brothers to say anything nice about me. Are they here? And could I ask who you are?"

" Yes, Ma'am. I'm Sherry, Rick's fiancée'. He works nights and is sleeping but it's almost time for him to get up." Her expression changed to one of caution. "I'm guessing that Carl is sleeping, too, but I don't dare bother him."

"I see, but I could talk to Rick?"

Sherry shrugged. " I guess." She unlatched the chain and opened the door.

"Would you like to come in? You can wait here while I get him if you like."

She pointed toward the living room. Alysse could see that the same worn furniture and carpet were still there, all worse for wear and soiled a couple of shades darker.

It was evident though, that someone had done what they could to make it neat…most probably Sherry, Alysse surmised. There was nothing out of place or stuff lying around. She didn't think she'd ever seen the room that way.

"Would you like something?...Uh…I think we might have a soda in the fridge…or some water," Sherry offered.

"Thank you, but I'm fine. I'll just wait for Rick."

For some reason Alysse felt a kinship with Sherry. Did she recognize in her the same desire to live better than the way life had dealt her? But she didn't want to think about that. She wanted to stay angry…to find a way to ruin Grace Morgan's life and make Zach Clayton sorry he chose Grace over her.

Soon she heard movement in the hallway and her youngest brother and Sherry walked into the room. Alysse was surprised to see that Rick had actually grown into a nice looking young man…scruffy and sleepy-eyed, but he had a gentle look about him.

"Hey, Sis. This is a surprise." He stood several feet away as though leaving it up to her to make a move to hug him or not. After all, she'd left without a goodbye and had been gone for years with no word whatsoever. Alysse didn't move so Rick and Sherry sat on the sofa across from her.

Alysse didn't expect the emotions that rose within her when she saw her brother. He didn't look like a scumbag, nor was there any indication that he was using drugs. She hadn't expected him to look like the nice kid next door. She swallowed hard, put a smile on her face and said, "Well, Rick, what are you doing now?"

"I work at a warehouse," Rick said "I drive a cherry-picker, loading and unloading freight. I'm looking for a second job, though. My car broke down and I need to buy another one."

He looked at Sherry, " And this is Sherry…we've been together for over a year now and we want to get married, and hopefully soon, to have our own place."

"I'm looking for work, too," Sherry said timidly, "but it needs to be within walking distance and there's not much available close by."

"Uh…We've seen the ads for your design business on TV," Rick said.

Sherry's eyes brightened. "The rooms they showed, they're all just beautiful. I wish I knew more about how to make a place look…not that fancy, for sure…but prettier."

'Looks like you've done well for yourself," Rick said.

" Yes, I have. I've worked really hard," Alysse said.

Sherry put her hand on Rick's arm. "See, Rick, I told you it's possible for us to make a better life for ourselves if we just keep working at it."

Rick sighed. "I know, but it seems we take one step forward and then something like the car breaking down happens and we're back to where we were, stuck in this rathole."

Unfamiliar remorse filled Alysse. Why had she just taken for granted that her little brother was content to stay in the environment that had driven her to find an escape.

She remembered how she was the one who took care of him as a baby and until he got old enough for Carl to make him his child slave. He was pretty much under the thumb of their older brother and did whatever Carl told him to do from the time Rick was five or six.

Apparently, he'd grown up enough to think for himself now, though.

Being the youngest, Rick probably suffered the most neglect and misery inflicted by their parents. At least she could remember a few pleasant times in her younger years before the addiction had totally consumed them. But by the time Rick came along they were completely dependent on alcohol.

" You said Carl was sleeping…does he work nights, too?"

Rick and Sherry looked at each other and Rick said wryly, "I guess you could say that."

Softly Sherry added," Whatever he does at night you can bet it's not legal. That's why we want out of here so badly. We're afraid if the cops come after him they'll think we're in on his illegal doings and we have nothing to do with them. I'm scared to death of some of the characters he brings over here, especially when Rick's gone to work. I stay in our room with the door locked most of the time."

"It's that bad?" Alysse asked. "I thought he probably just used drugs and drank."

"He does that too, but he deals all kinds of stuff and he must be in pretty deep because he carries a gun on him all of the time," Rick said.

When they heard the sound of a door opening down the hallway, Rick stiffened. He got up and walked toward the doorway. Alysse recognized the next voice as her brother, Carl's.

"Is somebody here?" he growled.

"Yeah… You won't believe it… Alysse," Rick answered.

Carl was obviously surprised. Then he frowned. "What does Miss High and Mighty want?"

"I don't know. She hasn't been here long. I think she wants to talk about something…"

Carl ran his hand through his already tousled greasy hair and cursed. Dressed only in boxer shorts he said, "I'll be there when I get some clothes on," turned and headed back to his room.

Rick took a deep breath as he returned to the living room. "Carl's getting dressed…he'll be here in a minute."

Sherry stood. "Rick, I've got to start cooking if you're going to have time to eat before you leave for work."

Turning to Alysse, she said, "It was nice to meet you. We don't eat fancy but you're welcome to join us."

Alysse was touched by the young woman's offer. "That's very kind of you, Sherry. I'm not sure that I'll have time, but we'll see."

After an awkward moment, she asked, " Rick, are you trying to find another warehouse job or something else?"

"I was hoping to get a warehouse job because it pays a little more than anything else I'd be qualified to do. But most warehouse jobs are full time and I just don't think I can work two full time jobs. It would help if Sherry could get something."

"She seems to be a really nice young lady, Rick."

Rick smiled. "Yeah, I got lucky when I met her. She's got a heart of gold and is always ready to help somebody. For sure, she's changed my life. I'd pretty much given up on getting out of here, but she's made me want more.

"Her family background is pretty much the same as ours was, but she doesn't let it get her down. I guess she's kind of like you. She keeps telling me we can do better, and we're really trying. I don't think Carl likes that about her, but he does like the fact that she cleans and cooks." He grinned. "'Which neither of us did much of."

Out of the blue Alysse asked, "Is my old room still empty?"

The question took Rick aback. "I don't really know, Sis. I haven't even opened that door since you left. Carl took Mom and Dad's room when they died, and I just stayed where I was. I never had a reason to go to your room, so…do you want to see it?"

"I think I'd like to," Alysse said, standing.

She let Rick lead the way, a little wary of what they might find and the memories that might assault her as well.

Rick had to push hard on the stuck door. When it came open Alysse was surprised to see that the room was just as she'd left it, but considerably dustier and stale smelling.

"Whew!" Rick said. "I think I'd better open a window."

Alysse walked over to the dresser and ran her finger across the scratched top that she had painted lavender. Dust rose and so she stopped. "I remember the night Rad and I carried this thing home from the dumpster on the corner. He couldn't believe I was going to paint it purple!"

"Do you still stay in touch with that guy? I remember you two were pretty close back then."

"Oh, we talk every few months or so and went to dinner recently. He's a private investigator now."

Rick laughed out loud. "'Ole Rad's a P.I.? I guess I shouldn't be surprised. You always had him checking out something for you."

Carl appeared in the doorway and Alysse could see that unlike Rick, he was exactly as she had expected him to be— swarthy, several days growth of beard, hair that hadn't been cut in months and the smell of last night's alcohol on his breath.

"What are you doing here, stranger?" He growled at her.

Suddenly, all of Alysse's vague ideas of getting both her brother's involved in something that was undoubtedly illegal were confused. She didn't want to involve Rick. Not now. He was trying so hard to be free of this environment and he had a nice girl who loved him. He might come from a rotten past, but he was good inside. Carl was a different story. If he wasn't doing an unsavory job for her he'd likely be doing one for someone else.

She turned away from Rick and said, "I wanted to talk to you about something, Carl. Is there someplace we could go…get a drink, maybe? I'm buying."

Carl eyed her suspiciously, but too curious about her showing up to turn her down. "Yeah, there's a bar on the next corner." He looked her up and down. "You'll be kind of out of place there, but then, I don't think you'd want to be seen with me at one of your ritzy hangouts."

"Your place it is," she said.

"I'll be gone to work by the time you get back," Rick said. He paused, still uncertain about how to act with her. "It was good to see you, Sis."

"You, too, little brother," Alysse said and hugged him briefly.

As they walked past the kitchen door Sherry stuck her head out and said goodbye to Alysse.

"I wonder what your sister could possibly want to talk to Carl about," she said to Rick.

"I'm as curious as you are, Sherr. We've not heard a word from her in probably twelve years." He put his arms around her from behind as she stirred the dish on the stove. "She said she thought you were really nice."

Sherry was surprised. "She did?"

"Yep, and so do I, " he said, kissing her neck. "Whatever you're cooking there sure smells good."

"It'll be ready by the time you get dressed for work."

He released her. 'Okay, I can take the hint." He smiled at her and she couldn't help smiling back. He was just too handsome, and she was sure glad he was hers.

* * * * *

Seeing the torn vinyl on the worn seat Alysse chose the side of the booth she felt was less likely to ruin her silk skirt. As she and Carl waited for a server to come she had to admit that her brother had been right. It seemed that everyone in the bar was looking at them, especially her. She rarely went to bars. There were times she had to take clients out for drinks, but she made sure it was an upscale place that was more restaurant than bar. This place certainly didn't qualify, even though they served food and honestly, she was hungry.

"What can I get you folks to drink?" a gum-chewing server with a swinging ponytail asked.

"A Lone Star," Carl said.

"I'll just have water…for now, and menus, please," Alysse said.

"Okay, I'll be right back," Ponytail said, swinging away.

Alysse was nervous. How did she start this conversation with a brother she never really liked and hadn't seen in twelve years? She still didn't like what she saw, but she needed him.

Carl was watching her, waiting, and finally said, "Okay, when are you going to tell me why you showed up after all this time and why do you want to 'talk' to me?"

Alysse took a deep breath and let it out. "I need you to do a job for me. I'll pay you well, but you've got to keep it quiet."

Carl gave a sarcastic laugh. " Oh, so my high society sister has some dirty work she wants done while she keeps her hands clean."

Ponytail returned with their drinks, handed a menu to each of them and said she'd return to take their order.

Carl took a swig of his beer, then said, "Okay, spill it."

Alysse toyed with her water glass. It hurt her pride to say that she was out to get a woman because a man chose that woman over her.

She took a deep breath. "Let's just say there's a woman I want to have removed from the picture."

Carl lifted his brows. "And just how 'far' are you wanting her…uh...removed?" He leaned across the table and with a hard stare said, "You've been gone a long time, but there's something you need to know. I haven't stayed out of jail by being stupid. If you think you're going to suddenly show up and expect me to do something dumb…think again!"

Alysse's face reddened. "I just want her away from a certain man."

"Well, there's only one way I know to guarantee that happens and I just told you…I don't do stupid! And I'm supposing that if she's in this dude's life it's because he wants her there. What makes you think that if she disappears he's going to run to you?"

Angrily Alysse raised her voice. "I know I can make him love me. If this woman isn't here I just might be able to persuade him to give me a chance."

"Sounds to me like you've been trying, and he's just not interested. When are you going to learn that you can't control everybody else, Alysse?

He sat back and folded his arms. Lowering his voice he said, "If you have this woman knocked off you won't get away with it. Somebody's gonna spend a lot of years behind bars. If you have her roughed up she'll just run back to her boyfriend, report it to the cops and again, somebody's going to jail. I don't want any part of it. I'm outta here!" He stood to go.

"Wait, Carl!" Alysse quickly rose and grabbed his arm. "If I can come up with a plan that wouldn't get you in trouble will you help me? I'll pay you five thousand dollars."

Carl looked at her for a few moments. "That's not enough, and I'm not takin' anybody out, is that clear?"

"Yes. I'll have to come up with something…some way to make her break up with him."

"And you really think you can do that? All you're going to accomplish is the two of them getting closer. Take my advice and forget this whole thing."

Angrily Alysse pounded her fist on the table. "I have to do something!"

The waitress neared the table but stopped when she heard the loud remark. Alysse saw her standing there and rudely told the girl to bring her a shot of whiskey.

"Oh…Okay, Ma'am. Do you want to order now?"

"I just did! Bring me the whiskey!"

"I'll order," Carl said. "Bring me a double cheeseburger with fries and another Lone Star," he told the waitress and frowned at Alysse.

" You probably need to eat something."

"I'm not hungry," she answered sullenly. The anger had so consumed her that she no longer felt the need for food.

The waitress couldn't leave quickly enough.

Carl kept looking at Alysse with contempt. "I don't know why I'm even sitting here with you. You left Rick and me high and dry to deal with the folks. It was bad enough with the old man when he got sick, but after he died, we had to take care of Mom by ourselves. That didn't create any warm fuzzy feelings toward you."

Alysse didn't know what to say. All she had thought about was her need to separate herself from her miserable family. Why couldn't any of them see her side of things?

Carl drained the first beer and sat the bottle down with a bang. With a sarcastic grin he patted her hand. "You know what little sister? I'm going to do this dirty deed for you…just to take your money. You can make it ten thousand in cash paid up front. And you'd better figure out a way that doesn't land me in jail or you're going to be in the cell next to me."

He laughed. "That might even make it worth it!"

Miss Ponytail brought their round of drinks before Alysse could think of a retort. All of the old animosity between her and Carl rose to the surface and she grabbed the shot glass and downed the drink in one gulp. "Bring me another one!" she ordered the waitress.

"Like mother, like daughter," Carl said spitefully and turned to the waitress. "Miss, would you have the cook make my burger to go? I don't think I want to eat it here." He stood and with that sarcastic smile that Alysse hated, thumbed her direction, and said, "She's paying."

* * * * *

When the green bus arrived back where the tour had begun Radford Connally departed as quickly as he could. He pulled out from the parking area as other tourists were still thanking the preacher and Grace for a nice day. That steak dinner with all the delicious side dishes and desserts was the best meal he'd had in ages, but his stomach still felt queasy from his guilty conscious that had bothered him all day.

Then that time around the campfire! The camp songs had been kind of fun, but when the preacher started singing *'Amazing Grace,'* the whole atmosphere changed, and it was like that beach became…like…like a holy place.

It had been all he could do to keep from crying, and he didn't know why. There was something about the music as Grace sang with Zach that moved him deep inside like nothing ever had before. He wanted to get up and leave, yet, at the same time he wanted to experience that feeling forever.

Radford knew Alysse was expecting him to call, wanting to know what kind of dirt he'd found that she could use against the preacher and Grace. He just couldn't deal with her tonight, though.

Zach Clayton and Grace Morgan were the most genuine, nice, folks he'd ever met, and he had decided that for the first time in his life he was going to refuse to do what Alysse wanted. Just making that decision brought relief. He knew she'd be calling him every few minutes when she didn't hear from him, but he could turn his phone off. She didn't know where he lived so there would be no way she could bother him. He'd pay for that later, but somehow he didn't care.

He had certainly been no saint but every time he left Alysse or talked to her on the phone he felt so dirty. The feeling that had washed over him there at that campfire was like a cleansing. He hardly knew how to describe it himself; he just knew it had been too special to allow Alysse to ruin it tonight.

* * * * *

Zach pulled his truck into Grace's driveway and turned off the ignition. Turning to her, he said, "Come here."

"I thought you'd never ask," she said as she slid into his arms.

"You worked so hard today, Babe. Thank you."

"No harder than you," she replied. "But it was a good day. The group really seemed to enjoy it, though I could tell some of them were dragging by the end."

"That's pretty much the way it always is. Tire 'em out but let them leave happy."

"Did George Williams say anything to you before he left?" Grace asked.

"No, did he talk to you?"

"I didn't even see him; he must have gotten out of there quickly. I think he's the only guest that didn't come up and thank me for an enjoyable tour. It really didn't surprise me, though. Something made him very uncomfortable in our presence."

" I believe there was a real spiritual battle going on inside that guy. He was there for a reason; I know that."

"We'll have to keep him in prayer." She smiled at Zach tiredly, "But right now I need a shower and some sleep."

Zach lifted his brows, "Oh, but Ms. Assistant, you're still on the clock."

Grace laughed. "I see, Boss. Just when do I get to clock out?"

Zach leaned in and tipped her chin up. "After I've kissed you a time or two."

"I get overtime pay for that," she managed to say before he covered her lips with his.

CHAPTER 25

Alysse feverishly wrote on her notepad as one idea after another came to her mind. The plan to get rid of Grace Morgan was falling into place. She felt her second shot of whiskey had stimulated her brain; the thoughts were coming so quickly. Surely Carl would go along with it since the chance of his being identified was unlikely. She didn't doubt that he would rat on her if he was to get caught, but she didn't intend for that to happen. She just wished he hadn't been so adamant about not taking the woman out for good. Her plan would work but it still depended on Grace Morgan's being intimidated enough not to talk. Somehow, she'd have to be convinced otherwise.

The next step was to make a list of the things needed to make this work. She'd go out and buy them after she met with Rad.

Rad…what was going on with him? It was evident that he had lost his enthusiasm for this job. Maybe it was taking too much time and he was missing work for paying clients. She might have to throw some cash his way. Anyway, she was eager to see what he had captured on camera when he went on the tour. He kept making excuses for not coming over and showing her the video. He said he caught a bug or something and didn't want to give it to her. It didn't ring true to her, but anyway, he was coming today. Alysse wondered if she should tell Rad about her plan, then thought better of it. If he wasn't totally on her side it was best he didn't know.

The first thing Radford noticed when Alysse opened her door was the smell of alcohol. Her appearance was as disheveled as when he'd last seen her and her bloodshot eyes had a frenzied look that caused him alarm. This was not good.

"Hey, 'Lysse," he said.

"Rad, Rad. Come in and join me in a drink," Alysse said, twirling around with a half-filled glass in her hand.

He frowned. "When did you start drinking? You never touched the stuff in all the years I've known you."

Alysse tossed her head as though Rad's question bothered her. "I don't want to talk about that. I just want to see what you got on your camera for me to take down Zach Clayton and Grace Morgan."

"Well, you're going to be disappointed, because there's nothing in a day's worth of filming that's any worse than a few hugs and a peck or two. " Rad felt a twinge of conscience thinking of the photos he had deleted of Zach going in and out of the bar. But he hadn't lied. There weren't any such pictures there now.

"The truth is, Alysse. I'm backing out of this situation. My opinion of Zach and Grace after spending a whole day with them is that they are two of the nicest people I've ever met. I think they truly care for each other and whether you want to believe it or not, that preacher is never going to fall in love with you. You need to drop this thing right now and forget whatever you're planning to cause them harm."

"No!" Alysse screamed in his face. "How can you do this to me? You're supposed to be my friend!"

Rad tried to calm her down, "I am your friend, 'Lysse. I've been there for you through all kinds of trash, but this is wrong. You're crossing a line and I'm not going to help you destroy them or yourself.

In fact," he said, picking up his camera, "There's no reason for you to look at the pictures. It will only make you angrier. I'm going, and I hope you'll stop with the booze before you end up like your folks."

He turned and headed back toward the door as Alysse grabbed him from behind.

"But Rad! You don't understand. I love Zach and I need him! You've got to help me before they get married!"

"I can't, Alysse. Please, just forget about Zach Clayton."

He opened the door and left, hearing her wild accusations trailing behind. When he got to his car he took his camera out of its case and turned it on to the file of pictures he still had of Zach and Grace. He began to delete them one by one, until he came to a great shot of the two of them laughing together and looking like the happiest couple in the world. It was too good to delete, so he kept that one for himself as a reminder of the most special day he could remember. Then he proceeded to erase all other evidence of his surveillance.

* * * * *

Zach awoke early and put the coffee on as usual. Although the sun hadn't completely risen, he took his Bible and went outside to the patio and sat enjoying the peace of the morning. Sunday morning, the day he would step into the pulpit of his church for the first time in three years. He thought he would be nervous about it when this time came, but he felt only excitement.

He wouldn't be preaching today, though he knew that was coming. But he would share his heart with his people and then introduce the congregation to the woman that God had sent to stand with him and love them as he did.

Jim Sheridan was thrilled when Zach told him he'd like to speak a few minutes this morning and introduce Grace to the people of Cornerstone Cowboy Church. People seeing them together would be wondering about their relationship so they might as well make their engagement public and end the curiosity.

"Lord," he prayed. "I believe that the people of the church will accept Grace, but I'm asking you to work in their hearts so that they quickly feel the kind of bond with Grace that they had with Sasha so she will be able to minister to them freely. Let my coming back to lead these people be a smooth transition, especially for those who have joined the body while I was away and have only known Jim as pastor."

Appreciation for his friend filled his heart. Jim had done an outstanding job and so had his wife, Sharon. Zach had already been thinking of some way to show them how thankful they were as a body. Maybe it was time to have another get-together at the ranch as soon as he and Grace got settled there. He'd have to talk to her about it.

Grace was awake early, too. She was so excited for Zach to stand before his church again and she really wanted to be there with him. There was just the uncertainty of how the church would receive a new wife with their beloved pastor. But only one person she had met from the church had treated her negatively, Alysse Stratton. The woman was determined to have Zach, but he was taken!

She heard Karen in the kitchen a little later and joined her friend over coffee.

"What does a woman wear to her introduction as the preacher's soon-to-be wife?" she asked.

Karen cocked her head and thought a minute. "Hmm...Clothes," she said with a grin.

"Big help you are, friend."

"Gracie-Lou, you always look ready to meet the queen, so I'm sure these cowboys and cowgirls are going to think you're beautiful no matter what."

Grace finished her coffee and put her cup in the dishwasher. "Okay, I'll go search the closet."

When Zach came to pick up Grace she thought she'd never seen a more handsome man in her life. He was wearing a dark, western-cut suit, string tie, really nice boots that she hadn't seen before, and as always, the black Stetson. How had she never noticed how nice a man looked in western wear? Of course, there weren't a lot of men dressing that way in downtown LA.

"California gals, you don't know what you're missing," she said under her breath as she watched him walk to the door. She opened the glass door as he approached and watched his eyes light up when he saw her. She would never tire of that sight.

Zach pulled her into his arms as soon as he was inside the house. "Good morning, my beautiful soon-to-be wife. You look absolutely amazing."

Grace smiled. " I was just thinking the same thing about you."

Placing a gentle kiss on her lips, Zach held her close for a moment then sighed. "We'd better not get started down that path. I'm running a bit late as it is…had an ornery heifer this morning that somehow managed to get out of the corral."

In a teasing voice Grace said, "But you showed her who's boss, didn't you, Cowboy?"

He gave her a faked hard look. "I did indeed. You might keep that in mind."

They laughed and headed toward his truck where Zach turned to her seriously and asked, "Are you sure you're ready for this? When our engagement is announced you're stepping into a new role. Up to now it's been just us, and I'm glad to have had this time when I didn't have to share you—though it's been really short."

Grace looked into his sincere brown eyes and knew that Zach's intent was to protect her. "I know things will change, but Zach, this is what we both are called to do. I'm sure there will be some bumps in the road, but I'm excited about our next step. I can't wait to get to know the people and share in their lives."

"All right, Beautiful. Let's go do it!"

* * * * *

The last thing Alysse wanted to hear was a group of people singing praises to God. She had awakened with a throbbing headache and not even the handful of pills she'd taken had completely eradicated it. She didn't want to be in church, but that was the only place that she might possibly get to see Zach. Even if he had that Grace woman with him. As long as he was in the same building there was the possibility.

She'd arrived at the church a few minutes after the service had started and found a place at the rear. The congregation was standing as they usually did during the musical part of the service. That made it harder for her to find Zach — if he had come at all. Maybe last week was just a fluke and he wasn't going to be coming regularly.

The song the praise team was singing was making her uncomfortable, but most of the people were singing it as though they really meant it

"Come like the rain and wash all of my sin away
Come Holy Spirit and Cleanse me
Cover me now with the blood of the Lamb
Wash me much whiter than snow

Purify my heart
Take all the things that are unlike You
Make me a vessel of honor
Ready to do Your will, O Lord
Ready to do Your will

Alysse wasn't ready to sing those words. Her agenda was all that mattered to her and she knew her plans would get no approval from any heavenly being. Slipping out of the row she made an unnecessary trip to the ladies' room, fussed with her hair to kill time, and hoped the music would be over by the time she returned to her seat.

Looking into the mirror she could see the effects that her drinking was already having. She saw her mother's face instead of her own and remembered for the first time in years what a pretty woman her mother had been prior to her addiction. Is that the way she would end up?

But she wasn't going to keep drinking. She was stronger than that. She was only using alcohol now to get through this ordeal that was consuming her life. She'd just have to put more effort into maintaining her image.

When Alysse returned to the auditorium the people were seated and Jim Sheridan was speaking.

"We are so glad to have each of you worshipping with us this morning. If you are a visitor we want you to know that you are welcome to become part of this church family."

He paused and seemed to be struggling with his emotions before continuing. "For those of us who call Cornerstone Cowboy Church 'home,' this is a day that we have been eagerly awaiting…will you come and take your rightful place at this podium, Pastor Zach Clayton!"

An exclamation of joy began to move in a wave across the congregation, becoming louder as people all over the auditorium stood to their feet and applauded. Zach squeezed Grace's hand and quickly stepped up to the platform. Jim grabbed him in a warm hug and pointed him to the pulpit.

The people continued to clap, some of the cowboys calling, "Welcome back, Pastor! We love you, Pastor Zach!"

Zach's eyes filled with tears at the love directed his way. Finally, he asked them to be seated. After drying his eyes, he looked down at the pulpit, grasping it with both hands and grinned, "Man, this feels good!"

Laughter and more shouts of affirmation filled the room for a few moments. "I'm just up here for a few minutes this morning, but it won't be long before I'll be giving Bro. Jim a well-deserved break. I don't think there are enough words to express my appreciation for Jim and Susan Sheridan and what they have meant to this church body."

The people again stood in agreement and applauded. After a moment Zach began to speak. "Most of you here know at least a little of my story…our story as a church family. In case you're new around here and don't know, I came here almost ten years ago with my precious wife Sasha. We knew the Lord was sending us to start a church, and that's what we did. We and the four friends who wanted to support us."

He laughed. "You might think that would be discouraging, but we were so young and ignorant and full of zeal…so sure that we were in the perfect will of God…that we were thrilled. We had started our church!

"I see some of you out there that joined us not long after that, and others of you who came along through all these years. We couldn't have done it without you. I love and appreciate you so much.

"Most of you also know that our dear Sasha lost her battle with cancer three years ago. To say that I was devastated would be an understatement. I've never prayed and believed so hard for anything in my life as I did for Sasha's healing. and when that didn't happen, your big, strong cowboy pastor crumbled. I wish I could say that I practiced what I'd preached to you about faith and standing in the time of trials, about believing that God can and will somehow bring good out of the difficult circumstances like He said He would.

" Instead, I allowed bitterness and doubt to rule in my life and I'll tell you now, those have been the most miserable years of my life.

"I couldn't see myself pastoring without Sasha. She was by my side through the entire journey. We loved each other so much and worked together so well. It was simply beyond my comprehension that there could be another woman that I would be able to love and work with, one who would share my heart for you and the lost souls in our city."

He shook his head. "I am so glad God sees beyond our limitations that we place on Him. And in spite of our lack of obedience, our lack of faith and even the lack of desire, He still works in our lives to fulfill the plan He'd had in the works all along. He didn't leave me in the miserable rut I was in, but gently drew me back to Him, covered me with His love ,and brought a new love to my heart."

He chuckled, " Someday we'll tell you our story of how we met, but today I just want to introduce you to the woman that God has used to heal my heart, one who has love simply flowing out of her to everyone, and I'm really glad it's flowing my direction. Sweetheart, will you come."

Zach stepped down to meet Grace and escort her up to the pulpit. "Church family, I am so very pleased to introduce to you my future wife, Grace Morgan."

The entire congregation stood and applauded. There was such love and acceptance in the atmosphere that any apprehension Grace had before was gone.

When the people had been re-seated, Zach asked Grace if she would like to speak. She nodded and he handed her the microphone.

"I am so glad to meet you, Cornerstone Cowboy Church family! It has been a joy to get to know just a handful of you in the past few weeks and to see how much you love this man.

"We truly believe that God bringing us together was a miracle. I was no more looking for a husband than he was looking for a wife, yet in spite of *our feelings*, here we stand, deeply in love and excited about serving God together.

"I am so eager to get to know everyone—please just give me a little time to learn all your names.!" The people laughed and applauded again as she and Zach moved toward the steps.

"When's the big event taking place," someone called.

"We're working on that," Zach answered. "As soon as possible!"

Alysse sat watching as a myriad of emotions raced through her mind. Anger, Jealousy, rejection, hopelessness. She couldn't sit there any longer, though she had hoped to see and speak to Zach after church was over. Most of the church people would come and make a big deal over that woman who had stolen Zach's heart. She couldn't watch that.

CHAPTER 26

At the end of services at Cornerstone Cowboy Church it was customary for the praise team to lead the congregation in one last song while the ministers made their way to the doors of the church to greet the people as they left. As the music began Jim Sheridan stepped down from the platform and motioned Zach and Grace to accompany him and Susan to the main entrance.

"Get ready," he said softly to Zach "They're all going to want to congratulate you two."

And they did. As she shook hands with the people and received hugs from many, there were some that she already knew she would at some time be praying for. That sensitivity to the needs of others was already bonding her to Zach's people.

As the last of the crowd had greeted them Zach and Grace made their way to his truck. When they were settled into their seats Zach pulled out onto the street and said, "I've been thinking about our situation and how we could spend time with your parents. Even if we went to California we could only spend a few days. I'd like to get to know them and for them to see what kind of cowboy has roped and hog-tied their daughter."

Grace laughed at that image. "So, what do you have in mind?"

"Do your parents have any obligations that would prevent them from coming here for an extended visit?" he asked.

"I don't know of any. They're not that active in their church, 'don't have pets or other animals to care for. They pay a lawn service to keep their yard mowed."

"This might be completely out of their comfort zone," Zach said, "but I was wondering if they would be willing to come and stay at my place for several weeks before our wedding. Lil and Jay will be moving to the mobile home soon but even if they don't, I have a third bedroom. I'll be moved in there by then and will see that they have what they need. It would give us time to really get acquainted and to show them around our area, go to church with us. You can spend as much time at the ranch as you'd like, too."

"Oh, Zach, I wish they would come. I really want them to have time to know you and come to the church, to see how we will be living," she laughed, "and to see me on a horse!"

Zach chuckled. " Who knows; we might even get them riding. Jay and Lil would love that! To have another senior couple to ride with."

Grace laughed a real belly-laugh. "Oh, my. I can't even imagine my parents on horses!"

Zach's eyes twinkled, "Seems like I remember you saying you'd never imagined yourself on a horse either."

"Okay, you're right. I'll call them tonight. There are a number of issues that I've been thinking we need to add to our list of things to decide about the wedding."

"Oh, no, can you make the decisions without me?"

"No, I really can't. They're more important than choosing the color of napkins."

They were pulling into the driveway at Karen's home now. "Can you put on a pot of coffee to help me through this?"

Grace assured him she could. After they entered the house Zach reached for her. "We've been surrounded by people all day and I couldn't do this," then he kissed her, long and sweet. "Oh, Gracie, can't we just elope and skip all this?"

"Yes, we could, but I think people close to us would really be disappointed. Weddings bring joy and that's a good thing."

"I guess you're right. Am I being selfish?"

"You're just being an impatient cowboy," she said. "Now let me get the coffee going."

The smell of fresh coffee brewing filled the room as Grace laid "The List" on the table. "Okay, what can we cross off as being done?"

" I don't think there's much else I can say is completely done. Jay and I have to repair some fences before I can move my cattle from Jim's. I've packed some of my things, but I need a couple more boxes. So what are the new things to be added to the list?"

"This is probably a given, but who's going to marry us?" Grace asked.

"Jim, of course," Zach said. "I haven't mentioned it to him, but I think he'll expect to do the honors."

"That's what I thought," Grace said, "but this next one may be a little harder. We rode to the meadow on horseback, but the terrain looks like it might be difficult to travel in a car. How are guests going to get there?"

Zach laughed heartily and reached out to take her hand. "Sweetie, have you noticed what all of us drive?"

She thought a moment. "Big pick-up trucks."

"Yep, and they all have four-wheel drive that will have no problem getting them to the meadow. The few people coming that don't have trucks can ride with those who do. Problem solved!"

"Oh," Grace said, as though she couldn't believe it was that simple. "I guess I have a lot to learn about the way Texans live."

"You're doing great, Beautiful. And your concern was a legitimate one. If we're going to do something on a full-time basis there I will have to build a road, but we can by-pass that expense for now."

"I'd really like to have another look at the meadow. I wasn't thinking about having a wedding there when I saw it the other day. Could we go back again soon?" Grace asked.

Zach looked at his watch. "If you'd like to go now we could get back by the time I need to feed the stock."

"Oh, Zach, that would be great. Thank you!"

"I don't see Jay's truck," Zach said as they neared the ranch. "He and Lil must be gone."

When he just kept driving through the yard area and across the land. She giggled. "This is so weird to me…I've only ridden on roads!"

Zach grinned. "I'm having fun providing you with all these 'first time' experiences. You just have to watch for holes and rocks driving across the open land"

"And rabbits!" Grace added as a large-eared one scampered out of the truck's path.

"Oh yes, we have plenty of those."

Soon he came to a stop at the place where they had viewed the meadow from their horses.

"It is so beautiful, Zach," Grace said. It's perfect for a wedding. Can we go down there to the pond?"

"Sure, hang on."

The ride was bumpy as Zach slowly maneuvered the truck down the incline and soon they were parked in the center of the meadow. "Let's go take a look."

Hand in hand they walked toward the pond and through the wildflowers that grew around it. Zach pointed to an area. "This is where I thought the gazebo should sit," and I talked to Glenn, the builder, about a couple of walkways, actually bridges, coming from either side over the water up to the gazebo itself."

"Like pretty white picket fencing?" Grace asked, her eyes shining."

"Yes. I'll get a crew of guys in here to do some clean-up around the pond…add a little more landscaping."

"It doesn't need much, though," Grace said. "It's just so naturally beautiful. We could rent white chairs and set them up at the lower curve of the pond, so everyone has a good view of the wedding."

Zach was looking around the entire meadow, again sensing that God had a purpose for this lovely piece of land.

Grace took his hand and together they walked slowly . "There's love here, Zach," she said quietly. "and healing."

They stood quietly for a few moments, then Zach exclaimed, "Grace! That's it! That's God's plan for this meadow! A place of healing for troubled marriages. And for people hurting and broken from divorce."

He looked in a full circle, counting under his breath. "We can build at least ten separate cabins and a large central meeting place with kitchen and dining room. We'll need quarters for the counselors and teachers, too."

"Oh, Zach, I know you're right. We've both been through so much that the Lord can use for us to help couples who are struggling. This feels so right. I can see them renewing their vows at the end of the weekend in the beautiful gazebo."

Zach shook his head. "My mind is spinning with ideas, mostly with how to get it all together as quickly as possible. I've got some money, enough to get started, but it's going to take a lot more. I know God is going to supply what we need, though. I feel this so strongly."

"We'll have to have other people to join with us, too," Grace said, "not just financially, but workers, counselors, people who have hearts to minister."

"They're going to come, Grace, I can see it. I see maybe an older couple living here to oversee things. We'd need to build a larger cabin for them."

"I think we need to have sitting areas set up around the grounds where the couples can talk privately, " Grace said.

"That's a good idea," Zach nodded.

"It needs a name," she mused. "'Love Meadow…" What do you think of that?"

Zach stopped and turned to her, softly repeating, "Love Meadow…Love Meadow Retreat Center. I like it! I think you did it, Grace, we have a name!"

He picked her up and swung her around, both of them laughing. "We have a name, we have purpose, we have a wonderful future ahead of us!"

"And we have a wedding to go through so we can get to work on it!" Grace added.

"Oh, yes, that," Zach said, teasing her. "I still think we should elope."

"I know, love. If it wasn't for all these other things that need to come into place I'd agree. I promise to keep it as simple as I can so we can get married in a few weeks."

"That's my girl," Zach said, pulling her into his arms. "My beautiful partner and gift from God. I love you, Grace Morgan. I think there's something significant about our being the first couple married here in this meadow. It's as if our love is seed planted to grow and nourish relationships for the couples that will come here."

"Can we pray for them, Zach? I know they won't be here for a long time but they're out there, perhaps struggling in their marriages even now."

"Yes, certainly. What better time to pray than when God revealed His plan to us," Zach said and took both her hands in his.

"Heavenly Father, Grace and I bring before you every couple, every single person, all of those that You will someday lead to the Love Meadow. We pray for protection over their lives and that each of them would experience Your love. As we plan and work to create the buildings, the grounds, the necessary natural things, we ask that You give us wisdom.

"We thank you in advance for bringing the people You have chosen to join with us in this vision. We look to You as our source of supply for the funds it will require to establish this ministry and we give You thanks for making it possible. Amen."

Zach and Grace rode back over the bumpy ground with cheerful hearts. " And Lord, " Grace said, "Please help us get a road built quickly!"

CHAPTER 27

Grace awakened slowly and rolled over to check the time on her alarm clock. Nine o'clock! She sat straight up. How long had it been since she'd slept that late?

She had called her parents last evening to invite them to come and spend several weeks in Texas so they would already be here for the wedding. She had talked to her mother for a long time; there was just so much to share about the vision God had given them. Her Dad listened in on most of it through the speaker phone, but when his wife and daughter got into the wedding details, he told them he was checking out to watch a rerun of a ball game on TV. He did say, "Mom and I will pray about the trip and let you know."

Grace wasn't sure if they could see themselves staying on a ranch for weeks, but she felt they would enjoy it as much as she had. She knew they'd love Zach and the fellowship with Lil and Jay.

Quickly, she tried to think if she and Zach had made any plans for this morning, then she remembered that he would be supervising the work being done to prepare the space for the mobile home for Lil and Jay. Her calendar was blank for the first time since she'd come to Karen's, and she found herself missing spending time with Zach. They'd soon be together every day and night though, and she couldn't wait.

Her phone rang and she smiled when she saw the caller was Zach. "Good morning, my love," she said.

"Man, I can't wait to be greeted in person like that every morning ."

Grace flopped back on the bed. "I was just thinking along those lines myself. I'm imagining us living in your ranch house and loving every minute of it."

"That reminds me, I've been meaning to tell you that we don't have to keep the same furniture and décor…all that stuff that's really important to you ladies. If it's an issue at all that Sasha chose that style we can start new with your plans."

"That's so understanding of you, Zach, but I love your house just the way it is. Sasha did an amazing job making it beautiful while blending with the ranch life. My question is, are you comfortable with leaving things the same, or does it bring memories that would be difficult for you?"

Zach was quiet for a moment. "I hadn't thought of that." He paused again. "You know, I think I would like for you to re-decorate the bedroom. Is that all right with you?"

"Absolutely. I think that would be nice for both of us. I'll start thinking about that. Do you have any ideas in mind?"

Zach chuckled. "No Babe. I have the same feeling about furniture as I do food…anything will do that meets the need. But I might mention that I do need the extra-long, king-sized bed!"

"Okay, you've got me excited now. I have to do some laundry, but I don't have anything planned after that. I could go furniture shopping this afternoon."

"You do know I'm paying for this? So don't buy anything until I'm with you. I love that you're saving me from having to look and choose, though."

"Maybe I'll call Lana and see if she's available to go with me. I've been wanting to spend some time with her anyway."

"That would be great. Well, I see the concrete truck pulling into the drive, so I'd better get out there. Have fun shopping, Beautiful, and remember I love you."

"I love you, too, Cowboy. Give Lil and Jay hugs for me."

"I will. Can I take you to dinner tonight?"

"Yes, you may. Seven o'clock?"

"That works. See you then."

Grace went to the kitchen, popped bread in the toaster, and called Lana Caldwell's number.

"Hey, Grace!" Lana answered the phone. "I've been thinking about you and was going to try to reach you today. How are you?"

"Absolutely wonderful, Lana. I've been thinking about you, too. In fact, I want to ask if you might possibly be free to spend some time with me today."

"Funny you'd ask. Bruce had some vacation time today and decided to take the boys fishing. So I was trying to decide which thing on my "Free Day List" to do. You have made that decision for me and I'm delighted. What do you have in mind?"

"Well…Zach asked me to re-decorate the master bedroom in his house and I need to go shopping for furniture. You know that's always more fun with a friend."

"Oh, that's exciting. I'd love to come along. I have a few necessary chores here to keep the house livable, so maybe in an hour and a half-ish?"

"That sounds good. I've got some quick laundry to do, then I'll be ready to go. Oops, I forgot…I don't have a car. Zach and Karen have been taking me everywhere."

""Not a problem," Lana said. " I'll pick you up. There's a new sandwich and salad place I've been wanting to try. 'Want to do lunch before we shop?"

"Yes, definitely! Okay, 'see you in a bit."

"Bye."

Lunch at the sandwich shop was pleasant, and Lana and Grace caught up on the latest events of their lives

"Is working the tours with Zach going well?" Lana asked.

"It's been amazing," Grace answered. "By the second day things were just moving along easily. I'm enjoying being with people and of course, with Zach, too."

Lana smiled. "So things are really going well with you two, aren't they? Jim Sheridan said he hadn't seen Zach so happy in years."

"If anyone had told me six weeks ago that I would find love and be this happy—and so quickly—I wouldn't have believed it," Grace said. " I thought I had experienced love before, but my relationship with my former husband was nothing like I've found with Zach. Almost every day I realize more about how I was really living a lie that my husband perpetuated."

"As horrible as this whole thing was for you to go through, you wouldn't have come here if it hadn't happened," Lana said. "And I'm so glad you're here."

Grace took her hand. "I am too. Lana. Not only have I gained new love, but all of you wonderful friends."

Lana squeezed her hand in return. "Okay, now before I get weepy, I have a surprise for you."

"Oh, really," Grace said. "I love surprises."

"There is a couple you haven't met at church yet that own a huge wholesale business for home goods. Since they are wholesalers and normally sell only to businesses, I called and told them I'd like to bring you in because you and Zach are updating some things in his house. They are so happy about Zach finding a new wife and they want to give you guys a discount above what the business owners receive."

"Oh, Lana, that's wonderful! How sweet of you …and them! What are their names?"

"They are Ben and Rebecca Reynolds, and their business is Reynolds Wholesale Interiors. It's just on the outskirts of Houston, about a half hour from here. They carry beautiful furniture and décor as well."

"Are we ready to go?" Grace asked, rising.

Lana laughed as she placed money in the server's folder. "We are!"

"My, this place is huge!" Grace exclaimed as Lana pulled into the parking lot of Reynolds Wholesale Interiors.

"It is," Lana agreed. "We probably shouldn't try to cover it all today. We'd be exhausted."

"I'm sure I'll get distracted but I'll try to stay in the bedroom section." Grace decided.

But when they walked in the door and she saw the almost endless supply of home interior products she sighed. "This is going to be harder than I imagined."

A pretty, auburn-haired woman with a wide smile approached them. "Hello, Lana, and you must be Grace," she said. 'I'm so glad you made it. I'm Rebecca."

"I'm always amazed when I step in here," Lana said. "I really can't do it very often because it makes me want to replace everything in my house!"

Rebecca lowered her voice, "Believe me, I know. I refuse to tell people how often I do that!"

Grace shook her hand. "Thank you so much for letting me shop here, Rebecca, and I know Zach will appreciate it, too. He doesn't know about this yet, but I'll tell him tonight."

"You're welcome, Grace. Ben and I are just so happy that Pastor Zach has found someone to love and stand with him in ministry. We're eager for him to be back in the pulpit as soon as the Lord leads.

"But now, we need to get you started looking for your furniture. If you could give me any ideas about what you have in mind that might narrow things down a bit."

"I am a blank slate," Grace said. "I guess I'll just have to look and see what stands out to me. Zach's only opinion was that it needed to be an extra-long king-sized bed."

Rebecca laughed. "Yes, he will need that. Let's go this direction."

After a few minutes, the sense of being overwhelmed with so many choices settled into focus and Grace was able to categorize features she preferred over others.

The design job Alysse was working on was almost completed. She just needed three or four more decorative pieces to go on a mantle and an end table then she could call it done. She could always find what she needed at Reynolds Wholesale Interiors and the Reynolds were nice to deal with.

She quickly chose the pieces she needed and wheeled her cart to the counter. The thought came to her that she still needed to add a bedside table to her guest room. Not that she'd ever had a guest in her townhome. But she was a designer after all, and the room was incomplete. That wasn't good.

"You can go ahead and write these pieces up on my account, Charla," she told the familiar clerk. "I'm going to check on something right quick."

As she neared the bedroom section she heard voices laughing and talking and saw two women with the store owner, Rebecca. Seconds later, she recognized the women as the Caldwell woman from church and *Grace Morgan!*

Instantly, anger rose up within her. Now Blondie was invading *her* territory. Was there no place free of this woman who was destroying her life?

She couldn't help overhearing their conversation and it was obvious that Grace was choosing bedroom furniture for Zach's house which meant only one thing—they were getting married soon. The fact that another woman was re-designing Zach's home was almost more than she could bear. Now the anger turned to fury, and she didn't know if she could contain it. She turned her back and hoped that no one would notice her standing there.

"I really like this set," Alysse heard Grace say, "and I think Zach will like it, too. He said he doesn't really care what I choose. He is so easy to please."

Alysse could hardly stand there. Zach certainly had not been easy to please in regard to her. She could feel her face getting redder and she needed to leave. Somehow she couldn't make her legs move though because she wanted to hear everything Grace Morgan said.

"Okay, I think this is my choice," Grace said. "Zach insisted that I let him buy it, Rebecca, so can we set a time for us to come in. I'd like for him to see what I chose before he pays for it, in spite of what he says."

"Anytime Monday through Saturday during business hours works for us, so why don't you check with Zach and let me know."

Grace was looking at the calendar in her phone. "Monday's are catch-up days for us since we have the tours on the weekends. Tuesday I have to be at home to receive a package that I need to sign for. We'll likely make it Wednesday or Thursday since the tours begin again on Friday."

Alysse heard every word and a plan instantly formed in her mind. She turned to exit that aisle only to come face to face with the woman she had come to despise.

Grace had stopped walking when a woman almost ran into her, then quickly recognized her as the one who had thrown herself at Zach at the church. Her expression that day had been haughty when she looked at Grace. Today there was pure venom in the stare she gave her. A shudder went down Grace's spine and she felt Lana beside her, taking her arm and guiding her toward the front of the store.

Sensing something amiss, Rebecca stopped and engaged Alysse in conversation. She wasn't aware of any reason there might be a problem between the two ladies, but Alysse looked ready to attack Grace. The designer had been a good customer for several years, but Rebecca had never felt a personal connection with her as she had with most of her regulars. She recalled seeing Alysse at church a few times as well.

"Wow!" Lana exclaimed when they were out of earshot. "Talk about shooting daggers!"

Grace took a deep breath to still her uneasiness. "I know, Lana. That was pure hate in her eyes."

"I think Rebecca's trying to detain her there. Let's go ahead and get your order written up and get out of here."

Grace agreed, so they walked to the counter and gave a clerk the ticket from the furniture. "Please mark this as 'Sold' and my fiancé and I will be in to pay in a few days."

The young lady took Grace and Zach's information and gave

her a smile. "It's all done, Ms. Morgan. We'll see you when you come in."

Grace and Lana looked toward Rebecca as they walked toward the door and she waved to them from across the showroom. Alysse only gave Grace another stone-faced glare.

* * * * *

"Tell me about the happenings at the ranch today," Grace said to Zach as soon as they given their order in the restaurant that evening.

"Everything went so well," Zach told her. "The concrete slab was poured and it's big enough for the mobile home and to have a patio where Lil can grow all her potted plants. Jim's brother's crew got the sewer line completed in a couple of hours and the electrician set the pole and hooked everything up by two o'clock."

"That's great! Are Lil and Jay excited about it?"

"Yeah, I can see that they are. As much as they've enjoyed living in my house, it's mine, not theirs. I think this will feel more like their own place. Even though it belongs to their daughter and her husband, they'll be leaving soon and could be on the mission field for years. I heard Lil say that the kitchen is large and so she's looking forward to working her magic in there."

"Don't forget I want to pay for the permit to move the home. Can you find out how much that will be?" Grace asked.

"Yes, I'll do that tomorrow. It's really sweet of you to pay this for them."

"It just feels good to help someone. I miss that."

Zach reached across the table and took her hand. "I know your life is very different and you're not ministering to someone every day, but you're still touching more lives than you know, and mine for certain."

The love in his eyes made Grace's heart do that little flip-flop thing. The server came with their drinks just then and broke the moment.

Zach smiled and said, "Well, tell me, Babe, how was your day? Did you find us some new furniture?"

An excited expression lit Grace's face and then before she spoke, a somber look took its place.

"What…? Did something happen?" He asked in concern.

Grace smiled at him. "Let me give you the good news first." She told him about the discount they were given by the Reynold's, and that she had found bedroom furniture she thought he would like as much as she had.

"And then?" he asked.

Grace took a deep breath and said, "We ran into Alysse Stratton. Apparently, she's a regular customer there."

Zach leaned back in his seat and ran his hands over his face. "I'm so sorry. Did she say something to you?"

"No, but Zach, if looks could kill I would have dropped dead on the spot. There was pure hatred in her eyes."

Zach reached across the table to take her hand. "I'm so sorry, Love. Are you all right?"

"Yes. Lana kind of pushed me forward and out of the area, and Rebecca Reynolds started a conversation with Alysse."

"You know, I think that woman could be dangerous. For sure, she can be relentless. I had to absolutely forbid her to come to my place. I was really close to filing a restraining order against her. I just didn't want to do something that might bring negative attention to the church, nor to her. Alysse is a respected businessperson in this area and I didn't want to create a problem for her, even though she was definitely a problem for me. I wish I could do something to prevent any more chance encounters with her, but there's just no way to do that."

"Don't worry about me, Zach." Grace said. "So far, at least, I haven't been out in the town alone. I don't see that changing, and I don't think she's going to do anything more than give me her hateful glare. I'm not going to allow her to steal the joy of my new life."

"Speaking of that, I met with the carpenter to discuss the gazebo for the wedding. I think you'll like what he came up with. He said he'd fine-tune the drawing and show it to us before starting to build. So that's one thing we can partially cross off our list," Zach said.

"Oh, Zach, it's really happening, isn't it? Tell me it's not just a dream?"

"I'd be terribly disappointed if it was, my sweet Grace. We have so many good things before us."

*   *   *   *   *

Alysse had been in a state of rage ever since she left the church yesterday, and then to make matters worse, running into Grace Morgan at Reynold's was simply too much. She could not tolerate losing. And if she did lose, someone was going to pay. Zach's announcement made it clear that she was never going to be his wife, but if she could help it, neither would Grace Morgan.

She'd already loaded a number of things in her car and was driving to her old home to leave them with the brother she despised. She hated that she was having to pay him so much money to do this, but it would be worth it if the plan worked. If it didn't they'd both go to jail, but at this moment Alysse couldn't care less. Everything that had been important to her had taken a back seat to her efforts to marry Zach Clayton and since that wasn't going to happen nothing else mattered.

A couple of shots of whiskey had bolstered her courage before meeting with Carl. She hated the vulnerability, but she had to admit, she was afraid of him. She had seen a depth of evil in him that possibly exceeded her own if it benefitted him, and ten thousand dollars was no small benefit.

When she drove up to the house Carl was working under the hood of the beat-up car that had been in the driveway before. He looked up when he heard her car and gave her an unfriendly glare. He put his hands on his hips and simply said, "What?"

"I've got a plan," she said as coldly as her stare. "And there are things in my car that you'll need to carry it out."

"And the dough?"

"It's in there, too."

Carl started walking toward the car and Alysse joined him. They carried boxes into the house and an hour later, she arrived back at her condo where she took the liquor bottle to her bedroom just as she'd seen her mother do so many times.

CHAPTER 28

"I'll be home early today," Karen told Grace as they were eating their breakfast waffles. "We got a notice that repairmen will be working on the roof in our building at UH. One of the classrooms sprung quite a leak in that last thunderstorm we had, so now that it's supposed to be sunny for a few days they're repairing it."

"I just have to be here to sign for some final papers regarding the sale of the house in California. I can't believe how many things have to be signed, and though I hate to admit it, I didn't read them all!"

Karen laughed. "I did the same thing when I bought this place. I think there should be classes offered in "Legaleeze for Dummies."

"Hey, maybe we could find something to do this afternoon," Grace said. "We've been so busy we haven't had much time together."

"That would be great. Think of something and I'll be ready to go. I'll be back by noon, so we could do lunch."

"Okay, I'll figure it out. I'm going to hit the shower, so I'll see you in a few," Grace said.

Karen had been gone a couple of hours when the doorbell rang. Expecting the paperwork from California, Grace opened the door. A stocky deliveryman in a khaki uniform stood there. She opened the glass storm door and said, "Yes?"

The deliveryman looked down at the paperwork in his hand and said, "Are you Ms. Grace Mor…Mor- something…I'm sorry ma'am but we have a very large package that we think belongs at this address, but the shipping label has been torn and the name is incomplete. I really hate to have to carry it up here if this is not the right address. Would you mind stepping out to my van and checking it? I thought you might recognize the name of the sender."

"Oh, I guess so. I was expecting a delivery, but only a large envelope," Grace said. She started down the sidewalk with the man.

"I sure do appreciate this. That package must weigh seventy pounds," he said. A younger man, also in uniform opened the sliding door of the van which bore a magnetic sign saying, "A-1 Delivery Service."

"It's right here, Ma'am," the first man said, and Graced leaned in to see the package."

Suddenly she felt a cloth being clamped firmly against her nose as a hand at her back shoved her roughly into the empty van. The sickening smell of the cloth immediately made her ill as she heard the van door slam shut before everything went black.

The first conscious thought that came to Grace was that she was in a completely unfamiliar place. She was lying on her side on what felt like a very bad mattress that smelled old and musty. It seemed she was slowly emerging from a place of deep darkness. She tried to move and found that her hands were bound behind her back and her feet were restrained at the ankles. Something had been placed over her head and she was gagged as well.

Terror filled her. "Where am I?" she questioned. She struggled to regain her thinking. A vague memory of being shoved into a van flashed through her mind. What happened before that? Somehow, she was aware that it was important to know, but she couldn't remember.

Grace became aware of voices whispering. It sounded as though they were just outside the room she was in. One voice was that of a woman, a young woman, she thought, and the other sounded like a young man. Straining to hear what they were saying, Grace could tell that the young woman was extremely disturbed.

"Ricky, this is bad, really bad!" the woman said.

"I know, I'm sorry, but I didn't know what else to do. Carl said if I didn't help him, he'd throw us out of the house. It belongs to him, so he can do it. He said he'd give me five hundred dollars to help us buy a car, too," the young man said. He also sounded disturbed and remorseful.

"What are we going to do?" the young woman cried, now obviously in tears. "We could go to jail for years and it's not even our doing. Why did Carl kidnap this woman, anyway?"

"It's all Alysse's doing. She wants this woman out of a guy's life that she's infatuated with. I'm pretty sure she paid Carl a bunch of money to do it if he was willing to give me five hundred."

"I don't understand. How is kidnapping the woman going to accomplish that…Oh, my God, Ricky! Is he going to kill her? We need to get out of here, away from this whole mess…Now!"

The door to Carl's bedroom opened and he stepped into the hallway. With one hand on his hip he leaned against the wall. "I don't think so, missy. You're not going anywhere. You know why?" He walked toward them. "Because if you say a word to anybody about this or leave this house, I will put you away. Rats get shot!"

For emphasis he pulled the pistol from his waistband and lifted it up. "And if it ever comes to me having to talk to the cops I'll say that you two were in on this from the beginning."

Ricky moved to stand between Sherry and Carl. "Look, Carl, I did what you told me to. We don't want any part of this. But I swear, if you hurt Sherry in any way, you will be sorry."

He stepped closer to Carl. "I've done a lot of things just because you're my big brother and you told me to. But not anymore. If you don't get this woman out of here we are leaving."

Ricky had never stood up to Carl in his life and it obviously surprised him now.

"How long she's here depends on Alysse and how willing the woman is to go along with her demands," Carl growled. "Believe me, I want her out of here, too. Alysse should be here any minute, so hopefully this can all be over tonight."

He turned to go back to his room, pausing at the door and waving the gun. "I meant what I said."

Grace heard the whole conversation. So, this was all Alysse Stratton's doing. Zach had been right; the woman is dangerous. Does she intend to kill me? Fear gripped Grace as never before in her life. She was helpless. Lying in the same position with her limbs bound she could feel the cramping of muscles beginning. The gag in her mouth had absorbed all moisture and she desperately needed a drink. Her head hurt and she was sure she had bruises from the rough tumble into the van.

This situation was beyond anything she had ever experienced, and she knew there was only One who could help her. "Oh God, I know you're aware of all things. I am counting on you to bring me out of this." The thought that she could possibly not be alive to marry Zach, that all their plans for the future might not be realized, filled her with dismay. But the worst of it was her concern for Zach. She didn't think he could survive losing another woman he loved. She knew he would blame himself for not seeing the true potential of Alysse Stratton and preventing this.

"Lord, please let somebody find me and stop this. Keep me alive to be with Zach and to help all the people that need us."

Even in the terribly uncomfortable state she was in, a peace beyond her understanding fell over her and she went to sleep.

Karen drove into her gated community wondering what sort of plans Grace had made for their afternoon. She missed the "sister" time they used to share.

As she neared her home and started to pull into the drive, she noticed something lying on the curb of the street. It looked like one of Grace's house slippers. That was certainly strange. She glanced toward the front door and was surprised to see the glass storm door slightly ajar and the heavy wooden door open.

Hurrying into the house she called, "Graci-Lou! Gracie, where are you?" She went to Grace's room and the door was open, but the room was empty. A terrible feeling of unease was churning in her abdomen now. She looked throughout the entire house and Grace was not there. She walked out of the partially open door and went to the street where she verified that the object she had seen was indeed Grace's slipper.

Something was terribly wrong. She needed to call Zach and see if Grace was with him. But even if she was, she would never have left the door open and her slipper in the street.

Careful not to touch the door, she made her way into the house and went to Grace's bedroom. She knew her friend would never leave the house without her purse and phone.

Karen froze in fear when she saw that both those items were still there. "Oh, God, please protect her."

She picked up her phone and called 911. She explained the situation to the dispatcher who tried to tell her that Grace had likely stepped over to a neighbor's house. At Karen's insistence she said she'd send an officer out.

Karen then called Zach. He answered with his usual cheery greeting. With a trembling voice Karen asked, "Zach, is Grace with you?"

Hearing the fear in her voice, Zach immediately went on alert. "No, Karen. I'm moving cattle today and I haven't seen her. What's wrong?"

Karen couldn't hold back the tears now. "Zach, I came home and found the front door partially open and one of Grace's slippers on the curb at the street. Her purse is here, so I know she didn't go somewhere on her own. I called the police and they're sending out an officer."

"Try to stay calm, hon. I'll be right there," Zach told her.

Karen looked at her watch. It was ten minutes after twelve. She guessed she had been home about ten minutes. She couldn't imagine what Zach was feeling. He had been so frantic when he couldn't find Grace at one of the Galveston mansions, and that was the first day they had spent together.

"Oh God, help Zach," she prayed. "And keep your hand on Grace and protect her from evil. Bring peace to her wherever she is ."

CHAPTER 29

Zach stopped only long enough to tell Jay of the situation and to wash the smell of cattle off his hands. In the house he quickly told Lil and she assured him they would all be praying.

"Please don't let me get stopped for speeding, Lord," he prayed as he drove as fast as he safely could. The vision of someone taking Grace tormented him. Who could possibly want to do something so evil to such a pure, sweet, woman? Immediately, the image of Alysse Stratton came to mind. Could she possibly have something to do with this?

Grace had been visibly affected when she spoke of the way Alysse had glared at her with hate. Zach didn't doubt for a moment that the woman was capable of wrongdoing, but would she actually go so far as to physically harm Grace?

"Lord, please protect her. Wherever she is, don't let the enemy's plan succeed."

Zach speed dialed Jim Sheridan as he drove and told him what little he knew. Jim said he'd get the prayer chain at church going and then he'd check in with Zach again.

Zach and a city police officer arrived within seconds of each other at Karen's home. The officer walked toward Zach and extended his hand.

"Hello, I'm Lt. Sloan. I understand you've reported a missing person?"

Zach shook his hand. "I'm Zach Clayton. It's my fiancée that we're concerned about, but I don't know much of anything."

Looking at his phone Lt. Sloan said, "Apparently, the report was made by her roommate. I guess we need to get inside and see what we can find out."

"Oh, Zach, I'm so glad you're here," Karen said as she opened the door. He reached out to hug her.

"Karen, this is Lt. Sloan. Officer, this is Miss Karen Scott, and this is her home."

Sloan shook Karen's hand. "Can we sit, Miss Scott, and have you tell me everything you know about this situation?"

Karen told him how she had seen Grace's slipper at the street, how the house doors were not secured, and how Grace's purse and phone were not taken.

After eliminating the dispatcher's theory that Grace was simply visiting a neighbor, the officer looked through the house and found everything in order. He took the slipper as evidence, and carefully noted where it had been found. He also bagged a cigarette butt found a few feet from the curb in that location.

"I'm going to cover the doorbell in case there might be a print on it that could be evidence. I'll ask my supervisor to send out a team to check the door for prints, too. So try not to add any of yours to those areas until we've been able to get that done," the officer said.

He stood, "Since this is a gated community, if someone did forcibly remove Ms. Morgan they would either have to be a resident here, a vendor that has gate privileges, or someone who has gained entrance illegally. I have to say I'm leaning toward the last option."

He turned to Karen. "Did you say Ms. Morgan's phone is here?"

"Yes, it's still on the charger on her dresser."

"Would you get that for me?" he asked. "If we can find any calls made or received this morning it could at least give us a time frame to place the abduction."

Karen brought the phone and handed it to him. Lt. Sloan quickly brought up the call log. "It seems that a call from you, Mr. Clayton, is the only phone call Ms. Morgan received today, and that was at seven o'clock.

"Miss Scott, you said that you left for work at around eight and she was here at that time. Since she didn't receive or make any other calls, we can only conclude that if there was an abduction it took place between eight and twelve when you returned home and found her gone. "

Zach couldn't remain seated any longer. "Lieutenant, is there anything we can do? I don't think I can just sit here."

"I do understand, sir," Lt. Sloan said. "That is truly the most difficult part of a situation like this. If you would like to ask neighbors if they saw anything you can do that. If you get any information at all let me know."

"All of the neighbors here would normally be at work during that time," Karen said. "But I'll try to contact them."

"Do either of you have a picture of Ms. Morgan?" Sloan asked. "We need to get this on the air and hope that someone will come forward with information."

"I have pictures we took the day we were on your tour, Zach," Karen said reaching for her phone. "All others I have show Grace with dark hair."

Officer Sloan downloaded the picture into his phone and sent it to headquarters as well.

"Okay," Officer Sloan said. "I'm going to speak to the guard at the gate and ask the management to allow me to look at their security video during our timeframe. There's only one way to enter and exit the property, so the culprits should be on that video. I'll let you know if I find out anything."

Lt. Carter Sloan drove back to the entrance of the community and parked his police car inside the fence. He walked through a gate for pedestrian traffic and stopped in front of the guard's window. Sloan remembered that as he entered the property just a half hour earlier, the guard had not even looked at him nor shown any awareness that a police unit had gone through the gate. But when he looked up from his comic book now and saw the uniformed officer there was stark fear on his face.

Trying to put him at ease, the officer said cordially, "Hi, how ya doing today?"

Turning red-faced, the teen stuttered, "I…I'm fine."

"I'm Lt. Sloan with the Friendswood police department and I'd like to ask you a few questions if you don't mind. Could I get your name?"

He nodded, "Matt Benton."

"Okay, Matt. There's a lady who lives here that seems to be missing, and I'm just wondering if you've noticed anything suspicious or unusual. You know…out of the ordinary?"

Matt shook his head negatively, but his face reddened even deeper.

"You haven't had anybody trying to get through the gate without a legitimate gate code, have you?"

The teen looked at the officer as if frozen and didn't say anything.

Sloan stepped up to the window. "Maybe I'm wrong, Matt, but I believe you know something you're not telling me. This lady could be in peril of her life, so if you know something, you could be charged for withholding evidence."

Matt covered his face with his hands and broke out in tearful sobs. "I'm afraid I'll lose my job," he managed to say.

"All right," Sloan said gently. "'You want to tell me what happened? What time did you come on duty?"

Matt wiped his eyes. "At eight o'clock."

"Okay, and what happened after that?" Sloan was writing down everything the teen said.

"About nine o'clock these two guys drove up in a white van. It had a sign on it that said …I think it was like… 'A-1 Delivery Service.' The driver said he really needed to make an important delivery, but he'd lost the code the resident gave him. He pulled out a twenty-dollar bill and waved it at me, said it was mine if I could let him in so he could make that delivery."

Matt started crying again. "I know I shouldn't have done it, I shouldn't have taken the money or let him through the gate, but I did."

"Is there anything else you can tell me about the men? Can you give me a description of them? Were they wearing uniforms?"

"They were wearing khaki colored clothes, I guess they were uniforms, I don't know."

"That's good, Matt. How about a physical description? What did the driver look like?"

Matt thought a minute. "He was kind of heavy-set, dark hair…but it looked kind of weird, like it might be a wig, and I swear he was wearing a fake mustache. It kind of drooped on one side."

Sloan said, "You're doing great, Matt. What about the other guy? Did you get a good look at him?"

When he hesitated, Sloan nudged him. "Okay, Matt, don't close up on me now. Get it all out and things will go better for you."

Matt swallowed and began to speak. "I didn't really pay any attention to the other fellow when they came through the gate, but I got a good look at both of them later."

"'Wanna tell me how that happened?"

Matt shook his head back and forth. "I'm gonna lose my job for sure."

Sloan didn't say it, but he was pretty sure the job was already gone!

"Go on," he encouraged.

"I got up late and didn't have time to eat before I came to work so I was really hungry about the time those guys came through. There are snack and coke machines over by the pool. Guards are not supposed to leave the gate except to go to the restroom or to take our breaks. We have to call the office and one of the employees there has to come out and man the gate until we get back. They don't like to do that and always act mad at us, so we don't ask them any more often than we have to."

"I get it," Sloan said. "You figured going for breakfast snacks wouldn't be a good enough excuse to upset the office staff, so you thought you'd make a quick run over there and get your goodies and no one would ever know."

Matt's eyes lit up, surprised the officer understood his actions.

"Yeah."

"So what happened next?" Sloan asked.

"I went over to the pool area, got my snacks, and started to come back to my post. Then I saw something. I was already kind of feeling bad about taking that twenty and lettin' the guy in the gate, so when I saw the van just down the street there I guess I was checkin' them out."

Matt dropped his head. "I swear, I feel really bad about this. I just hope that lady's all right."

"Well, you're helping her a lot, so come on, Matt, don't leave me hanging. What did you see?"

"I saw the driver guy and the pretty, blonde lady that lives there walking from the house to the van. The taller, light-haired guy got out of the front seat and opened the sliding door.

"The lady looked in and I saw the big guy push her so hard that she fell up into the van. They slammed the door quick, jumped in the front, and drove out.

"When I saw what they had done I jumped behind the concession building . I thought they might do something to me if they knew I saw them. I'm still afraid of that, Officer."

"Okay, Matt, gather up your comic books and any other personal items you have here. I don't think you'll be coming back. Is your shift about over?"

"Yeah," Matt said, looking at his watch. "I just have another half hour."

"Well, I'm afraid we're going to upset the office staff because you're leaving early. I'm going to have someone pick you up and take you to the station so we can get a formal report of what you've told me."

"I've got to go to the police station? Am I being arrested?" Matt trembled at the thought.

"You did withhold information about a crime when you first saw it, but you also gave that information to me. Hopefully, it's in time to find and save that lady. How old are you, Matt?"

"I'm eighteen."

"Okay, is there anyone you need to make aware of this situation?"

"My folks would be so ashamed of me; I don't even want to tell them."

"Well, that's up to you, but you'll have to tell them sooner or later. I've got to talk to the manager here and to some other people, but I'll get to the station as soon as I can."

Matt gathered up his belongings and stepped out of the booth.

"I'm scared," he said.

"Yeah, I know, but there's just one thing you need to do and that's tell the truth, even the ugly truth, because it all comes out in the end. I can tell you now, there are some people who love Ms. Morgan very much and they will be very grateful that you told the truth today."

He put his arm around Matt's shoulder and guided him toward the office. "Let's go face the music, buddy."

A few minutes later Lt. Sloan was sitting with Karen and Zach sharing what he had learned from Matt.

"I've already had someone check on the A-1 Delivery Service and there's no such company licensed here in the city. Matt said the sign was only on the front doors of the van so I'm guessing that they are the magnetic signage that can be quickly removed. There are hundreds of white vans in this area, so that could take some time to process."

He looked at his notes. "A detective is now checking with all the companies that create those magnetic signs. He's also checking with uniform companies to see if they've had an order for just two suits in the sizes of these guys. Another detective is checking the costume shops for fake hair and mustache purchases in the past few days."

"I do wish that young fellow had called your department when he saw this happen, or reported it to the manager, but he did give you a lot to work with," Zach said.

"Yes, he did," Sloan said. " I think he's really a good kid that simply thought and acted like a kid. It's too bad that his poor judgement had such terrible consequences." He looked around at them, "Do any of you have any idea why someone would want to kidnap Ms. Morgan?"

In the quiet that followed Officer Sloan noticed that Karen and Zach exchanged a look he couldn't decipher. "Even the smallest thing could be important, Miss Scott...Mr. Clayton."

Zach stood and paced the floor. "I hate to bring this up, Officer, if there's nothing to it, ...this is kind of embarrassing, but..."

"Why don't you let me decide if it's nothing, Mr. Clayton," Sloan said.

Zach took a deep breath and sat down again. "My first wife and I started a church here ten years ago. She was diagnosed with cancer and passed away three years ago."

Lt. Sloan said, "I'm sorry to hear that, sir."

Zach nodded his acceptance of Sloan's remark. "There was a woman who had begun attending our church that developed...I guess you could say, an infatuation with me. Not once did I ever give her the slightest reason to think that I was interested in her. I dearly loved my wife and was praying and hoping with everything within me that she would recover."

"What is this woman's name?" Sloan was writing again.

"Her name is Alysse Stratton. She has a successful interior design business here. "

"So, what actions did Ms. Stratton take toward you?"

"She would show up wherever I went. She made overtures toward me anytime she could catch me without other people around. All the church members had my phone number, and she would call and try to set up meetings with me. I can't tell you how many times I have refused this woman's attentions. After my wife died she assumed that I would turn to her, but even then I refused to have anything to do with her. I have never known of any person so determined to force a relationship."

"When did your relationship with Ms. Morgan begin?" Sloan asked.

Zach smiled. "We met on the plane the evening that she flew here to be with Karen about two months ago."

"How did Ms. Stratton become aware of your relationship with Ms. Morgan?"

Officer Sloan continued to ask questions regarding Alysse and eventually closed his tablet

"Thank you for your candor, Mr. Clayton. I'm sure this is difficult for you to make public, but it is definitely important information."

"I just want Grace to be all right and back with us," Zach said.

"The manager of the community here is setting up the video footage of our time frame. It will show any vehicles coming and going through the gate. If you'd like to come watch that with me, it shouldn't take long. Thanks to Matt we can narrow the time to just minutes before and after nine A.M."

"Yes, I'd love to do that." Zach said. "Sitting here waiting is a nightmare!."

The security video was set to begin at 8:50 A.M. as Lt. Sloan and Zach began to watch it. Most of the traffic seemed to be residents leaving the community. Only one vehicle, a small car, had entered the property. Then at 9:06 A.M. a white cargo van pulled up to the guard shack and there was obvious conversation between the driver and the attendant. The camera clearly showed the dark-haired man handing a bill to Matt and proceeding through the gate as it opened.

At 9:07 Matt was seen leaving the gate area and walking toward the pool which took him out of the camera's viewing range. At 9:10 the van pulled up to the exit and as soon as the gate opened enough to allow it to pass, the van went through and exited the property quickly to the left. The license plate was in plain view, but the numbers were not discernable.

"Yes!" Both men exclaimed and exchanged a fist pump.

"I've got to get this to the department now," Sloan said. "They can blow that up and we'll have the license number in minutes."

Outside the manager's office Sloan and Zach shook hands.

"Thanks for letting me come with you. It makes me feel better knowing we have some evidence to work with," Zach said.

Sloan shook his head. "I'm sure you've heard the statistics about the necessity to find people quickly. Normally, when a person is kidnapped, unless it's a ransom situation, the end is not good for the victim. I assure you we are working this as quickly as possible. So, I'll get Grace's picture and info to the TV stations to be aired this evening and we'll hope for the best. I'll also try to talk to Alysse Stratton."

"I don't want to be accusatory or presumptuous about her involvement in this, but I can't think of another person who would wish Grace harm," Zach said.

"Jealousy is a powerful emotion," Sloan said. "You wouldn't believe some of the things I've seen done by a spurned lover." He clapped Zach on the shoulder, ""Need a ride back to Miss Scott's ?"

"Thanks, but I'll walk. Just go find my girl!" Zach told him.

"I'll call you when I have some news," Sloan said as he got in his vehicle.

CHAPTER 30

Back at the house Zach shared with Karen what they had seen on the video and what the police were doing to find Grace. She was encouraged to hear that there was solid evidence to work with now.

"They came while you were with Officer Sloan and did the fingerprinting work." She said. They were able to get a few good prints. Of course, they could be some of ours instead of the kidnappers, so we'll have to wait until they run them through the system."

Zach had given Jim Sheridan directions and the gate code to come to Karen's house. He and Susan arrived, carrying a casserole dish, salad, and homemade bread.

"That is so thoughtful of you," Karen said.

Susan gave her a hug. "Well, people still have to eat in crisis situations. We love Grace, too and want to help in any way we can."

"I don't think any of us had lunch, so I'm sure the guys are ready to eat, and now that I've smelled that casserole I realize I'm hungry, too."

"Well, let's get it on the table, then," Susan said.

There was a somber air around the table as they ate. The lack of Grace's presence hung over them like a dark cloud.

Zach stood when they'd all finished. "Folks, I can't tell you you how much I appreciate you and all the church people who are praying for Grace. I just need to get home and spend some time with the Lord. This is bigger than I can handle on my own."

After hugs all around Zach left. He was glad he'd moved his things to the ranch that morning, so he really was going home. He knew Lil and Jay would be eager to hear any news of Grace's situation, too.

* * * * *

Grace was awakened by voices again. She tried to move her cramped body and she needed to use the restroom. How long were they going to leave her like this? If they planned to kill her they might not bother to loose her at all. She remembered now how she had been enticed to come out to a van on the pretense of looking at a package, and then was shoved into the van. It must have been chloroform on the cloth he held to her nose that made her black out.

The conversation was getting louder now. She recognized the voices from the earlier conversation. Chills shook her when she realized that Alysse Stratton was speaking. It seemed that the younger man and woman were not in agreement with Alysse and the older man in regard to Grace. What connection did they have with Alysse? Were they relatives?

The door opened causing Grace's heart to leap. What would happen next?

"Well, well, if this isn't a pretty sight!"

Grace recognized Alysse's voice. "All bound up like one of Zach's cows. I wonder if he'd think you're so desirable like this."

Suddenly, the blindfold was jerked off Grace's head. For a moment, the light bothered her eyes then as they adjusted she saw Alysse standing over her with her hands on her hips and a sarcastic grin on her face.

"I guess I'll have to take the gag off, too if you're going to talk to me…and you're not only going to talk to me, you're going to say what I want to hear or pay the consequences."

She bent down close to Grace's face. "Do you understand me?" When Grace didn't respond she slapped the side of her head and angrily repeated, "Do you understand me?"

"Do whatever she says," Grace heard the Voice say.

Alysse roughly started untying the cloth that gagged her. "I want to hear you say it. 'Yes, Alysse, I understand'."

Grace's throat and mouth were so dry she could only whisper the words Alysse wanted to hear.

Alysse laughed wickedly. "That wasn't loud enough, Bimbo. I want to hear it loudly!"

Suddenly, a man appeared in the room. In spite of the difference in appearance Grace recognized him as her kidnapper.

"That's enough, Alysse! Cut the nonsense and get down to the reason you brought her here. We need this over and done with."

"But I'm having fun, Carl." Alysse said giddily.

"Alysse, I'm not kidding you. Cut it out!" he had stepped up closer to her and the anger in his eyes caused her to flinch. "Now get the tape off her hands and feet and get on with this."

Sullenly, Alysse complied. Grace wanted to cry out when the tape was pulled away from her skin so quickly. Then the tingling pain of blood suddenly being released back into her arms and legs consumed her.

"Lord help me," she prayed silently. She began to move the cramped limbs and slowly felt them returning to a semblance of normal.

Carl had left the room and returned with a bottle of water. He handed it to Grace with a growl, "Here." Grace was thankful for the water, no matter how unpleasant the giver.

After she had drunk almost the whole bottle she looked up to Alysse who had stood glaring at her the entire time. "What do you want from me, Alysse? Why are you doing this?"

"Do you really have to ask?" Alysse snarled. "You have ruined my life. Why did you have to come here and mess with Zach Clayton's heart? I have been waiting for him for four years, and just as he decides he's ready to finally move on from his dear Sasha, *YOU* come along and bat your big blue eyes and he fell for it!"

"That's not the way it happened, Alysse. Our being together wasn't really my doing, or Zach's. Neither of us was looking for a mate. Zach didn't just decide he was ready to move on after Sasha. He was still struggling with that even after we saw each other a few times."

"Then why didn't you just go back to California and your cheating husband?"

Grace was surprised that Alysse knew about Damien and his affair. "There was nothing for me to go back to, Alysse. As you evidently already know, my husband had found another woman he preferred to me. I was looking to start a new life because mine was destroyed, but I wasn't looking to add another man to it. This whole relationship with Zach is God's doing."

"Well, why wasn't it God's doing to cause Zach to move on before you came along?"

"I don't think God was responsible for that. Zach had loved Sasha so much he didn't think it was possible for him to love another woman. He was determined to keep things that way. He was miserable in his anger toward God, but finally had enough of living so unhappily.

Maybe that's what made him lay aside his anger and become ready to move on."

Alysse was thoughtful. "But you said you didn't want another husband in your life. So what changed your mind?"

Grace smiled and shrugged. " I was attracted to him the moment we met on the plane in California. I had never felt that kind of attraction to a man ever, not even my husband. We didn't exchange any contact information and never expected to see each other again. But my friend had booked us to go on a tour of Galveston a couple of days later and it just happened to be Zach's.

"So when we saw each other that day I think we both knew there was something between us. I loved being a pastor's wife but couldn't be that without a pastor husband. Zach felt he couldn't pastor again without a wife by his side, so I guess we just made a good fit."

As she talked Grace forgot she was speaking to the woman who had arranged for her to be kidnapped and maybe worse. She found her heart going out to this lonely woman who had everything the world could provide but was so empty without love.

"Alysse, why do you go to Cornerstone Cowboy Church?" she asked.

Alysse seemed surprised at her question. "Because of Zach. I have wanted him from the first time I saw him, and I would do anything to have him love me."

"I did everything I could possibly do to make my husband love me, too, Alysse, but no one can make someone love them. The feeling is either there, or it's not. I'm sure there's a man out there that will love you for who you are. It's just not Zach, and as long as you keep him in that place in your heart you don't leave room for the man who's best for you."

"But I don't know how to stop loving him," Alysse said.

"The best advice I have is to give your life totally to the Lord. His love fills so many broken places in us. It's only when we allow Him to be the true love of our lives that we make the best mates for earthly men."

"I have had to scrape and fight for everything I've gotten in life. I can 't just give over that control to someone else, not even God." She seemed saddened but determined.

Grace sensed that their conversation was over but hoped to keep the rapport that had begun.

"I really need to go to the restroom, Alysse," she said.

"All right, but I haven't decided how I'm going to handle this, so no trying to get away, understand?"

Grace agreed, and Alysse led her across the hall to the bathroom and stayed by the door until Grace came out.

The young woman whose voice Grace recognized as Sherry, appeared in the hallway. Timidly, she said, "I've made some soup, Alysse. Do you want some for yourself and …her?"

Grace looked to her captor and said, "I haven't eaten since breakfast and I'm really hungry."

Alysse nodded to Sherry. "You can bring her some. I'm not ready to eat." Sherry turned toward the kitchen and Grace went back to the room where she had been.

"Just so you know, the window in this room has been nailed shut from the outside. I'm going to be in the living room, but I will hear if you open the door."

Grace shook her head in agreement. She could see that Alysse was confused about how to handle her but felt she should just remain submissive and allow God to free her.

In a few moments Sherry came with the bowl of vegetable beef soup and crackers. It smelled delicious. Sherry sat the bowl and a glass of tea on the nightstand. Instead of leaving the room immediately she looked cautiously at the door and came closer to Grace. "I'm Sherry, and I think what Alysse is doing is wrong. I'm going to try to help you."

They could hear the door from Carl's room open and Sherry left abruptly.

Grace couldn't wait any longer to start eating the soup, but she wanted to hear whatever was said in the household if possible. Carl had joined Alysse in the living room and plopped down heavily into a chair.

"So what are you going to do, just sit here and drink?" she heard him say. "You need to be getting rid of that woman. Have you decided what you're going to do with her?"

"Not yet," Alysse answered.

"That's some answer." Carl growled. "I knew this was a bad idea."

"Turn the six o'clock news on," she said.

A few seconds later Grace heard the music that preceded the beginning of the newscast. A few stories of local interest were given then Grace stopped eating as she heard:

"The Friendswood Police Department is asking for any information regarding the apparent kidnapping of a thirty-two year- old woman who recently came to live in this area. Grace Morgan was found missing under suspicious circumstances around noon today. These two men driving a white van with a sign saying 'A-1 Delivery Service' were allegedly seen forcing Ms. Morgan into the van and leaving the Sun and Sea gated community just after nine o'clock this morning. Anyone with information regarding this situation is encouraged to contact the police department at…"

Grace was stunned. Apparently, they had shown a picture of her and also of the van as it came and went. From the broadcast it sounded like they had a picture of Carl and Ricky, too. How was this going to affect her situation now?

Carl cursed and threw the remote control across the room. Of course there had been security cameras. He'd always lived in this same house and never had any reason to think about them. But he was sure that Alysse would live in some fancy place that had them.

"'Forgot something didn't you, Miss Brilliant? Now what are we going to do? That picture could put me away."

Alysse looked frozen. She had not thought ahead to what she would do if things went wrong. She was so consumed with her hatred of Grace Morgan and planning retribution for Zach Clayton that she had not planned well at all. And strangely enough, she didn't hate either of them anymore. What had she gotten herself and her brothers into?

She had already sipped on one drink as she sat in contemplation. She poured another and drank it quickly.

Carl stood in front of her now. "So…What are you going to do? You need to get that woman out of this house, and any of the stuff that would tie us to her!"

"And just where would I take her?"

"How am I supposed to know? Where were you planning to take her if she agreed to split with the preacher? Did you think she'd just go home like a good little girl and not tell anybody we drugged and kidnapped her? Not to mention how you were slapping her around."

He paced the floor in angry frustration. "I wish you'd stayed away another twelve years instead of bringing all this on us!"

Starting to cry now, Alysse said, "I thought it would work out."

"You haven't even told her you want her to leave town and forget about the preacher, have you?"

Alysse ignored the question and drank another gulp of the liquor.

Carl bent down and looked her in the eyes. "I really thought you were smarter than this. I don't know how you're going to get out of this mess, but I'm leaving before the cops show up at the door." He gave her a sarcastic smile. "And thanks to your money I can go anywhere I want!"

He quickly headed down the hall toward his room. Grace was listening intently and could hear Carl apparently throwing things together.

Carl's leaving brought a measure of relief to Grace. She felt that Alysse was not as likely to harm her now without someone putting pressure on her. From their remarks she believed that both Ricky and Sherry would be on her side.

* * * * *

A few miles away Radford Connally was watching the evening news when he froze in horror at the announcer's story. Grace Morgan had been kidnapped! He knew immediately who was behind this and fear gripped him. Alysse had become absolutely deranged over her inability to gain Zach Clayton's love. But was she really evil enough to harm Grace?

He tossed aside his half-eaten burger and grabbed his keys, trying to think where Alysse might have taken her. Would she have her hidden somewhere at her business? That didn't feel right. He practically ran to his car and drove out of the apartment community, then stopped. Where was he going?

Radford couldn't remember ever praying in his life, but he paused and said out loud. "God, you probably don't even know who I am, but the way the preacher talked the other evening around that campfire, you hear people like me that haven't done one single thing to deserve any favors. So, if that's true, would you help me figure out where Alysse might have taken Grace?"

Barely three seconds later the thought came: "*Her family home.*"

"Yes!" Radford exclaimed and quickly headed in that direction. So many questions raced through his mind. Would Alysse go so far as to kill Grace? How else could she make sure that Grace would not have Zach? He had to stop her!

Rad hadn't seen or heard anything about Alysse's brothers since he had moved out of that neighborhood years ago. They weren't exactly the kind of people you'd want living next door to you as best he could remember. At least, the older one. Rad had heard that he was already dealing drugs before Rad left the area.

Like Alysse, he was so glad to be out of that environment he'd not gone back there even once. He couldn't help but wonder if her brothers were involved in this.

He found himself praying for the second time in his life. "God, please don't let them harm Grace. Help me get there in time to stop whatever Alysse is planning."

Sherry busied herself in the kitchen, trying to act as though everything was normal. Ricky had gone to work but hated leaving her there in that volatile situation. She had tried to think of some legitimate excuse to leave the house but knew Carl would shoot down anything she would say.

She was glad Carl would be leaving, but what was Alysse going to do? She'd been drinking heavily for the last hour. Sherry peeked into the living room and saw that Alysse appeared to be asleep. She walked out of the kitchen and Alysse started. "Where are you going?"

Timidly, Sherry said, "I'm just going to the restroom." Alysse grunted, fell back onto her seat, and took another drink.

Sherry quickly made her way to the restroom, locked the door, and pulled out her phone. She dialed 911 and when the dispatcher asked, "What is your emergency?" Sherry whispered into the phone, "I can't talk out loud…can you hear me?"

"Not well, but I'll try to understand. How can I help you?"

Grace whispered again, "The lady, Grace Morgan, that was kidnapped. She's here at this house."

The dispatcher had already seen the address pop up on her screen and recited it back to Sherry. "At this address?"

"Yes, Ms. Morgan is all right just now but I'm afraid of what they'll do to her. They're talking about taking her somewhere else."

"What is your name, hon?"

"It's Sherry Martin."

"All right, Sherry, I need you to stay on the phone a little longer if you feel safe doing so. I want to ask you some more questions, but I need to get an officer headed that way. Can you hold for me?"

"I think so, but not for long. They'll get suspicious."

Sherry could hear the dispatcher in the background as she contacted an officer on the radio and gave him the address.

"Okay, Sherry, do you know if anyone in the house has weapons?"

"Yes, Carl, my boyfriend's brother always carries a gun in his back waistband."

"Thanks , Sherry, can you tell me how many people are in the house? "

"Carl's sister, Alysse is here and then just Ms. Morgan and me. I think I should get back to the kitchen."

"Okay, you've done a good job, Sherry. The officers will be there soon."

Sherry flushed the unused toilet and ran water in the sink. She was afraid of what would happen to her if Carl or Alysse realized she'd called the police, but also felt relieved that she had done the right thing. A glance at Alysse as she passed the living room let her know that the woman was likely passed out.

The sound of a car screeching to a halt in front of the house quickly caused her heart to beat rapidly. A car door slammed, and Sherry slipped into the kitchen and stood there in fear. A loud knock at the door was quickly followed by a man calling, "Alysse! Alysse, it's Rad, let me in."

"Rad"... Sherry thought. That name sounded familiar...Ricky and Alysse were talking about him the other day. Should she let him in?

The knocking continued even louder. "Alysse, let me in, it's Rad!"

Alysse stirred, looking around to see where the noise was coming from. Sherry heard Carl coming from the back and saw that he had his hand on his gun. When he heard Radford identify himself he cursed and opened the door.

"Hey, Rad," Carl said in a fairly pleasant tone. "Long time, no see. What's up?"

"I need to talk to Alysse."

"Well, I think she's kind of under the weather right now."

"It's important, Carl. I need to talk to her."

Alysse appeared behind Carl, leaning unsteadily on his shoulder. "Rad...sweet old Rad," she slurred. "You couldn't stay mad at me, could you?"

Carl backed out of the way, knowing it was useless trying to prevent Rad's entering the house now.

"Alysse," Rad took her by the shoulders, "Where is Grace Morgan?"

"Grrraaace?" Alysse staggered and Rad lowered her into a chair. "She's the one that…that stole my…my Zach away from me."

Carl stepped up to Rad. "I think you ought to leave now," he said in his tough guy voice."

Radford squared his shoulders and looked Carl in the eyes. "And I think you need to tell me what you've done with Grace Morgan and quickly before I call the cops."

Carl cursed the fact that he'd hadn't gotten out of there before Rad came, but now that somebody else knew–however he'd found out–that they had taken the Morgan woman he'd have to get rid of him or bring him in on it.

"All right, Rad, we go back a long time, so I'll tell you the truth. The woman's in there in Alysse's old bedroom."

"Have you harmed her?"

"No, man…we just had to make sure she couldn't get away…you can see for yourself, she's fine. We even gave her something to eat."

Alysse seemed to be growing more cognizant of what was going on. "We weren't going to hurt her, Rad. I…I just wanted her …gone."

"'Lysse, Lysse," he said, using his old nickname for her. "What have you gotten yourself into? There is no good way out of this." Taking a deep breath, he turned to Carl. "I want to see Grace for myself."

"Why, Rad?" Alysse asked. "Why are you so worried about her? You were supposed to be helping me."

"I just need to see that she's all right, 'Lysse."

"Go on," Carl said sourly, nodding toward the hall.

Radford walked down the hall to the bedroom where he had spent so much time with Alysse when they were kids. Who ever thought he'd be coming here to see a woman his friend had kidnapped? He tapped lightly on the door. "Grace? Can I come in?"

Grace had listened at the door and heard the conversation. Apparently, the new man's name was 'Rad.' She didn't know anyone by that name; why would he be so concerned about her? But the voice sounded familiar. She was still trying to place it when he spoke to her.

He sounded nice but she didn't know what to expect. "I won't hurt you. I promise," he said as though he'd read her mind

"Come in," she said warily.

The door opened slowly, and a familiar face brought a surprised smile to her lips. "George…George Williams…What brings you here?"

Rad's face reddened. He had actually forgotten that Grace would know him as the imposter he'd been on the tour.

"I'm sorry, Grace," he said. "My name is really Radford Connally. I hope you'll allow me to explain all this later. I don't know how I'm going to get you out of here, but I'm going to try."

In her relief Grace threw her arms around him. "Oh thank you, I was so afraid."

Just then Alysse entered the room with Carl beside her. She was startled to see Radford with Grace in his arms. She screamed, "Isn't taking Zach enough for you, Grace Morgan? I hate you! You almost had me fooled, but here you are stealing Rad's heart, too while Zach's probably out there worried about you!"

Grace could see the hatred in Alysse's eyes that had pierced her previously. "Rad has been mine since we were kids, but you can't stand me having anyone, can you? Well, this will be the last man you steal from me."

No one expected Alysse to grab the gun she knew her brother wore in his waistband. In an instant she had it pointed directly at Grace and without a moment's warning pulled the trigger. Rad wasn't aware of thinking about his action, but in a split second he threw himself in front of Grace.

It all seemed to transpire in slow motion as the sound of the pistol echoed in the small room. Rad fell to the floor and bright red stains began to flow into the old, worn carpet around him.

Every other person in the room seemed frozen in horror, until a strong voice commanded, "Ma'am, put the gun down slowly and lift your hands…Now! Do you hear me? Put… Down…the Gun and raise your hands or I'll have to shoot you."

In a stupor, Alysse laid the gun on the floor at her feet, looking at it as if she was surprised to see it in her hand.

Another officer was calling for an ambulance and reporting the shooting to the dispatcher.

Grace flew into action when she saw how much blood was flowing from Rad's body. She grabbed the sheet from the bed, wadded it up over the wound and applied pressure firmly to his chest. The officer who had just handcuffed Alysse nodded his approval and thanked her.

Grace looked down at the bleeding man. "Oh, George…Rad . Thank you for saving my life. You've got to make it. I couldn't bear it if you don't. Just stay with us!"

Rad wanted to speak, to tell her it was all right if he didn't, but for some reason the words wouldn't come out. He managed to nod briefly, though.

Grace kept the pressure on Rad's wound until the paramedics arrived. One of them complimented her on her actions. "You probably saved this man's life, Ma'am."

"I was returning a favor," she said.

As soon as Lt. Carter Sloan got Alysse handcuffed and read her rights, he handed her over to another officer to take her to headquarters. He then turned his attention to Grace who had just returned from washing Rad's blood from her hands.

"Ms. Morgan, I'm Lieutenant Sloan. I've been working your case since early this afternoon and I can't tell you how glad I am that we have found you. Your fiancé, Mr. Clayton, has been informed of your situation and he'll meet us at the station as soon as we can get there. I'll need to hear from you just how this whole thing played out. Since I've been looking for you all day I'd like to personally escort you if you don't mind my clearing up a few details here."

"Officer. I don't even know myself how all this came to be. I guess I can ask you questions too when we get to the station. But not until I hug Zach!"

Sloan grinned. "I assure you that will be a priority. That man has been out of his mind with concern for you."

CHAPTER 31

Zach was already standing outside the police station when Carter Sloan pulled in. Grace opened her door almost before the cruiser came to a stop and Zach met her with open arms. He could hardly speak as gratitude for her safety filled his heart.

"My darling, Grace! I'm so glad you're safe! I can't tell you how sorry I am that this happened. I should have foreseen it…done something to prevent it."

"Zach, please don't feel guilty about this. It's not your fault. I'm just so glad to see you!"

Zach held her so close he was afraid he might be crushing her, but he never wanted her out of his sight. He didn't think he could live through the horror of this day ever again. After kissing her gently, he realized that Officer Sloan was standing to the side, but patiently waiting.

He laughed and acknowledged the officer. "I can't thank you enough, Lieutenant Sloan for bringing Grace back to me."

Carter Sloan came and shook his hand. "I am very glad for the positive outcome here, too, Mr. Clayton. Had it not been for the intervention of Mr. Connally, we would very likely not be celebrating Ms. Morgan's safe return."

Zach looked between Grace and the officer with questions in his eyes.

"He's talking about the man we knew as George Williams…on the tour. The fellow with the camera that acted so strange?"

Zach nodded. "I remember him, but how does he come into this?"

"Quite honestly, Mr. Clayton, We're not really sure until we can interview the other persons that were there in the house. I'm going to need to get Ms. Morgan's take on the day's events, too, so why don't we go inside and get started."

The officer led them down the hall to a room where he had Grace begin with the fake delivery man coming to her door. Other officers were interrogating Alysse, Ricky and Sherry, and Carl, who had been intercepted by officers arriving just as he was trying to run with a bag full of cash.

Grace was exhausted when Sloan's report was completed, and Zach just wanted to take her home.

"Thank you again for your diligence in the search for Grace. We'd like to have you out to our ranch sometime when everything slows down a bit. Do you ride?"

"I do every chance I get. I grew up riding horses and I miss it…just can't keep one in an apartment!"

They all laughed as they walked toward the door. "Well, I've got several horses and lots of acres to ride them, so we'll do that soon."

Grace turned to Sloan. "I was wondering if you had any information about Radford Connally's condition. Do you know which hospital he's in?"

"I heard them say they were taking him to Physicians' Hospital over in Webster, but I don't have an update on his condition. As soon as I get that I'll let you know."

"Thanks, I would appreciate that," Grace said.

As soon as Zach and Grace were in his truck, he took her in his arms and held her close. "I was so afraid, Grace. I don't know what I would have done if something had happened to you…not that it didn't…this was horrible enough," he said.

"I know, love. I was more concerned for you than for myself. But I'm fine. A little sore, but thankfully this ordeal didn't last but one day. God gave me His peace and here we are together again."

"I'd love to keep you to myself, but I know Karen is so eager to see you. She's been sick with worry all day…Oh, Grace! I forgot…here."

He handed her his phone. "Call your parents. I spoke with them earlier and told them I'd let them know as soon as I heard something."

"You spoke with my parents?" Grace asked, surprised.

"I felt I had to let them know that you were missing, and I wanted to know if you might have called them."

Grace was dialing their number. "Oh, Zach, they must be so worried."

"Mom, it's me," Grace said when her mother answered. "Yes, I'm all right." She took a deep breath, then said, "I'm too tired right now to go into it, but I'm safe. Zach is here with me and the police have the people responsible for taking me. If you don't mind, I don't think I can go over it all right now. Can I call you tomorrow? We haven't gone into the house yet to tell Karen that I'm here and all right."

She paused, listening to her mother. "You're where? Why…Oh, Mom, that's wonderful! Okay, I'll tell Zach. Give my love to Dad and thanks so much for your prayers. We'll see you soon."

Grace handed Zach's phone to him with a smile. "Mom and Dad are at a motel in Arizona…on their way here! 'Looks like God is taking care of the number one item on our list."

Zach walked Grace to the door and held her close again. "After what we've been through today, I can hardly bear to leave you. I wish we were married so I could take you home with me."

" I feel the same way, But I know your love is with me and I'll see you tomorrow, won't I?"

"Right now I can't get my head around what I need to do tomorrow , but seeing you will definitely be on my list."

With a kiss that promised so much more he said goodnight, and once again she watched until his truck was through the gate.

Karen squealed and came running to hug Grace when she walked in the door. "Oh, Gracie, are you all right?"

Grace hugged her warmly. "I'm definitely not 100 per cent, but I'm okay. I'm still trying to process the events of this day."

"I doubt that you'll manage to complete that for a while," Karen said. "I'm dying to know details, but I'm not going to demand them tonight. You've got to be exhausted."

"I am, KK. I just want to shower and hit the bed," Grace said.

"Then you do that. We can talk tomorrow."

The hot shower seemed to relax all the tense muscles that had been holding Grace together and afterward, she could barely make it to the bed. She quickly fell asleep, though it was troubled by memories of the day.

When she awoke sunlight was streaming in the window. Grace stretched and found that her body was still struggling with the impact of being bound for those few hours from yesterday. There were bruises, now a blue-purple in color, as well. She got up and moved around, bending and stretching in spite of the discomfort.

A few minutes later she followed the aroma of fresh coffee to the kitchen and found Karen pouring coffee for the two of them.

"I heard you rumbling around in there, so I put some cinnamon rolls in the oven. I know they can't compete with Mama Lil's, but they're the best you're going to get in my kitchen," Karen said with a smile. "I'm dying to know what happened; are you to up to telling me now?" she asked.

"I think so," Grace said, and began with Carl Milton's coming to her door as a deliveryman. Karen's eyes filled with tears as Grace told of waking up and realizing that she was helpless to free herself.

"I think the worst of it was when I became conscious and couldn't see anything, say anything, or move. I had no clue where I was, or why someone would do this to me. That was terrifying."

"Later though, there seemed to be a change in Alysse after I talked to her and I think she might have let me go if she could have found a way to do it without getting into trouble herself. I wish I hadn't hugged Rad when he said he was there to help me. That's what triggered her anger again. She so misunderstood what she saw, and now she's in jail for shooting the friend who has stood by her since childhood."

"Gracie-Lou, before you start feeling too sorry for Alysse you need to remember that she's the person who arranged to have you drugged, kidnapped, tied up and slapped around, and then tried to shoot and kill you!"

To emphasize her point Karen just stood looking at Grace with her hands on her hips, until Grace said, "You're right."

Karen turned and opened the oven door. "Hmmm, these smell good." She removed the pan of rolls from the oven and began spreading the icing over them.

"I do hope they go easy on the girl, Sherry, though. It's her call to the police that got them there so quickly. Apparently, they heard the shot just as they got to the front door and raced in to intervene. As bad as this ordeal was, it could have been worse."

"I was thinking about that, too. You know, Rad was a witness to their kidnapping you, and then you were a witness to Alysse shooting Rad. If the police hadn't arrived when they did, that guy Carl would probably have decided it was better to get rid of both of you."

Setting a cinnamon roll in front of Grace, Karen smiled. "But thankfully, you're still here and we're drinking coffee in our pj's and your folks are headed our way."

"Yes! I will be glad to see them," Grace said. "Mom's supposed to call around three o'clock and let me know where they are. It's such a long drive and they're taking it easy now that they know I'm okay."

They heard Grace's phone ringing from her bedroom, and she hurried to answer it.

"Ms. Morgan?"

"Yes, good morning, Lt. Sloan," she said, recognizing his voice.

"How are you today? I know it's too soon to expect you to be over your ordeal, but I hope you're doing all right."

"I am, Lieutenant. Some sore muscles remind me of yesterday, but I'm just glad to be alive and well."

"We are all very pleased with that outcome, too. I wanted to tell you that Radford Connally is doing well. The bullet passed close to his heart…that's why he was bleeding so heavily. But he was one fortunate guy; he probably would have bled to death if you hadn't staunched that blood with the sheet and pressure."

"I'm so glad to hear that!" Grace cried. "I don't know how I could bear it if he had died saving my life. Is he allowed to have visitors?"

"I asked about that and the doctor said to give him another day or two. They just want him to rest right now. He gave me the okay to come tomorrow and interview Connally, but just for a few minutes," Sloan said.

"Lieutenant Sloan, I am concerned about the young couple, Alysse's younger brother and his fiancée. Are they going to be charged with anything?"

"The young lady was released last night. She obviously didn't know anything about the situation until you were brought to the house. She risked the wrath of the older brother and Alysse, too by calling the police. The decision is still out on what to do about the younger brother. I believe his story that he was forced into helping his brother, but he still participated in a kidnapping."

"I could hear their conversation when I was bound in the bedroom, " Grace said, "and Ricky was telling Carl that what he was doing was wrong and that he needed to let me go. I think Ricky's a good young man that has been trapped in a negative situation that wasn't of his making. I hope his life is not ruined because of this."

"I'll pass that information on to my superiors, Ms. Morgan," Sloan said. "I need to get back to reading all the interviews and we still have more investigating to do. Give my best to Mr. Clayton. I'll be in touch later."

"I'll do that, Lieutenant. Thank you so much for calling."

Grace shared the officer's comments with Karen as they ate their cinnamon rolls. "I need to call Zach and let him know about Rad, too, " she said." We want to see him as soon as they will allow us to visit."

Zach was in the kitchen with Lil when Grace called. " Hello, my lovely," he said. "I've been wanting to call, but I was hoping you were sleeping in."

After Grace assured him she was doing well, she told him about Lt. Sloan's call. "I'm really glad to hear that Radford is going to make it. I've got to personally thank him for taking action so quickly and likely saving your life," Zach said.

"You know, Zach," Grace said, "I heard him talking to Carl and Alysse when he came in and he was so concerned about me. I felt that was a little strange, but he really put himself in a dangerous position even before the gun shot. Alysse and Carl had committed a serious crime and somehow Rad knew about it. Still, he was determined to help me and I'm wondering why."

"I believe it had something to do with the Lord working in his heart that night around the campfire. I could tell that there was a battle going on in him. Maybe can learn more when we visit him."

Lil called out to Grace," I'm so glad you are all right, Sweetie. Jay and I were praying."

"Give her my love, Zach, and thank her for praying," Grace said.

"I was just telling her that your parents are on the way and will likely be staying with us a while," Zach said. "The mobile home is being moved here tomorrow, so I guess she'll be turning the kitchen here over to your mom in a few days."

He winked at Lil and said to Grace, "She's making a list of things to buy before they get here so your mom will have a full pantry."

"If you think of any foods that they especially like, Grace, please let me know," Lil called.

"Tell her I'll think about that," Grace told Zach. "It's so sweet of her to do that."

"We want to treat them right, so they'll let me marry you," Zach teased.

Grace laughed. "Is there any way I can help? I can launder bed linens, dust, and clean house. I don't want Lil doing all that."

"That would be a good excuse to have you over here, wouldn't it?" Zach asked.

"Hmm, let me think…do you have time today to go to buy our new furniture? If you can pick me up to do that, then I can go back to the ranch with you and help Lil in the house."

"'Sounds like a plan. Pick you up in an hour?"

"That works for me, see you then."

Rebecca and Ben Reynolds were both behind the counter when Zach and Grace walked into their business. Their faces lit up with smiles as they came out front to greet them.

"Pastor Zach, Grace! We're so glad you're here." Rebecca said. "Of course, we saw on the news the awful thing that happened and it's wonderful to know that you came through it so well."

Ben stepped forward to shake Grace's hand. "Welcome to our world here, Grace. I'm Ben. We are happy the Lord sent you to Pastor Zach. It's great to see him smiling again."

After a few minute's conversation Rebecca led them back to the area where Grace showed Zach the furniture she'd chosen. As she expected, he was pleased with it.

"We have room on our schedule for one more delivery late this afternoon if you'd like it brought out today," Rebecca said.

"I think that would work, Rebecca. I can get Jay to help me move out the furniture that's there now and the room will be ready for the new. That will be one more thing we can cross off our list, Grace."

"All right! Things are really moving quickly."

Lil was feeding the chickens when they drove up to the ranch. Jay came out of the barn when he heard Zach's truck. They were both smiling with welcome and again Grace felt the love from them.

Tossing the last of the chicken feed Lil called to them. "You're just in time for pie and coffee, kids. Come on in."

When they walked into the kitchen Zach spotted a big pot on the stove. "Oh my, is that the chili pot, Mama Lil?"

"Yes, it is," Lil replied. "I didn't think to ask if you've had lunch."

"We kind of skipped that to go buy our new bedroom furniture," Grace told her. "I have to admit, though, I'm hungry now, and you know Zach's always ready to eat."

"Well, Mama outdid herself on that chili today; you're gonna have to have some of that," Jay said.

As Lil heated the chili Grace set out the bowls.

"If you don't have something more pressing going on this afternoon, Pops, we've got new bedroom furniture being delivered later and I could use some help removing the things that are in there now."

"Well, that sounds more important than my afternoon nap, so I guess I can help you," Jay said with a twinkle in his eyes. "Do you have a place in mind to put it?"

"Not yet," Zach answered. "I thought I'd clear a spot in the barn until we can find someone who needs it."

Lil came and put her arm around his shoulders and smiled. "Well, you don't have to look far, son. The kids never did get a second bedroom set up in their mobile home, and since they won't be leaving for the mission field for a couple of months they'll still be needing theirs. So, Jay and I were going to have to come up with furniture."

Zach grinned and patted her cheek. "I love it when problems get solved so quickly."

"Well, if your new stuff is coming today where are we gonna put the pieces we're taking out until the mobile home gets here tomorrow?" Jay asked.

"I think we can deal with it pushed into the living room for one night," Zach said. "I'd rather not take it to the barn if we can help it."

"All right," Lil said, "Just as long as it's out of there by the time Grace's folks get here. I don't want their first impression of their new son-in-law's home to be that of a junked- up thrift store."

They all laughed at the fervency of Lil's comment. Zach gave her a hug and said, "I promise. We'll have the furniture out of there in time. Now, where's that chili?"

Lil brought out a beautifully baked apple pie when Zach and Grace had eaten their fill of the spicy chili. After they'd all had pie and coffee Jay turned to Zach.

"Okay, son, let's keep these gals happy and get that stuff moved."

After the men had left Grace turned to Lil. "I forgot about bedding, Lil. I should have gotten new things, but I didn't even think about it. Would there happen to be any extras the right size?"

Lil smiled and put her arm around Grace, "Honey, the Lord takes care of everything. You see, Sasha was always buying things when she found a good sale on items that she felt would be used sometime in the future. She put them in the closet in the third bedroom…the one your parents will be using… and rarely even mentioned those things to Zach. Mostly because he wasn't interested! I know there's a new, complete bedroom set in there that Zach has probably never even seen. The only question is, will it be something you'll want to use."

"Can I see it while the fellows are busy with the furniture?" Grace asked.

"You sure can; let's go take a look."

When Lil pulled the large, clear plastic bag from the closet Grace was pleased to see that the turquoise, gray and black pattern was exactly what she would have chosen if she'd purchased it herself.

"Oh, Lil! This will work perfectly. Our furniture is the new gray/washed look that's popular now and this be so pretty with it."

Lil was still going through things in the closet and brought out another large bag. "How about these throw pillows? Will they work?

Grace couldn't help laughing as Lil pulled out decorative pillows that obviously had been purchased to go with the bedroom set. "They're beautiful, Lil! I love them."

"Does it bother you at all, Grace, that Sasha chose these things?" Lil asked gently.

Grace reached out to take her hand. "No, Lil, not at all. Maybe it's strange, but I have this feeling that had I known Sasha I would have loved her as much as everyone else. And I have this crazy idea that if she is aware of what's happening down here with Zach and me, she's completely happy for us."

Lil had tears in her eyes as she hugged Grace. "I don't doubt that for a minute, hon, and as much as Jay and I loved Sasha, we are absolutely thrilled that you are marrying our Zach. We love you just as we did her."

"That means so much to me, Lil, and I love being part of his 'family.' She gathered up the bedding and pillows. "I don't think I've ever been so excited to make a bed!"

Two hours later the master bedroom was bare, all dust that had managed to evade Lil's broom and dust cloths had been removed, carpets were vacuumed, and tile floors mopped. Bed linens were on their last spin in the dryer and the house was sparkling.

Lil smiled at Grace, "Well, sweetie, I think we're ready. For the new furniture and for your folks…as soon as that stuff is out of the living room."

Grace laughed. "Even if it has to stay there until my parents arrive, I assure you it won't bother them nearly as much as it's worrying you!"

* * * * *

Lt. Carter Sloan walked up to the glass window in the jail and smiled at the young woman working there. "Hey, Teresa."

"You're back," she said. "You must really like our place, Lt. Sloan," she bantered.

With a sardonic grin he replied, "Yeah, a real home away from home."

Cocking her head Teresa said, "You know, we have about seventy-five people here that say the same thing. Which one of them do you want to visit?"

"That would be Richard Milton, please."

"You got it." She picked up a phone and spoke to someone then smiled at Carter again. "Okay, Lieutenant, I'll buzz you in. They'll bring him to room three."

"Thanks, Teresa," he said and gave her a wave as he walked through the door .

Sloan walked down the familiar, drab hallway to the room marked "Interrogation Room 3," and opened the door. He laid the manilla envelope he was carrying on the table, pulled out the single chair on one side of the table and waited.

In a few minutes he heard the approach of steps in the hallway and Ricky Milton appeared in the doorway, handcuffed, with a guard guiding him from behind. The kid looked scared to death and Sloan couldn't help feeling pity for him. He smiled, stood, and nodded at the young man.

"Hey, Richard, how are you doing?"

"I don't think I'm doing so good, Lieutenant."

Sloan gave a slight smile. "I can see why you'd say that. Have a seat."

Ricky sat in the chair Sloan indicated across the table from where he also sat down.

"I'm just curious, Richard. How long had it been since you had contact with your sister, Alysse, before this situation with Ms. Morgan?"

Ricky shook his head. "We hadn't seen or heard a word from her since I was ten years old…that'd be twelve years. She just left. It was like we didn't even exist anymore. A few years ago we started seeing ads for her business on TV. Otherwise, we wouldn't have known she was even alive."

"And then she just showed up a week or so ago?"

" Yeah."

"Did she say why she had come after all that time, or why she'd stayed away?"

Ricky shrugged. "Not to me, but she and Carl left the house to go somewhere and talk. I guess it was then that she told him about wanting to get rid of the lady…Ms. Morgan."

"Did she talk to you later about her plans to kidnap Ms. Morgan?"

"No, and neither did Carl. All he told me was that Alysse wanted us to dress like delivery guys and pick up a package. I had no idea that the 'package' was a woman… that we were supposed to kidnap somebody. I would never have agreed to that."

"You're telling me that you didn't know before you went to the home where Ms. Morgan was staying that the plan was to take her?"

"I'm telling you the truth, I swear, Officer. All Carl said was that we were supposed to pick up a large package for Alysse. He said it was important and if I didn't help him he'd kick Sherry and me out of the house. I didn't know what else to do. We'd have been living on the streets and I couldn't do that to Sherry. Carl said he'd give me five hundred dollars to help him. I really needed the money to get my car fixed or get another one. I know he's done stuff against the law, drugs, and stuff, but I never thought he'd do anything this bad."

"When did you realize you had been duped into being party to a kidnapping?" Sloan asked.

Ricky shook his head. "Carl paid that kid to open the gate for us and we stopped at the lady's house. When Carl went to the door he told me to open the door of the van. I thought he was going to get the package, so I waited and then he and the lady came, and she looked inside. I was shocked when I saw him push her into the van and I didn't know what to do. He slammed the door shut, yelled at me to get in, and got in the driver's seat and took off. It all happened so fast."

Ricky had tears running down his face. "I just yelled at him, "What are you doing? This is wrong. I don't want any part of this."

"What did Carl say to that?"

Bitterly, Ricky said, "He just gave me that hateful grin of his and said that was too bad, because I was already part of it, and I would be as guilty as he was if we got caught. He said he would tell the police that Sherry and I were both involved in the whole thing."

"What do you think your sister will say about your participation in the kidnapping?" the Lieutenant asked.

"I have no idea," Ricky said. "I don't even know her anymore. My sister was really good to me when I was little. She took care of me more than my mother did because…because my parents drank a lot. I would never have thought that she could do something this bad. But then, I never thought she'd just leave without ever getting in touch either."

Lieutenant Sloan reached for the manilla envelope he had brought in with him.

"We found this on your sister's desk when we went to search her condo, Richard. It seems that in spite of your sister's actions toward Ms. Morgan she was concerned about how this situation would affect you and your girlfriend."

He pushed a handwritten sheet of paper across the table to Ricky. It was messy, but legible.

"Dear Ricky," it read. "I'm sorry I walked out of your life, even if I'm not sorry for leaving Carl and the folks. I just couldn't take the situation at our house any longer and felt like I would die if I had to stay there.

"I hope that the plans I made with Carl will not affect you and Sherry. I know I'm years late, but I want to help you now. Whatever happens to me, I want to give you a chance to make it out of that hell-hole and get out from under Carl's control. I'm really glad you have Sherry in your life. I can tell she's a good girl and she loves you. I only wish I had found someone to love me like that.

" I have written instructions to the supervisor of my business and to my lawyer. If you want the job they will put you to work at my company and train you from the ground up how to manage the warehouse and delivery part of the business. How quickly you will advance will be up to you. If you work hard, which I think you will, you can be successful.

"As for Sherry, she has the same opportunity. I have left instructions to pay her expenses to enroll in design school and for her to work on weekends at my business. When she completes her schooling she will have a full time position there. I see in her the same desires that I had to make things pretty and to get out of the trap of poverty. I made it out by fighting and scratching my way up, but I think Sherry is too gentle natured to do it my way. I have also left money for her to buy clothing to dress the way she will need to look to work in this type of business. My employees there are nice, and they will help her."

"If something happens that I'm not able to live in my condo for a while I'd like you and Sherry to live there. I just ask that you take good care of things, keep the utilities paid, etc. You won't have to pay rent so you should be able to do that. "

"I'd like it if you'd keep in touch. Let me know if you decide to work at my company…and for heaven's sake, marry that sweet girlfriend of yours! Believe me, when she gets all dressed up and confident in her abilities, she will be a knock-out, and you will have a lot of competition!

"I'm sorry for everything. I love you, little brother.

"Alysse"

Ricky's tears fell onto the letter as he looked at it in disbelief.

"I don't know what to say…whoever thought …? Officer, could I get permission to call Sherry and tell her? I'm worried about her, anyway. I don't think there's much food there in the house. Is there any way someone could check on her? "

Sloan smiled, "Well, if you think she'll be all right for the next hour and a half or so, I believe you'll be able to tell her yourself. Your brother admitted that he forced you into helping him, but really all you did was ride along and open a door. Ms. Morgan reported that she heard you trying to influence Carl to let her go and that you didn't support him in keeping her there.

"I have spoken with Judge McKinley and in light of your clean record and the testimonies from other involved parties, he has agreed to clear you of any charges regarding the kidnapping itself. There is one standing charge for not informing us, 'failure to report a crime,' but the judge is willing to have you report for four weekends of community service then appear before him again to clear everything."

Ricky looked as though a ton of weight had been lifted from him. "Wow, thanks, sir. I can't believe this."

Sloan walked to the door and knocked on it to let the guard know they were finished.

"They'll take you back to get out of that pretty, orange suit and give you your clothes back. I'll see you to the judge and then drive you home."

Within two hours Lieutenant Sloan pulled up in front of the run-down Milton home. He turned to Ricky and extended his hand. "I'm glad for you, Richard. Just make sure you turn up for your community service, get that done and put all this mess behind you. I wish you the best."

"Thank you so much, sir. You have been really nice to me through this. I assure you I will report on weekends to do my service. Will you be there at my last court hearing?"

"Probably so," Sloan said.

"Then I'll see you there. Thanks again for the ride." Ricky opened the car door as Sherry came running out of the house to meet him. Sloan couldn't help smiling as Ricky picked her up and swung her around, holding her close then kissing her.

As Sloan drove back to the station he thought back to when he'd walked into that bedroom with Alysse still holding the gun she had fired into her friend instead of Grace Morgan. Thankfully, Connally was going to be all right.

It seemed that once the police had reason to start looking into Carl Milton's activities there would be charges against him for several different offenses, so he wouldn't be getting out of jail for a while.

It seemed that Alysse Stratton's day in court would be delayed for a while at least. Her mental stability was in question and his superior officers had determined that she needed psychiatric evaluation before going any further. She had been transferred to a mental hospital in Houston.

At least things had turned out well for Richard and his girlfriend. It was a pleasant feeling to see a good ending in his job. Far too many situations in law enforcement didn't work out well. He found himself yawning as he headed home. At least, he'd sleep well tonight.

Chapter 32

Zach and Grace stopped at the front desk of the hospital to get the number of Radford Connally's room , then entered the elevator.

"I hope Radford feels up to visiting with us," Grace said as they stopped on the third floor.

"Yeah, we should probably keep it short," he replied as they located Room 310. He knocked lightly on the door.

"Come in," they heard Rad say weakly.

Zach opened the door then stood aside for Grace to enter before him. Rad's face was pale, and his eyes were red-rimmed, his chest completely wrapped in white bandages. Tubes on both sides of the bed were attached somewhere out of sight.

"Ms. Morgan…Pastor Clayton…I'm surprised to see you."

"How are you feeling?" Grace asked as they stood at his bedside.

"I'm not sure, to tell you the truth. They keep me pretty doped up. 'Want to pull up chairs?"

Zach moved the two available chairs, so they'd be nearer to Rad. "We wanted to come and thank you for risking your life to save Grace's, Rad."

"And I am so glad the doctors say you're going to be all right," Grace added.

Rad gave a small smile, "I'm kind of glad about that, too." He shifted in the bed. "But I owe you an apology. When Alysse asked me to do some private investigating on you I thought it was just another of her whims. But in a few weeks I could see that she was becoming completely irrational about getting you out of Zach's life, Grace. I was concerned, but I still didn't think she would go so far as to bring any bodily harm to you. I want you to know that I'm really sorry that I didn't see how dangerous she had become."

"Don't feel bad, you're not the only one that didn't see it coming," Zach said. "Her actions had become questionable, but like you, none of us saw the danger."

"I want you to know that I told Alysse a week ago I wasn't doing anything else to help her. Spending the day with you on that tour I saw what kind of people both of you are. I tried to get Alysse to drop whatever it was that she was planning against you, but it just made her angrier."

He paused to take a drink from the straw in a cup of water. "I deleted any pictures from my camera that she might have tried to use against you, and I didn't go back. I was listening to the news and when I saw the report that you had been kidnapped, I immediately thought that Alysse was behind it. I didn't know where she might have taken you, but...well...I prayed, like you said at the campfire that night, Pastor. I asked God to tell me where Alysse had taken Grace, and right after I prayed I just knew it was the old house where she grew up. I got there as quickly as I could. Carl didn't want to let me in, 'tried to keep me from sticking around, but I knew you were there, Grace. I was kind of surprised when he agreed to let me go back to the room where you were."

Grace's faced reddened. "I'm sorry that I hugged you when you said you would try to get me out of there. It gave Alysse the completely wrong idea and the next thing we knew she had the gun pointed at me!"

Rad gave a wry smile. "I really thought I was going to die there on that floor, but for some reason, I didn't mind...I wasn't afraid. I used to be scared of being killed in a car accident or something. I knew I wasn't ready to face God if that was what happens when you die. Something changed in me that night around that campfire. I still don't know exactly what it was, but somehow I knew things would be all right."

"Rad, God has a plan for your life, just as He does for Grace and me, and every other person on earth," Zach said. "That plan begins with our having a relationship with Him. The only problem there is that we are all sinners, and our sin is a barrier between us and God, who is holy.

"Fortunately for us, God wasn't content to be separated from us, so He sent His Son, Jesus, to earth in the form of mankind, to be a sacrifice, a payment, for our sins. So all we have to do is acknowledge that payment and let it totally wipe clean our sinful slates. Then we can step into that relationship that will bring more blessings than you ever dreamed. I believe God saw your willing heart that night on the beach and even if you hadn't gotten it all together, He was still protecting you."

"I want that relationship, Pastor; what do I do?" Rad asked.

"It's as simple as believing that Jesus is the Son of God , that He died for your sins, and then repenting of those things you've done wrong," Zach told him.

"Really, it's that easy?" Rad asked with hope in his eyes.

Grace and Zach both smiled and agreed, "Just that easy!"

As they drove home later Zach and Grace were rejoicing that they had a new brother in the Lord. And Rad had assured them that when he was out of the hospital and able to come, they had a new member of their church, too.

"I wonder if Rad would have found the Lord if I hadn't come here," Grace said.

"I guess we have to wait until we get to Heaven to ask the Lord, but it just reaffirms the scripture that tells us that God will turn to good what the enemy means for harm."

Grace agreed just as her phone rang. "Hi, Mom," she said, seeing it was her mother. "Where are you guys? San Antonio? Okay…Yes, we're ready for you…All right, we'll see you tomorrow afternoon. 'Love you."

She turned to Zach. "I guess you got the gist of that."

Zach grinned. "I think so, your parents are in San Antonio, they'll have a leisurely breakfast and be here with us in the early afternoon."

Grace reached up and kissed his cheek. "You're good."

He pulled her closer and said, "Have I told you today how much I love you?"

"Not in the past two hours," she answered.

" Hmm, I have some making up to do, don't I?"

"When we get home, Cowboy!" she said as she directed his attention back to the road.

"Hey, how are we doing on our list?" he asked. "I've got both my cattle and me moved back to the ranch, the mobile home got moved today, your parents are almost here, Jay and Lil just have a few more things to take to the mobile home, I have a crew lined up to clean up the area in the meadow. Oh, we have new bedroom furniture that's just waiting for us. What more is standing in the way of us getting married?"

"Lana called me this morning. She wanted to know if I would be all right with her gathering some ladies to put together a reception. She had already talked to Georgia, Susan, and Lil, and she wants to add Karen."

"Oh, my goodness! Those are the best cooks in the county…well, I don't know about Karen."

Grace laughed. "KK's talents lie in other areas, but she's a great helper and I know she wouldn't want to be left out."

"Then it sounds to me like we should be setting a date, huh? You know I need to call my dad and invite him and his wife. I hope it's not too short notice."

"I do, too. Do you have any idea when the gazebo will be ready ?" Grace asked.

"Sorry, I don't know. I've been so busy I haven't checked. I'll call Greg and see. He may need to build the bridge-walkways on site. I'll find out. "

Knowing that her next question could be sensitive, Grace gently asked, "What about your mother, Zach. Do you think she would come if we invited her?"

Zach sighed. "I wish she would, but I know that's not going to happen. I think she really meant it when she told me she didn't want me coming to see her anymore, to forget about her and go on with my life."

"We both know that's not possible. No matter what has happened, she's still your mother.'"

"That's exactly what I told her, but Grace, the whole situation with her is negative, frustrating, and unhappy. I don't want any of those things putting a damper on our happiness. I will keep on checking on her, even if it has to be through Joe, the bartender. He's a good guy and he'll let me know if something happens to her. I have finally realized there is nothing I can do to change her mind or her life, so I've placed her in God's hands."

"Okay, then let's do what we *can* do…plan our wedding."

"What's next? He asked.

"I think the ladies can have the reception plans together in a couple of weeks. I still need to find a dress, which hopefully won't take long. We will need to get a marriage license, I need to see a florist about flowers, and you still haven't talked to Jim about marrying us, have you?"

"No, I keep forgetting when I talk to him. Do we need to have people stand up with us?"

" I think we should have at least one person, a maid of honor for me, which will be Karen, and a best man for you." Grace said.

"Boy, every time we mark one item off the list we add two more. Where does it end?" Zach moaned.

"At the altar, Sweetie!," Grace told him.

Zach rolled his eyes at her and Grace laughed and punched him on the arm. "Buck up, Cowboy, it will be worth it all."

They had just pulled into the driveway at Karen's place. Zach killed the engine and took Grace in his arms.

"That I don't doubt, Beautiful," he said and kissed her like he'd been wanting to all day.

* * * * *

Zach woke early and looked around his bedroom. It felt so different. The new mattress was a bit firmer than the one he'd been sleeping on at the Sheridan's barn loft. The furniture was new and unfamiliar making the room smell "new." Kind of like when you buy a new car. He had never really noticed the barn smell in the loft, but now he was aware of the lack of it. Jim Sheridan kept a clean barn and Zach had helped keep it that way himself since he had horses there, too. He chuckled to himself, thinking what Grace would think of him missing the "Eau de Barn."

He was glad that he would get to meet Grace's parents today, but a little uneasy about how they would feel about staying at a ranch in Texas for a few weeks. They would probably be gracious about it, but he hoped they would enjoy being here and be convinced that their daughter hadn't really lost her mind planning to marry a cowboy she'd just met.

Zach missed Lil and Jay being there in the kitchen when he got up, and the fact that the coffee was always made when he got there, too. Should he get up early and have it going for Grace's parents? Would her mom prefer to do that? Who would cook? After all, they were his guests. It should be his responsibility to see to their meals. "Grace! I need you!" he yelled into the empty kitchen. "Zachary Clayton, you are being an absolute worry-wart!" he said out loud.

"For heaven's sake, stop talkin' to yourself and open this door!" he heard Jay yell from outside.

Red-faced, Zach opened the door to find Jay standing there with a plate of sausage biscuits balanced on two cups of coffee.

Holding the door Zach grinned and said, "So you heard me? See what happens when a man lives alone? No wonder God said it wasn't a good thing."

"Well, Lil felt sorry for you and sent me to rescue you this first morning. Here…he nodded toward the plate of biscuits for Zach to take them.

They sat at the table and immediately began to enjoy the delicious treats and coffee.

"You're not the only one feeling out of sync this mornin', son. Nothing in that mobile home feels like home yet. But it will. The most important thing is that Lil is there. It's a little different living with Crystal and Tom, but we'll be missin' them when they're gone overseas, so I'm not complainin'."

"Do we ever reach the point where God doesn't think he needs to shake things up a bit?" Zach mused.

"Well, if we do, it's past the age of seventy-five," Jay said, his eyes twinkling, "Cause I'm sure still being rattled."

"I remember my high school biology teacher telling us that 'Life means change.' I didn't really get that as a kid, but I can see the truth of it now. All living things are constantly changing, either for the good or the bad."

"At least with the Lord the changes are always for the good, even when it doesn't seem that way in the middle of the process."

"Grace and I saw that last night when we visited the man that took that bullet for Grace. We were able to lead him to the Lord, Jay. It was the neatest thing."

He reached for another sausage biscuit. "I sure hope Grace learns to make these. Her parents are supposed to be here this afternoon around two o'clock. I wonder if her mother bakes?"

Jay just rolled his eyes. "You and food! Okay, what do we need to do today to get this place ready for a wedding?"

They discussed plans for clearing better access to the meadow, and what Zach would like the landscape crew to do. "I've got a few phone calls to make after I help you feed the cattle." Zach said.

"Just do what you need to do. I've got the cattle feeding covered. You can catch up with me later." Jay stood and headed toward the door as Zach's phone rang.

"Zach here," he answered.

"Hey, Zach, this is Greg. I have your gazebo ready to bring out this afternoon if it's okay. I'm planning to install the walkways when I get there because I want to set them in concrete, so they'll be good and stable."

Zach laughed. "I was just telling Grace last night you might want to do that. Yeah, today works great. I need to do a little mowing in the spot where I think Grace will want it. Will a couple of hours work for you?"

"It does; I'll see you then."

Four hours later Zach straightened his back and leaned on the hoe he'd been using. He wiped the sweat from his brow as Jay looked up and paused, too.

"What's the matter, boy? A little manual labor gettin' to ya?"

Zach just looked at him, trying to come up with an answer, then grinned. "Okay, Pops, I can't deny it. I've become a wimp. Thank goodness I've got that crew coming in to do the rest of this."

He looked over toward the pond to see how Greg and his helper were coming along with the gazebo. It really did look pretty sitting near the pond. One of the small bridges was already in place and the men were installing the second.

Zach looked at his watch. It was almost four o'clock. He hadn't talked to Grace all day and he was missing that connection. Her parents should have arrived by now.

"Okay, Pops, let's call it a day. I need to check with Grace and see if her parents are here."

"Sounds good to me," Jay replied, gathering their tools.

As they rode back to the house Jay asked, "So you're gonna meet Grace's parents this evening?"

"I think so, we hadn't really talked about when that's happening, but I haven't seen my girl all day so I'm hoping we're on for dinner and a visit tonight."

"Are you nervous?"

"I have to admit, I am…a little," Zach said. "Texas ranch life has got to be so different from the LA metropolis."

"Well, I think they're going to find that this place beats the smog and the fast-paced life. They just may want to stay."

"Grace would love that, I'm sure, but I won't hold my breath," Zach said as he pulled up to the house. "Thanks for your help today, Pops. I appreciate it."

Jay just waved him off as he walked toward the mobile home. "See you tomorrow, son."

Zach headed for the shower as soon as he entered the house. His phone rang and he was glad to see it was Grace calling.

"Hey, Beautiful, I was just thinking about how much I missed seeing you today."

"I missed you, too, but when you didn't call I assumed you were busy."

"Yeah, I just walked into the house. Jay and I were cleaning up around the pond, and guess what's sitting there looking ready for a wedding."

"The gazebo?" Grace squealed.

"Yep, you're going to love it," Zach assured her.

"I want to see it!" Grace said. "My parents got in, so can we come out?"

"I was just going to call you and ask if we could get together for dinner this evening. Why don't you come as soon as you can, and we'll have a little time before it gets dark to show them the meadow. Then I'd like to take everyone to dinner."

"I know they'd like that, so we'll be out soon."

"I love you, and can't wait to see you," Zach said

"I love you, too, Babe. 'Bye," Grace told him.

After a quick shower Zach was dressed and ready when Grace and her parents arrived. Zach smiled when he saw Grace's mother. She looked like an older version of Grace with the same sweet air about her. Her dad was a handsome man, too, with silver gray hair and the air of a man comfortable in his own skin. He reached out to shake Zach's hand.

"I'm Bill," he said. "'Father of this little girl." Smiling, he nodded toward Grace.

Grace gave him an affectionate scowl, "Da-ad!" Moving to Zach's side, she nodded toward her mother. "Zach, this is my mother, Sarah."

Zach wasn't sure how to greet her, but Sarah made the decision for him. Reaching out to hug him, she said, "I feel as though we've already met, Zach; Grace has told me so much about you."

"And you still hugged me?" Zach teased.

They all laughed. "Did Grace tell you we're going to the meadow?" he asked. "I don't mean to hurry you, but we don't have long before the sun sets. We'll need to go in my truck, because as Grace pointed out to me, there's no road going that way…yet!"

A few minutes later Zach stopped the truck at the rise as he had when he showed the meadow to Grace the first time. Now, the beautifully designed gazebo shone in white elegance in the dimming light. The walking bridges curved gracefully over the water up to the gazebo itself and the overall effect was breathtaking.

"Oh, Zach!" Grace said. "It's absolutely lovely. I knew it would be pretty, but this is beyond words. The walkways coming out over the water are simply perfect."

"Thank you, Ma'am," Zach said proudly. "That was my idea. But Greg and his crew did an amazing job. 'Ready to go on down to the pond?"

Zach had to agree he needed to build a road for at least this last section of ground since it was pretty rough even in the four wheeled drive truck.

As they walked around the pond Grace's parents asked questions about their dreams and plans for the meadow. Since Grace had already shared the vision in general with them, they had really insightful comments and questions that impressed Zach.

Just before the sun retreated they left the meadow and went to Sam's restaurant because Grace insisted her parents' first meal in Friendswood should be Gulf Coast Shrimp. The conversation flowed easily, and Zach found himself completely at ease with Bill and Sarah Morgan. Since they were staying at his house, they went back to the ranch. The men carried their bags inside, and Grace led them to the room they'd be using.

"Do we need to take you back to your place," Bill asked Grace.

"Just stay and make yourself at home," Zach insisted. "I'll take Grace back to Karen's and be back later."

Zach drove just far enough to be out of sight of the house then stopped the truck and took Grace into his arms.

"I really like your folks, but I couldn't wait to get you alone," he admitted. "This is the first time I haven't seen you all day in…I think since we first met."

"I know, hon. I think we should set the date."

"Well, your parents are here, and the gazebo is ready, what about tomorrow?" Zach teased.

"Not quite that soon, but how about in two weeks?"

"That long?" he groaned

"I know, but maybe this will make it better," Grace said cuddling closer and kissing him with all her heart.

Bill and Sarah Morgan got their things unpacked and settled in their bedroom then came back to the living room. They sat quietly, content with the meeting with their daughter's future husband.

"There's a spirit of peace in this house, Sarah," Bill said.

Sarah nodded. "What a difference to Grace's home with Damien," she agreed. "I think she's going to be very happy in her marriage to Zach. They are both obviously crazy about each other."

Bill nodded. "Who would have thought just weeks ago that our little girl would be so happy…and with a man who is perfect for her?"

"And a cowboy at that!" They both laughed heartily.

"Well, we saw the meadow; what do you think?"

Sarah nodded, "I can see their dream fulfilled there, Bill. The cabins, the meeting and dining halls, couples renewing their vows and others marrying for the first time."

"Can you see us playing a part in the kids' dream?"

"I can, hon, and I don't think I've felt so excited about anything in years."

Bill chuckled. "We were really getting to be old sticks-in-the-mud, weren't we?"

Sarah laughed too. "Yes, but I've got a feeling that soon we're going to be too busy to get stuck anywhere!"

* * * * *

Zach woke up to the smell of bacon frying. Used to Lil cooking early, at first it seemed normal. Then with a start he remembered that Lil was no longer the chef in his kitchen. It must be Grace's mom, Sarah. Still, he should be in there trying to help. He dressed quickly and walked down the hall toward the kitchen. He was surprised to see Bill, not Sarah, wearing an apron and seemingly at ease with the skillets and bowls he had spread around.

"Wow, …uh, 'morning, Bill." Zach stuttered.

Bill chuckled. "I get that you didn't expect me to be the cook."

"Yeah, I guess." Zach really didn't know what to say.

"When I retired I still woke up early, but Sarah considered it her time in life to sleep later since I didn't have to be at work," Bill said. "So I decided to try my hand at cooking breakfast and found I really enjoy it. So that works well for both of us."

Zach frowned. "Do you think Grace will expect me to cook for her?"

"Well, I don't know," Bill said. Then he smiled. "There's one way to get out of that…just offer to cook for her once and make a real mess of it. She probably won't let you do it again."

Zach laughed. "I'll remember that." He poured himself a cup of coffee. "I can keep myself from starving, but that's about it. Please, you and Sarah are welcome to take over the kitchen. I wouldn't have to fake cooking up a mess, so you don't want me to do it."

His phone rang. "It's Grace," he said. "Good morning, Love. Isn't this a little early for you?"

"Yes, but Karen wanted to see Mom and Dad before she goes to the university, so I'll ride with her. I want to see if Mom will go wedding dress shopping with me today."

"Aha, one more thing to cross off our list," Zach said. "Why don't you gals come for breakfast…your dad's cooking."

"What? My Dad's cooking?"

"You didn't know your dad could cook?" Zach asked, grinning at Bill.

Speaking loudly enough for Grace to hear him, Bill said, "See, old dogs *can* learn new tricks."

"I've got to see this," Grace said. "We'll be there."

"I'd better add more bacon," Bill said. He smiled. "It will be like old times having Karen at the table. She spent many spring breaks and holidays with us in the college years. She's like a second daughter to Sarah and me."

"She's a great gal," Zach said. "Grace is blessed to have her for a friend. And if she hadn't come here to stay with Karen I wouldn't have met her."

"Well, the Lord sure worked that out, didn't he?" Grace's mom said as she came into the kitchen. "Good morning, guys." She walked over to Bill and gave him a quick kiss.

Bill slipped his arm around her while stirring gravy with the other. "Good morning, Sunshine. I thought you were going to sleep in."

"Well, the breakfast you're cooking smelled too good to stay in the bed."

"I was about to come and tell you that Karen's bringing Grace over, so we'll get to see her," Bill said

"I'm so glad," Sarah said. "I was disappointed that we didn't get to connect with her yesterday. I guess she's pretty busy as a department head at the college."

" Would you like to set the table, hon? The girls will be eating, too," Bill told her.

"I should have thought of that," Zach said sheepishly. "I just don't have these kitchen skills down yet."

Sarah patted his shoulder. "Just drink your coffee, son. You have plenty to do running a ranch. Don't worry about this…" She waved to Bill at the stove and the rest of the room. "Your kitchen crew has arrived."

Zach gave a sigh of relief. "You have no idea how glad I am to hear that. Believe me! Just make yourself at home."

The sound of a car arriving brought him to his feet. Trying not to act like an eager teenager, he walked outside to open the car door for Grace. His heart beat faster as he saw her welcoming smile. How he loved that! He hugged her and held her close.

"You look beautiful this morning," he whispered in her ear.

"Okay, lovebirds, I'm going in to see Grace's parents," Karen called and started walking toward the back door.

Zach hadn't shaved yet and the dark stubble made him look even more handsome to Grace. She reached up to stroke his cheek. "I never knew I needed a cowboy, but I'm sure glad the Lord said he'd give us what we need even before we ask!"

Zach chuckled. "And I surely never would have asked for a "California girl."

Playfully Grace tossed her hair and gave him a flirtatious look. "You wouldn't have asked for this?" She struck a pose and started singing the lyrics to the song, "California Girl."

Zach couldn't help laughing as he hugged her again. "We're going to be late for breakfast if we don't get in there. Wait 'til you see the feast your dad has cooked up."

Zach could see the mutual love between Karen and Grace's parents as they ate and bantered back and forth. Bill and Sarah revealed a few of the girls' antics that they thought had remained a secret, so it was humorous to see their reactions when the Morgan's told them they had known all along.

"I hate to leave, but duty calls," Karen said. "Grace, I'll meet you at the bridal shop a little after twelve."

"Okay, what's on our schedule for the day, Zach?" Bill asked. "I want to help in any way I can. I even bought a pair of jeans for the first time since I was a kid."

"Really, Dad?" Grace asked. "You are full of surprises today!"

" I bought some, too," Sarah told her. "We want to experience this ranch life to the fullest."

"We haven't gotten the boots and cowboy hats yet. I don't even know where we'd have bought them in LA!" Bill said.

"Don't worry," Zach said, "They're readily available around here, but as for what to do today. I think I need to install a partial roadway to the wedding site. The first part is just across flat pasture and won't be rough or too difficult for four wheel drive vehicles. But maybe you can help me determine the best place to put the road coming into the meadow.

"I never thought to tell you, Zach, but Dad retired as an engineer. He's great at that kind of thing," Grace said.

Zach stood and extended his hand to Bill. "That is the Lord answering our prayer to send us the people we need to get Love Meadow Retreat Center going. I'll find you a hat, though, there's a reason we wear them in this hot Texas sun."

"Grace and I can clean up here, fellows, then I'm taking her wedding dress shopping. Who's going to have the most fun? " Sarah said with a mischievous smile.

"To each his own, Darlin'," Bill imitated a Texas drawl, "I would definitely not call dress shopping fun."

"No comment," Zach chimed in. "But you have fun, love." Turning to Bill he said, "Let's go build a road."

When Grace and Sarah walked out to the car Lil was tossing feed to the chickens. She waved and headed toward them. "I just have to come and meet your mother, Grace."

Grace gave her a hug, "I meant to introduce you and Jay sooner, but we've been so busy since she and Dad got in. Mom, this is Lil. She and her husband, Jay, are the wonderful couple who have been taking care of Zach's ranch, and honestly, Zach, too!"

Lil reached out to hug Sarah. "I'm so glad that you were able to come. Zach is like a son to us and Grace has become like one of ours now, too."

"How are you doing in the mobile home?" Grace asked her. "Is it going to work out for you?"

"It's a bit different, just remembering what drawer or cabinet I've put my tools in. But it's going to be fine. In fact, I wanted to ask if I could cook supper for all of you this evening. I know you have a lot to do and I'd love to take that task off you if you'll let me."

"That is so sweet of you, Lil. Of course you can cook for us." She turned to her mother. "Mom, you, and Dad are in for a treat. This lady is a gourmet ranch cook!"

Sarah smiled. "Grace has told me about your cooking, and we will be delighted to get to indulge this evening."

"Will about six o'clock be all right?" Lil asked.

"I think that should be fine," Grace told her. "And please tell Crystal and Tom they are welcome, too. We're eager to hear more about their plans to go to the mission field."

"They love to talk about that, their hearts are so full of this new direction the Lord is leading them. I'll tell them they're invited."

"Okay, we're heading for the bridal shop to find our dresses for the wedding, so we'll see you this evening," Grace said.

Dinner that evening was like a holiday family gathering. They had spread Lil's wonderful meal out on the large dining room table and the conversation flowed as Crystal and Tom shared about their mission vision.

The guys talked road business. After tending to the stock Jay had joined Bill and Zach at the meadow and worked with them to lay out a section of roadway that would make the meadow accessible. Their plans would also provide a lovely view as drivers approached the meadow. Karen had met Grace and Sarah at the bridal shop on her lunch hour and all three ladies had found the perfect dresses.

"I've been meeting with Susan, Lana, and Georgia about the reception and we've pretty much got everything planned. I think you're going to love it, Grace. And the food Georgia has been bringing for us to sample and choose from has all been so delicious. I don't know how we can come up with one simple menu," Karen said. "I know you're busy, Gracie Lou, but I think you and Zach need to make the final decision."

Lil and Grace looked at each other and laughed. "Grace can do that," Lil said, and both of them together chimed, "Zach won't care."

"Okay, I'll get with Georgia on that," Grace said. "Really, to Zach, food is food. All good!"

"Grace, have you thought about having any children in the wedding…a ring bearer or flower girl?" Karen asked.

Grace's eyes widened. "You know I haven't thought of that at all. I guess because I know so few little ones here…just Lana and Bruce's boys. I don't know any little girls."

Karen smiled, "Well, when Lana and Bruce told the boys that you were getting married, the middle son, Max, immediately said he wanted to be the one that carried the rings. I guess they had been to a wedding in their family recently and the boys were really impressed with the children being in such an important event. Then their youngest, Carson, remembered the little flower girl that tossed the rose petals and he thought that was really neat. Lana said he wants to be a 'flower boy.'She didn't want to mention this to you in case you hadn't planned for children in the wedding. She isn't aware I'm telling you, but I thought you'd like to know. Those boys are so crazy about Zach and you, too."

"I love the idea," Grace said. "And who says only girls can toss flower petals. I'm sure Zach would like it; I'll give Lana a call. I think we've decided to do this on Saturday, two weeks from now. Zach finally thought to ask Jim Sheridan to marry us, and that works for him."

"Did you know Zach asked Jay to be his best man?" Lil asked.

"No, I didn't but that's great."

"Jay protested at first, mostly because he'd have to get dressed up," Lil said, "But Zach told him that Jim can't be best man and perform the ceremony, too."

"And I know how much Jay means to him," Grace said.

"I was thinking about how we're going to keep you out of sight of everyone until you start walking…well, I would normally say, 'down the aisle,' but I guess it's 'up the walkway' this time," Karen said. " I checked with the company that you're getting the chairs from and they have pretty, small, white tents they rent. How about getting one of those, Grace?"

"I hadn't thought about that, KK, but it's a good idea. You're a great maid of honor!"

A few more wedding details and road talk later, the guests began to depart, the kitchen was all cleaned up and only Karen, Zach and Grace were left with her parents.

"I know it's been a busy day, guys," Bill said, "but Sarah and I would like to talk to you for a few minutes, if that's okay."

"Sure, Bill," Zach said. "Want to sit at the table?"

Sarah joined Bill on one side, and Zach and Grace sat across from them with Karen on the end.

Bill slipped his arm around Sarah's shoulders and smiled. "Would you like to start, hon?"

Sarah nodded and looked at Zach and Grace. "Needless to say, as Grace's parents we were as devastated as she was at the outcome of her marriage to Damien. Until you become parents, you can't know how painful it is to see your child hurting so badly and not be able to do a single thing to make it better." She smiled.

"But on the opposite side of that, nothing makes parents happier than to see their children loving and being loved and cared for, to know they are walking in a Divine plan that will only bring good to them and to others." She looked to Bill and nodded.

"About a year ago," he said. "Sarah and I came to the realization that we were following the path of most of our friends who had retired and were just 'taking it easy,' thinking about how to entertain ourselves in our boring old age. But as Christians, who are supposed to be thinking about how we can be a blessing to others, we became convicted of our selfishness and for slipping into that mindset that our lives were basically over until we die and our kids bury us. We have been blessed to still be in good health, so we began to pray about what the Lord has for us in this new season of our lives."

Sarah spoke again. "We began to evaluate…I guess you could say…the tools we had to work with, what we could use from our life experiences. We began to hear about young couples in our church who were struggling in their marriages. They face so many challenges in our fast-paced world today. God gave us wonderful counselors in the early years of our marriage. My parents and Bill's, too, had poured wisdom into our lives. They never criticized our mates or got more involved than they should, but their little comments at times gently guided us and we worked out our own way of making marriage work.

"We didn't say anything to anyone, but last year we began to prepare for a ministry to couples. We signed up for a course at a Christian college and learned even more ways to help those who are struggling in their marriages.

"When you told us of the vision God has given you for Love Meadow, Grace," Bill said, "your mom and I both immediately felt this was the direction that the Lord has for us. When you said that you were believing for an older couple to live there at the meadow and help in the ministry to the couples that come…"

"We knew that couple is us," Sarah finished.

Bill nodded. "If it witnesses in your hearts that this is God's plan for your ministry as well, we'd like to build the house that we'll be living in. We'll pay for it entirely, including getting the utilities run to the area. We'd just like to feel that we'll be able to live there as long as we need to, then it will be deeded to your ministry."

He gave Sarah a squeeze then looked at Zach and Grace. "So what do you think? Are you ready to have us in your hair for the foreseeable future?"

Both Zach and Grace had tears in their eyes. "Excuse me," Zach said, "but I'm speechless. The vision just came to us and yet, God is already bringing it to pass. This is huge! Not only to have a wonderful, godly couple to join with us, but to have the home for them to be built without expense to the ministry…I can only say, "Yes!"

"Mom and Dad," Grace said, "There's no couple better that God could have sent to fill this position. I lived with you, I know how you treated each other, how you always put God at the center of your marriage and our family. All I can say is, 'thank you.' And I am absolutely thrilled to have you this close."

Bill looked at Sarah, "Well, hon, I guess we can buy those boots and hats now."

"We're going to get you riding horses, too," Zach said.

"That sounds like fun," Bill said, and Sarah agreed.

"What about your house in California?" Grace asked.

Both Bill and Sarah smiled. "We've been clearing out the years of clutter," she said, "and Dad's been doing the little repairs that make it sale ready. We've already got it listed with a realtor; she's just waiting for our final go-ahead to put it on the market. She's has several clients waiting for homes now, so it will likely sell immediately."

Bill added, "As you know, Grace, the house was paid off years ago, so when we sell, it will all be profit. The way prices have escalated through the years we'll be able to live on that and my retirement very well. So we don't expect any kind of salary from the ministry. In fact," he stopped and pulled a folded check from his shirt pocket, "we want to give you our first gift for the Love Meadow ministry. I think this should cover most of the cost of that roadwork we planned today."

He handed the check to Zach who unfolded it and showed it to Grace. "Five thousand dollars!" she said, "Oh Dad, Mom, thank you!"

She stood and went to them, hugging them both at once. Zach was right behind her.

"Sarah, Bill," he said, "As wonderful as this is, the money and your wanting to become part of this ministry, it's so much more than that. When God starts bringing it to pass it's confirmation that we're on the right track. Just think, God was preparing you for this before Grace and I even met." He chuckled, "Even when both of us were still mad at Him for our first marriages not working out."

"It's really a lesson in trust, isn't it?" Karen said, "to keep believing in the hard season that He's still in control and is working things for our good."

"It certainly is," Bill said.

"I hate to break this up," Grace said, "but KK has to be up early in the morning, so we'd better head for her place."

"Yeah," Bill said with a yawn. "If I'm going to cook breakfast again I'd better get to bed."

Zach quickly grabbed him by the arm and pulled him toward the hallway. "Then go, Bill! Breakfast is important!"

They all laughed as they went their ways. Zach walked Grace out to Karen's car and held her in his arms. "Just two more weeks, my beautiful Grace." He gave her a quick kiss then told Karen goodbye, too. This time he was the one watching the tail lights of the car as Grace left.

"Just two weeks, Zach," he said to himself.

He turned to re-enter the house and his phone rang.

"Hey, Dad," he said when he saw the caller ID. "I was just about to call you."

"Well, I guess I beat you to it, didn't I?" His dad chuckled. "What's going on in Texas?"

"I can't speak for the whole state, but things have been hopping here at the ranch." Zach told him.

"Oh, you're living back at the ranch?" the senior Clayton asked.

"I've been back for about a week, Dad, but I'll be here permanently now."

I'm really glad to hear that, Son. Are things looking up for you?"

Zach smiled. "You could definitely say that."

"Well, tell me about it…Oh, does this have anything to do with that young lady from California you mentioned to me?"

"Everything, Dad. We're getting married in two weeks. I was going to call you to invite you to the wedding."

Walter Clayton paused a minute, "Zach, this is such wonderful news. I don't know how to say this…I was calling to tell you that Vera and I would be gone for at least a month. Her youngest daughter is having a very difficult pregnancy. She's in the hospital right now but will be coming home when Vera can be with her. The baby's not due for another month, and she has to be bedridden until it's born. We're just praying there won't be any more complications before then. We're really not sure when we'll be able to come back to California."

"I'm sorry to hear that Dad. Grace and I will be praying for the daughter and the baby."

"Well, while you're praying you could include Vera and me. Her kids live on a farm in Oregon, and there are animals and some crops that need tending. Her husband was called away in the National Guard, so they are desperate for help. We're just hoping that he'll get to come home when the baby's born."

"That's really generous of you and Vera to step into that big a situation, Dad. We will definitely be praying for all of you. I would love to have you here for my wedding and to meet this wonderful woman God has sent to me, but I can see you are needed far more in Oregon."

"So you're not upset with me, then? I'd really like to be there."

Zach's eyes misted with tears. "Dad, you have been there for me all of my life. Believe me, you've got credit in your account! I don't know a man on earth with a bigger heart than you, so give my regards to Vera and keep us updated on the situation."

"Thank you for understanding, Son. I love you."

"I love you , too, Dad."

Zach put his phone in his pocket and raised both hands to the heavens. The night sky was clear, and the stars shone brightly. His heart was full…full of love for Grace and full of her love for him. Already loving his new in-laws and the way they had blessed him and Grace. Thrilled that others had caught the vision and would be standing with them to see it fulfilled. So grateful for the unwavering love his father had shown him all of his life. He would have been pleased to have his father here when he married Grace, but he was even more pleased that Walter Clayton was a man willing to go the limit to help others in need.

What a legacy! One worth more than all the silver and gold a person could acquire. "Lord, if you bless Grace and me with children I want to be able to say that I have passed that same godly legacy to them,“ Zach prayed.

Then he prayed for Vera's daughter and for the baby in her womb that God had already destined for His purposes, for the husband who was distraught at having to be away when his family needed him, and for Vera and Walter to have the strength and wisdom they would need.

Bill and Sarah had already retired when he entered the house and suddenly he felt the busy day catching up with him, too. As he turned back the new comforter and bed linens and lay on his bed, he thought of Grace and her smiling face. "Zach Clayton, you are one blessed man," he whispered as he drifted to sleep.

CHAPTER 33

The next two weeks passed quickly as everyone was busy with wedding preparations for a venue that had never hosted a wedding. Somehow, Bill and Zach had managed to get electricity to the site which would accommodate the sound system and any lighting they might need.

When Sasha was still in good health she had made certain that Covenant Cowboy Church was well equipped with everything used to host nice events, so Lana and Susan had chosen everything they needed from the church and had the guys deliver it on Friday. Due to the ever-present concern regarding rain showers in South Texas they left as much as possible to be completed on Saturday.

People began to arrive in the early afternoon to put the last of the wedding decorations in place, driving up the newly built road which made it so much easier to reach the meadow.

Rows of white folding chairs encircled the side of the pond opposite the gleaming gazebo with its gracefully bridged walkways. The florist crew was setting in place the pale pink and ivory floral arrangements. Even real pink and white water lilies floated in the pond.

A white Bride's tent stood waiting on the left side, surrounded by large potted palms provided by the landscaper for free. A ten-foot swath around the pond had been cleared for the chairs, but the rest of the meadow remained in its natural glory with the many Texas wild flowers and their variant colors.

The temporary sound booth had been set up by the church tech team but was almost hidden by decorative foliage. Already, instrumental classic love songs were playing and filling the meadow with ambiance as the ladies put the final touches on the bride and groom's table. Silver chafing dishes were lined up on the food table, just waiting to be filled. A round table, beautifully decorated with the pink and ivory roses would bear the wedding cake which would be the last thing set up due to the warm weather.

Lana and Bruce Caldwell and their boys pulled into the parking area. "All right, boys, this is a 'be-on-your-best-behavior" day. No running, and no rough-housing," Lana said.

"You can walk around and look, but don't touch anything," Bruce told them. "And don't go onto the little bridges or the gazebo, hear me?"

Max and Carson looked adorable, identically dressed in their long sleeved white shirts, new jeans, western boots, and cowboy hats.

"But Da-ad," Carson said in alarm. "I'm supposed to throw those flower things on the bridge for Ms. Grace."

Max joined in, equally concerned, "And I'm supposed to carry the rings up there for Pastor Jim to give to Ms. Grace and Pastor Zach."

Bruce looked at Lana, who was laughing at him. ""Guess you need to clarify those instructions."

Bruce knelt down to the children's level. "Okay, I didn't mean you can't throw the flowers and produce the rings when it's time. I just meant that you're not supposed to be up there before the wedding. Okay?"

"Okay, Dad," they said in unison.

The Sheridan's drove up in their big truck just then and the boys headed their direction.

"Hey, David, come play with us."

The older Caldwell son Robbie, grinned at David and exchanged a fist bump with his best friend. Nodding toward his younger brothers he said, "They're not supposed to be playing. Both of them are in the wedding and they need to stay presentable."

Susan Sheridan gave Lana a hug then turned to the boys. "Well, I think it would be a good thing if you two older boys helped them do that while we adults are getting things ready, okay?"

"Yeah, we'll babysit," Robbie said.

David reached out a hand to Max. "Come on, Max, you're my buddy today."

"I can help watch them, too," Danette Sheridan said.

"You can watch me," Carson squealed, holding his arms up. He had idolized Danette since he was a toddler.

"Okay, Carson," she said, giving him a hug. "Let's go see what we can find."

As the children walked away, Bruce smiled after them. ""Got some good kids there, don't we?"

"Yeah, buddy, just chips off the ole' blocks," Jim said.

Susan patted him on the shoulder. "Okay, Ole Blocks, if you still have it in you, we need some help carrying things."

Karen, Georgia, and Lil were already at work and welcomed the Sheridan's and Caldwell's.

"What's the plan for Grace to get to the bridal tent without Zach seeing her?" Lana asked.

"Her parents are bringing her from my house, "Karen said. "When she's inside the tent someone will call Zach and tell him he can come on up."

"If I know Zach, he's pacing the floor right now," Lil said as she arranged silverware. I'm glad Jay's with him. I told him to keep Zach there until he got the call."

Karen looked at her watch, then around the meadow. "Where is the photographer? He's supposed to be here by now."

She turned to Bruce, "Grace's mom will be in the Bride's tent with us until just before the wedding begins and you can meet her there and walk her to her seat on the front row of chairs on the right."

Bruce nodded, "Got it!"

Checking her list, Karen looked to Jim. "You can be standing off to the right, Jim, with Zach and Jay. When Mrs. Morgan is seated you guys can come up the walkway to the gazebo. Jim, you'll take your place in the center and Zach and Jay will stand on the lower level facing the walkway.

She continued with her directions and as she finished, the Morgan's car drove into the meadow with the photographer just behind.

"Okay, guys, that's my cue to go," she said. "The bride has arrived!"

Grace couldn't refrain from looking toward Zach's house as they passed it, knowing he would be there anticipating this wedding as much as she was. She hadn't seen the meadow since all the decorations had been put in place and she gasped in awe when they arrived. Not only was it beautiful, but her friends were there, all new acquaintances who had so quickly found places in her heart.

"Grace, honey, this is absolutely lovely," Sarah Morgan said. "And the feeling is just as wonderful."

"I know, Mom. I think that was what touched Zach and me the most. We could feel God's love and His peace in this little meadow that day He revealed His plan for this place. I'm so glad we're able to be married here."

Bill Morgan's cell phone rang just as they drove up to the white tent. He answered it, then happily said, "You're here? Oh Son, Grace will be delighted. We all are!...All right. I'll drive up and meet you at the house."

"Was that Josh, Dad?" Grace asked in surprise. Her brother had told her he wouldn't be able to attend the wedding due to a long-scheduled work conference.

"Yes, it was! He caught a cab from the airport so he's on his way. He said he'd give us the details later."

Sarah was fighting back tears at the thought of her complete family being together for this occasion. "I am so happy!"

"We can start a little late if we have to," Grace said, thrilled that her only sibling would be here after all.

"Okay, let's get you in that tent, sweetie," her dad said.

Karen appeared at the car door and helped lift Grace's long gown until they were inside the tent. Even the floor had been fitted with white carpet, and Karen had furnished it with everything she thought Grace might possibly want or need in the short time she'd be there.

Karen stood behind her, both looking into the mirror. "You were a beautiful bride for your first wedding, Gracie-Lou, but this time you are stunning!"

Grace turned to face her. "This time is real, KK. That may sound strange, but my wedding with Damien was like a show that had to meet his standards for proving to some unknown persons that he was successful. I wish I had been able to see that then."

"Well, that's behind you and a wonderful future with Zach is ahead," Karen said. She chuckled. "And just think, it all came down to which type of entertainment I decided to book when you came here!"

"Was that when you went on Zach's tour of Galveston?" Sarah asked.

"Yes," Grace said. "Neither Zach nor I expected to see each other again after meeting on the plane. But obviously, God had other plans."

"And what a plan that has become," Sarah said, "even including your dad and I."

"Oh, KK, I forgot to tell you, Josh is on his way here from the airport!" Grace said.

"Really? That's wonderful," Karen said. "What happened that he was able to come?"

"We don't know yet; he called from the cab and said he'd tell us later. Dad's gone up to the house to meet him when he arrives."

With a glance at her watch, Karen shook her head. "He's cutting it close, but it's great that he got to make it. I can't think when I saw him last. Whenever it was he was still a kid wanting to tag along with us!"

Grace laughed, remembering how irritated they were when her younger brother insisted on going places with them.

Jay sat relaxed at the kitchen table with a cup of coffee while Zach paced the floor. "What are you so nervous about, boy? You're just getting' married."

"I'm not nervous about that…I guess I'm just excited. I hate being up here when everyone else is there at the meadow," Zach answered.

"'Everyone else being Grace, right?" Jay said with a twinkle in his eyes.

Sheepishly, Zach answered, "I guess so."

When a car pulled into the drive, he hurried to the door and looked outside. "Who would be coming by cab?" he asked with a frown.

The young man taking his bags from the cab was a stranger to Zach. He was tall with dark, wavy hair and handsome in a familiar way. He paid the driver and looked around as the cab headed back out the driveway. Just then Bill Morgan drove up and pulled to a stop. He quickly walked toward the young man as the stranger began striding toward him. The two embraced warmly and then Bill waved toward the house.

Zach stepped out to meet them as Jay watched from the door.

"Zach," Bill called. "Come and meet Grace's brother. He was able to make it after all! This is my son, Josh."

Zach was delighted to meet the young man who would be his brother-in-law in less than an hour. "Josh, I'm Zach Clayton," he said, reaching out to shake his hand. "It's wonderful to have you. I know Grace will be thrilled. Does she know you're here yet?"

"Yes," Bill said, "Josh called just as we got her to the Bride's tent."

"I'm sure the cabbie was speeding, but fortunately, he didn't get stopped. I told him to get me here as soon as he could," Josh said.

"Well, we still have about…" Bill looked at his watch, " twelve minutes. Do you need to freshen up or change clothes ?

"If I could have just a minute I can be ready to go," Josh said. "I wore dress clothes so I could slip right in, but I'd love to wash off the travel grime."

"This way, then," Zach said leading Josh to his bathroom. "This is my best man, Jay," he told Josh as they hurried by the older gentleman on their way.

"You and Jay can go ahead to the meadow if you like, Zach, " Bill told him. " Josh and I will be right behind you."

Jay laughed. "He's been itchin' to hear those words, Bill, almost wearin' a hole in that kitchen floor."

"Well, get on down there, Son," Bill told him.

"Okay, Gracie-Lou, let's get your headpiece on," Karen said. "Your dad was going to tell Zach he can come now, even if Josh needs a few minutes to freshen up."

"Okay, Grace said with excitement in her eyes. "This couldn't be more perfect, having all my family here."

"The hairdresser certainly did your hair beautifully," Sarah said.

"Yes, Lana recommended her to me," Grace said. "I'm sure I'll use her again."

The stylish updo swept part of Grace's hair into large defined curls as the rest of her hair fell in soft waves onto her shoulders. It was perfectly styled to accommodate the headpiece of pink satin roses anchoring a mid-length veil of barely pink illusion that fell softly down her back. Grace wore the diamond and pearl earrings that had been a gift from her Grandmother Morgan when she graduated from college.

"Grace?" They heard Bruce speaking outside the door of the tent.

"Yes, Bruce?" She answered.

"I just wanted to let you know that Zach and Jay are onsite now and your dad and brother will be here in just a couple of minutes."

"Thanks, Bruce, " Grace answered, then Karen said. "We'll give them a minute for Josh to say hello to his mom and Grace when they get here, and then we should be ready to start."

" Okay, I'll be back to escort your mom to her seat," he said.

"Knock, Knock, Ladies, Can we come in?" they heard Bill Morgan ask.

Sarah pulled back the tent flap with a huge smile for her only son. "Get in here, you!" she cried with her arms open to hug him.

Grace was next in line. "Wow, Sis, you look absolutely gorgeous! " Josh told her.

Grace hugged him tightly. "I'm so glad you could come, Bubba!"

Josh laughed and pulled back. "Nobody's called me that in years.!"

Then he looked to Karen who was standing there as though starstruck. "Karen, come here. I haven't seen you in ages. You're still as beautiful as ever." He pulled her into a warm hug. When they parted she couldn't take her eyes away.

"I..I don't think I would have recognized you on the street, Josh." She blushed. " I guess I was expecting you to still look like you did the last time I saw you."

Josh laughed. "Well, thankfully that gangly kid is gone!"

Bill noted the time and reminded them that he had a daughter to escort to get married. He pulled back the tent flap to see Bruce waiting for Sarah. "Come, love,"

"All right, I'm ready. Josh, you can follow behind us." She gave Grace one last hug and kiss on the cheek. "I'm so happy for you, Dear." Then looking almost as lovely as her daughter, she stepped out and took Bruce by the arm.

The friends who had come to celebrate with Grace and Zach were already seated when Bruce led Sarah to her chair. He then joined Lana as Josh sat next to his mother.

The music paused then began playing a different, sweet melody. Jim Sheridan took his place in the center of the gazebo and Zach and Jay stood side by side on the right.

"Oh, my!" Lil whispered , "Don't my fellows look handsome! I haven't seen Jay that spivied up in years."

Everyone around her laughed softly and agreed that the men did indeed look handsome.

Then a happy "Ohhh," swept over the group as Max in his new western outfit began to walk over the small bridge, carefully holding the ring pillow as though it was a treasure that might break. He then went to stand by Jay, receiving a well-done pat from Zach on the way.

Another exclamation came when little Carson stepped onto the bridge with his basket of rose petals. Apparently proud of his assignment he looked to his parents, grinned, and waved before beginning to toss his cargo with abandonment to the laughter of the crowd. He also got a high five from Zach as he went to stand beside his brother.

Karen came next, lovely in her pale sage green gown that complimented her auburn hair.

Josh leaned in toward his mother and whispered. "She really is beautiful."

Then the music quieted before the wedding march began, a recorded symphonic rendition that filled the meadow as Grace and her dad stepped from the tent. Everyone stood for the bride as Bill escorted her to the gazebo, and the look on Zach's face left no doubt that his heart was filled with love for Grace. "A vision in pale pink," he thought as he watched her walk toward him. When their eyes met, and Grace smiled at him it was just as obvious that she loved him deeply, too.

When Jim Sheridan asked the age-old question, "Who gives this woman in marriage?" Bill Morgan said, "Her mother and I do." Then he quietly said to Grace, "I give you as a woman to this godly man, but you will always be my baby girl."

"Oh, Dad, I love you. You'll always be my daddy, too!" They hugged and Bill said to Zach, "Take care of my little girl, Son," to which Zach assured him that he would.

Jim then began a touching message regarding marriage and the blessing it was when God brought a couple together in His plan. He said that the couple standing before him were a perfect example to prove that the story is not over in the midst of the hard times, but that God has promised to bring joy out of that sorrow.

Grace and Zach had decided to write their own vows to each other, so Jim now called on Grace to share those with Zach.

"Zachary Bryant Clayton…" Zach couldn't help smiling at her use of his full name. That usually meant he was in trouble, but the look of love in Grace's eyes told him that wasn't the case today.

"I thought I knew what love was, but after our relationship began I realized that what I had known was simply a surface emotion with no foundation or stability. I can look back through the pain and be so very grateful that God allowed it to come to an end. Otherwise, I might never have known the depth of true love that I share with you.

"Zach, I vow to you today that I will do everything I can to nurture this love, that it will only grow deeper and stronger. That we can continue to receive Godly wisdom to share with others. I promise to stand beside you as you lead us and the ministry God gave first to you and now to me as well. I will be here with you in the good times and the bad, believe with you for the fulfillment of the vision God gives you," she paused, "and promise to indulge your ever hungry appetite."

Zach threw his head back and laughed heartily as did the guests. Grace reached up and touched his cheek. "I love you, Zach, and I always will."

Zach wanted so much to reach down and kiss her, but he didn't think he was supposed to do that until later.

Jim grinned at Zach. "That's a hard act to follow, but Zach, will you share your vows with Grace."

Zach looked down as he held both Grace's hands in his. Then he met her eyes and said, "You know, our relationship began with me holding your hand, Grace. That plane took off and all I could think at that moment was how right it all seemed. In spite of my absolute certainty that I could never love again, in spite of the fact that I didn't get your number and thought I'd never see you again, here we stand. I'm holding both your hands and more importantly, I know that I hold your heart. We both know there are no guarantees in life, but I'm pledging to be here, connected to your heart as long as I live. Our love is a gift from God that I cherish and I vow to you this day to fulfill the command in God's Word that tells husbands to love their wives, even as Jesus loved the Church enough to give His life for it. I give you my life, Grace, as you have given me yours and I can't wait to see what God has in our future as we partner with him."

He smiled at her. "I hope you don't get tired of me telling you how much I love you, because I never tire of saying those words. You are my treasure, Grace." Then he broke the emotional moment with, "And I never get tired of eating your good cooking, either."

Everyone laughed, even Jim as he wiped tears from his eyes. "You know, most of us here today have been close to Zach in these past few years. We have shared in his heartache and pain. Those of you who were close to Grace have done the same thing as she went through her valley of suffering. But today, it brings me indescribable pleasure that we are all sharing in their joy and looking forward with them to the future that God has planned for them."

He paused as a wave of agreement rose from the wedding guests, then looked at the couple before him.

"Zach and Grace, I speak every good blessing upon this marriage. I now pronounce you husband and wife. Zach you may kiss your bride."

And he did, sweetly, thoroughly, and possessively.

"Okay, folks," Jim said when the kiss ended, "It is with pleasure that I introduce to you for the first time, "the Reverend Zach Clayton and Mrs. Grace Clayton!"

Everyone stood and applauded as the music began and the Claytons walked down the pretty little bridge arm in arm. Before joining their guests they paused to look around them. The sense of joy filled the naturally beautiful area. Excitement rose in their hearts as they again envisioned the buildings that would be built and the couples who would come and be touched by God's presence there in the Love Meadow.

After a few special moments Zach grinned at Grace and gave her a squeeze. "Hey, Beautiful, let's go eat cake!

Credits

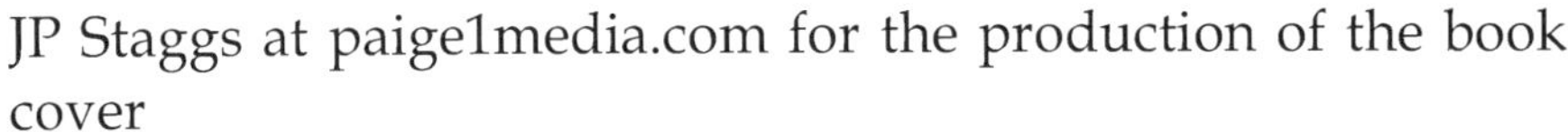

JP Staggs at paige1media.com for the production of the book cover

Dakotalynnphotography.pic-time.com for the cover photo

AUTHOR'S PAGE

I grew up on the Texas Gulf Coast in a small town south of Houston. My upbringing was in a Christian home with a houseful of musical instruments that my five siblings and I were encouraged to learn to play. The local library was just around the corner and since reading was my favorite pastime, next to playing the piano, I was delighted that books were always available.

My adult life has been filled with Christian service, especially in creative ways as I have written many skits, plays, musical performances and have been involved for years with women's ministries.

On January 1st…New Year's Day, 2008, a new chapter began in my life. Early that morning I became aware that in a way somewhat like dreaming, I was "receiving a book." It played out like a movie, but I knew I was to write this story. I had just joined the writers' group at my church, and the timing was perfect. The two ladies who led the group worked in the writing industry, teaching in local colleges and ministries. It seemed that each lesson on their agenda at our bi-weekly meetings was just what I needed for what I was dealing with in the writing of my book at that time. Thanks again, Cindy and Dagny!

Creating this first book was probably the most difficult thing I'd endeavored to do but it was also the most enjoyable. It was such a delight when new characters and situations I wasn't smart enough to think up on my own just appeared as I typed! So many times I was encouraged to believe it truly was God's direction for me to write these books when things I wrote as complete fiction turned out to be true!

Eventually, *Search for the Whole Heart* was completed, but I had a problem…it was way too long! I didn't think even a good friend would be willing to read a first-time author's book of over 800 pages! So I then had to learn to divide the book and create a sequel. Just as I was wrapping up the second book I was impressed to take one incident from the first book and write a third one that tied up everything for the series and has been the favorite of several of my readers. So, *Search for the Whole Heart* became a trilogy, and the volumes are *Change, Discovery, and Restoration.* The story is set in the historical period just following the Civil War. It begins in Missouri, and ends up by wagon train in the wild west as the characters find each other and a love-filled life in the new, untamed Dodge City, Kansas.

My fourth book, *Treasure from the Storm,* actually began with my having pastry and coffee at a delightful little café called "Sugar Magnolia's" in Lompoc, California. I hadn't begun my writing career yet, but I loved the name, so years later, after completing my trilogy I decided I should write a book and name the main female character "Sugar Magnolia." I thought with that name the book would have to be based somewhere in the South. I was awakened in the middle of the night, hearing, "Biloxi," so that became the foundation to start with. I found the fascinating history of Biloxi's trademark lighthouse, the only one of its kind existing, and incorporated its story and the three generations of one family who faithfully kept it sending beams of light out over the waters of the Bay.

I felt Sugar should have some sort of establishment which she inherited from her family, so the Magnolia Hotel was birthed in my imagination. To my surprise, I learned there really was a very popular Magnolia Hotel in Biloxi, Mississippi in the 1890's, (my time period for the book) and it still stands, having weathered many hurricanes through the years. There are actual records showing the cost of building the hotel, (just a few thousand dollars) and all the initial furnishings down to the number and cost of chickens and pigs. (We Southerners do love our bacon and eggs!) After renovations due to excessive storm damage the hotel is now being used as the Mardi Gras Museum. An overnight stay in Biloxi allowed me to actually view the hotel, and I discovered that it looked exactly as I had imagined it in my story before knowing that a real Magnolia Hotel had ever existed.

Lots of "Life Happenings," composing music, and conducting women's ministry made it difficult to be still and write consistently for a number of years, but I kept plugging away at *Receiving Grace*, Volume I in the Love Meadow Series, my first book written in a contemporary time setting. When I was forced to occupy the recliner for three months in order for a severe foot injury to heal, I made use of that time to complete the story. This one also came to me as I slept, just taking a nap one afternoon. Characters in this book had both been married previously, both had been in pastoral ministry, and both of them had lost their spouses in negative ways, leaving them doubting their purposes in life and even their faith in the goodness of God. I think you will enjoy seeing how God brings them together and learning how their struggles lead them into new direction, fulfilling love and a unified purpose they would never have imagined. There IS LIFE after divorce or the death of a spouse!

Love Wind is a fascinating story of a British sea merchant who decides to give his loyalty and the use of his ship to the struggling American colonies just as the war with England begins. This full-of-history love story has so many delightful surprises. It is almost finished and will be published soon.

In all of my books the stories contain characters who struggle with real-life issues. The solutions to their problems lie in knowing that God is always loving, always wants the best for us, and is always faithful to perform His Word. I have found these truths to be the foundation of my life, not just in stories. And yet, I have many comments from readers who have told me how reading about fictional characters finding their way to a place of trust in God have actually helped them to make it through their real-life problems. That keeps me writing!

I am so appreciative for all of you who find my books enjoyable. I trust that these stories also leave you feeling closer to the God who loves us all.

Ellen Sherrill

P.S. I love to hear from my readers. I can be reached at **ellen.sherrill@yahoo.com**.

Made in the USA
Middletown, DE
29 December 2022

18396377R00166